S0-GQE-948

This report is dedicated to the memory of all the victims of the genocide in Bisesero in 1994. Their defiance in the face of genocide, against impossible odds, is a standard which both the nation of Rwanda and the international community should uphold.

The struggle for life on the hills of Bisesero, in which all the refugees had a part, was guided by the bravery of men like Aminadabu Birara, his son Nzigira, Segikware, Habiyambere and Paul Bitega. All of these men are now dead. Siméon Karamaga, Aron Gakoko and Vincent Munyaneza, who are still alive, also instilled the will to fight in the frightened refugees and sustained them through three months of suffering. The names of these leaders will never be forgotten by survivors.

Resisting Genocide is based on testimonies given by 71 survivors of the massacres. Many may not have wished to visit their memories in such detail; it is one more sign of their courage that they have done so. It also includes the beginnings of a census which we hope will serve as a reminder of both the individuals who died and the scale of the atrocity.

Glossary

FAR — Rwandese Armed Forces
RPF/RPA — Rwandese Patriotic Front/Rwandese Patriotic Army

Local Administration: Rwanda is divided and subdivided into administrative units known as préfectures, sous-préfectures, communes, sectors, and cellules, the cellule being the smallest of these. The préfet is the highest local government official, with sous-préfets, bourgmestres, councillors, responsables and Nyambukumi respectively in charge of the smaller units.

"Refugee": this term has been used, as by the Rwandese themselves, to mean the people who fled their homes in search of sanctuary, even though they would not be considered refugees under international law, since they did not cross any national borders.

Rwandese names: Each family member usually has his or her own individual surname as well as first name. Hence siblings can have different names, and having a common surname is not a sign of being related, but of coincidence.

"Massue": refers to a nail studded club, a weapon frequently used in the killings.

"Interahamwe": the militia who carried out many of the massacres.

"Inyenzi": insult referring to any Tutsi. Literally means "cockroach".

"Inkotanyi": RPF soldier.

Contents

Introduction

The killings on the hills of Bisesero in April, May and June 1994 have a unique and important place in the history of the genocide of the Rwandese Tutsis. The many people who fled to this range of hills in Kibuye, in fear and in hope, fought a brave battle for existence. Initially they succeeded in defending themselves against local militiamen, killing a number of them in the process. However, news of the refugees' defiance soon reached the ears of prominent local authorities and experienced génocidaires. It became a principle of almost national significance that they should all be killed.

Most of those targetted by the 1994 genocide tried to defend themselves as best they could. Many fought in what survivors describe as "the war of stones against bullets" before they died in their thousands.[1] What distinguishes Bisesero is the organised nature of the resistance, and the fact that it lasted as long as it did, given the strength of the opposition.

Some of the most ruthless killers in the region and beyond were summoned to Bisesero to eliminate the refugees. They supervised militiamen, soldiers and local people in the killings, collaborating to ensure that their task was completed. A significant number of the génocidaires indicted by the International Criminal Tribunal for Rwanda participated in the killings in Bisesero.

As courageous as they were, the refugees were ultimately no match for the forces of the genocide. Indeed their struggle prolonged and intensified their suffering, and only an estimated 1,000 out of some 50,000 survived. This unified attempt at resistance, which was embarked upon in confidence and determination, tragically ended in despair and defeat. It says everything about how relentless and comprehensive the 1994 genocide was.

Today, the hills of Bisesero are still covered with skulls and bones. Where cows once grazed and children played there are now, said one survivor, "bones in practically every corner of the village". Human remains impossible to identify, or even to count accurately, are scattered irreverently and are occasionally trampled on by local people who conspired in the slaughter. These are the nameless dead; most of them were undoubtedly Tutsis, some of the native Abasesero people, others from the communes of Mabanza, Rwamatamu, Gitesi and Gisovu in Kibuye, Kayove in Gisenyi or from neighbouring parts of Gikongoro. Alongside them are some of the corpses of their tormentors. All of them were, either directly or indirectly, the victims of genocidal ideology. In the silent horror of the massacre site it seems certain that the souls of the dead would all testify to the consequences of hatred and speak in favour of peace.

On 7 April 1994, news of the first attacks upon Tutsis in the area reached Bisesero. The Tutsis of Bisesero, the Abasesero, were well-known for having defended themselves during earlier periods of organised violence. When people in neighbouring sectors first began to be killed, they called upon the Abasesero for help, but soon Bisesero itself was overcome by the genocide. Most of the local Tutsis were driven out of their homes and took to the hills to seek refuge. Initially, some of the Hutus and Twa of Bisesero joined them, unaware of the nature of the violence, but before long, they were made to understand who was being targetted and why. Over a period of three months, the refugees fought for their lives. Groups of survivors from other massacres were drawn to Bisesero by the reputation of the Abasesero, the strategic location, or news of their battle for survival. At its height, their number is estimated to have reached about 50,000. Bisesero was the last outpost of hope in Kibuye, the préfecture with the largest Tutsi population in Rwanda.

A well-organised and brave resistance kept the bands of soldiers, gendarmes, trained interahamwe and villagers at bay for around a month. Until the end of April, the refugees fought pitched battles against their killers, all armed to the teeth and supported by businessmen who provided weapons, vehicles, encouragement and financial incentives. They fought not only against assassins from Kibuye and Gikongoro, but even from Cyangugu, Gisenyi and Ruhengeri. They held out until the end of April, and killed a number of their adversaries—including policemen and militiamen. Their achievement is all the more remarkable given the scarcity of food, heavy rainfall and their exposure to the cold. While the majority were killed by gunshots, grenades, machetes or massues, some also died from untreated wounds, hunger, cold and exhaustion. On the open hillside, the men had the advantage of speed over women and children. Most of the survivors of Bisesero are male; this is rare in a genocide in which male Tutsis were identified as the first target.

Unable to defeat the refugees, the génocidaires suspended their campaign for the first half of May. They used this apparent "ceasefire" to re-equip their forces, re-organise, re-group and to mobilise reinforcements from other préfectures. Then they returned to battle. The number and array of weapons available to the killers now weighed the odds heavily against the refugees. Soldiers and militia came from Bugarama in Cyangugu, under the control of Cyangugu's best-known génocidaire,

John Yusufu Munyakazi. Others came from Gisenyi, Ruhengeri and Gikongoro. There were also local militia, as well as a substantial number of soldiers and Presidential Guard. From 13 May onwards refugees began dying in their tens of thousands. There was another massacre on the 14th, principally to finish off the wounded and to hunt for survivors. More than half the refugees—between 25,000-30,000—are thought to have died in these two attacks alone.

By late June, only about 2,000 emaciated people were still alive. These few survivors risked coming out of their hiding places to call for help from French reconnaissance troops who were driving by on 26 June as part of Operation Turquoise. The French troops promised to return in three days. In the meantime, the interahamwe, anxious to destroy the evidence of their crimes, set out to murder every last survivor. They had killed nearly a 1,000 of them by the time the French soldiers, alerted by a foreign journalist, returned to organise their evacuation.

The memories of the killings at Bisesero haunt the few survivors. The consequences for their lives have been so profound that there is little hope that any of them will ever fully recover. Most have lost their entire family and their friends, as well as their health, homes, and possessions. Many of them have returned to Bisesero and are trying to piece together the fragments of their former existence. Every glance towards the hills is painful—the skulls that are scattered all over them are a horrific display of all they loved and have lost.

---

1 For details about resistance to the genocide, see African Rights: Death, Despair and Defiance, August 1995, pp. 1024-1061.

The Exodus to Bisesero

Kagali hill in Bisesero.

Bisesero is a range of steep hills, straddling the communes of Gishyita and Gisovu in Kibuye. Covered with clusters of thick forest and blessed with many streams, they make up a beautiful green mosaic. All along the lower slopes are the farms and homes of the people who live in the fifteen cellules of Bisesero.[1] At one time they were mainly occupied by Tutsis.

The region is the historical homeland of the Tutsis known as the Abasesero, people from three clans—Abanyiginya, Abakono and Abahima—who lived as a community in solidarity and relative isolation. The Abasesero are traditionally cattle breeders, used to defending themselves and their livestock from outsiders. Efesto Habiyambere, from cellule Bisesero, sector Rwankuba in Gisovu, recalled life in Bisesero before the genocide.

There were many young girls and boys in Bisesero. They would gather on the hill during the day and play sport. They also played when they were looking after the cows. Few of the Tutsis from Bisesero studied. Their occupation was looking after the cows. So we remained isolated in our region, and no-one could attack us.

Siméon Karamaga, also from cellule Bisesero, spoke of how their reputation as a warrior people—whose "characteristic is a club in one hand"—attracted other Tutsis to the region when the first organised killings against Tutsis were launched in 1959.

In 1959, I was an adolescent. We made sure that we were able to defend ourselves in order to protect ourselves and our cows. Nobody could find a way of either stealing our cows or burning our houses. In 1962, the Tutsi massacres began again, but we managed to chase the enemy away, even though they had guns. In 1973, the killers returned. They burned two of the Abasesero houses. We were furious and took our spears and bows. The killers were afraid of us and they left us alone. The Tutsis from other regions were killed and their houses were burnt down. The surviving Tutsis left the country but all of us, except for a few families who went to Zaire, remained in Bisesero. We later killed the thieves who had tried to steal our cows. People from other regions who saw how we managed against the slightest resistance, believed that we were very strong men who could not be defeated by anyone.

At the beginning of the genocide in April 1994, many Tutsis came to Bisesero from other regions because they thought that the area was safe. Because we were known as warriors, everyone thought that the militia would be unable to attack the Bisesero area. However, this was not so. The militia attacked us at the very beginning of the genocide.

[1] The area includes fifteen cellules, eleven in sector Bisesero, Gishyita, namely Nyarutovu, Kigarama, Jurwe, Kazirandimwe, Uwingabo, Gitwa, Cyabahanga, Muhingo, Gatsata, Regete and Nyagafumba, as well as the cellules of Bisesero, Cyamaraba, Ruronzi, also known as Rubonzi and Gitabura in Gisovu.

Siméon Karamaga was one of the men who inspired and led the resistance in Bisesero in 1994.

Daphrose Mukankundiye

Daphrose Mukankundiye, then fourteen, and her brother, sixteen-year-old Niyitegeka, left their parents and six siblings in commune Gitesi and made their way to Bisesero. Daphrose explained why.

We had decided on Bisesero because it was often said that the Abasesero were very strong in battle. We didn't think that the militia would be able to attack us in such a place.

Emmanuel Gahigiro was also confident that the Abasesero would, once again, challenge their enemies. He remained at home in cellule Nyarutovu in Bisesero and watched the events as they unfolded.

Despite the fact that other Tutsis were extremely panicked, we, the Tutsis from Bisesero, were quite relaxed because we believed that no-one was capable of attacking us, due to our strength.

But not everyone in Nyarutovu felt at ease when the genocide began. On 7 April, Chadrac Muvunandinda was in the fields near his home when the news of the death of President Habyarimana reached him.

At about 9:00 a.m. people started to flee. They felt insecure due to widespread rumours that were going around. It was said that President Habyarimana's death could lead to the massacre of many Tutsis. We spent the night in the bushes because we were in such a panic.

The same day, Anastase Mushimiyimana from Musenyi sector, Gishyita commune received a warning from someone who had attended a meeting of the local authorities.

After he was informed of the death of President Habyarimana, Ezéchiel Muhirwa, councillor of sector Musenyi, chaired a meeting of the responsables of the cellules and the shopkeepers, which had as its subject the extermination of the Tutsis. He was accusing them of the assassination of President Habyarimana.

Anastase left his home for the hills. It was not long before Tutsi houses were being burned and the killings began. Gishyita was one of the first communes in the area to be affected. Elizaphan Kajuga said that the few educated Tutsis were the first victims.

The educated Tutsis were the first to be hunted down. Charles, the communal police officer in Gishyita, was killed. He was mutilated and his sexual organs were hung on an electric pole in front of Kabanda's shop in Gishyita.

Although Tutsis were the targets, not everyone realised who was behind the violence and what it meant.

On Friday 8 April, Tutsis began to be tortured, especially educated Tutsis. Emmanuel Murindahabi and Charles Nkundiye, agronomists from the commune of Gishyita, as well as all other Tutsis, were arrested and put into the prison of the commune. Their motorbikes were stolen. Kazungu from Bisesero was seriously beaten but he managed to escape.

On Saturday, 9 April, the people from the cellule of Karama, came to ask for our help as they said that they had been attacked by gangs of thieves. After this, we decided that we would have to start defending ourselves. At that time we were allied with our Hutu neighbours.

As soon as news of Habyarimana's death spread in Gishyita on 7 April, preparations for the killings got underway. Nathan Gatashya was living in sector Ngoma; he witnessed the distribution of weapons.

On 7 April, Obed Ruzindana, a businessman from Kigali, brought two lorries full of machetes. Obed unloaded these machetes at the home of Assiel Bazambanza, who had a welding workshop. Assiel sharpened the machetes because he had machines for sharpening metals. Assiel was a member of MDR PARMEHUTU, and he had been bourgmestre of Gisovu when Kayibanda was president in the 1970s.

At the meeting, Obed Ruzindana took the opportunity to hand out these machetes, grenades, etc... to the Hutu. After the meeting, each one had his machete. The interahamwe began to terrorise the Tutsi, telling them that they had killed Habyarimana, their President. They looted and burned the houses of the Tutsi. Then they began to kill them. So the Tutsi fled their houses to seek refuge in the Parish of Mubuga, the Parish of Kibingo and Mugonero hospital, while others went to the summit of the mountains.

Nathan's family split up; he went to Mugonero hospital and his wife left for Bisesero, where he would later join her.

Aron Gakoko lived in Kibingo, sector Gitabura in Gisovu. He was one of the first to be threatened on 7 April.

Munyampundu, a militiaman who was the responsable for Kibingo cellule, came to my house with his assassins. They came with machetes, guns and grenades. When we saw this group of well armed assassins coming, we ran out, taking nothing with us. They started taking my cows, looting the house. We reached Muyira hill, also in Bisesero, where we found other Tutsi refugees.

We stayed on this hill with nothing to eat. It was raining. The children started dying of hunger.

"The children moaned at us, asking why we had chosen to be Tutsi. We didn't reply".

Claver Mushimiyimana from sector Bisesero remembered how the people of Bisesero came together in an effort to prevent the violence from reaching their homes.

From the very start we lived in harmony with the Hutus and Batwa of Bisesero, which is why we believed it was the interahamwe who were responsible for the massacres following President Habyarimana's death, when we saw the houses set alight in Mubuga [situated] below. The burning began on 8 and 9 April. Along with Bisesero's Hutus and Batwa, we jointly agreed not to let any interahamwe into our sector, so that when the assassins began to move up towards Bisesero, we went down to the borders of the sector to prevent them from entering. Unarmed, every man and boy, without exception, remained firm against the interahamwe.

They were not able to contain the violence. Although they had fought back against massacres in 1973 and 1992, said Siméon Munyakaragwe, "We didn't know that this was genocide, which had been well prepared."

Ndayisaba from cellule Nyarutovu, sector Bisesero, is another surviving member of the Abasesero. He described the first time the militiamen arrived in sector Musenyi, on 9 April, and told of how he fled.

We were amazed because we were people who were feared. The militiamen first went for the sector of Musenyi. We staged a counter-attack. When we set off, we thought that they were thieves who wanted to steal our cows. However, when we got to where they were, we realised that what they wanted to do was to kill us. They said that their mission was to kill all the Tutsis. This occurred just a few days after the President's death. The militiamen had killed a few Tutsis that day with grenades and guns. Despite the fact that they had brought all these arms, we still managed to chase them away with stones, swords and clubs.

That evening, we decided to get together on one hill.

This group of Tutsis would soon be joined by others from the surrounding area, especially after it became apparent that the violence in Gishyita was officially sanctioned. The bourgmestre, Charles Sikubwabo, disarmed the Tutsis, assuring them that he would use his authority to rein in the "thieves." Emmanuel was on Kururebero hill with a group of refugees. From there they could see the homes of their fellow Tutsis being burned.

Suddenly we saw a lot of people who were carrying machetes, swords and guns. We took our clubs and went to defend ourselves. They had guns and so they shot several people in our row. Just as we were trying to repulse them, a group of soldiers arrived. When we saw them, we thought that they had come to help us. Instead, they surrounded us and told us to give them our weapons—clubs and spears. Following this, they told us to go and bury the people who had been shot.

Chadrac was also forced to surrender his arms.

Shortly afterwards, a group of people, headed by the bourgmestre of the commune of Gishyita, some gendarmes and the policeman of the commune, Ruhindura, arrived and declared a cease-fire. Our arms were taken away from us and given to our enemies. These were our traditional arms—machetes, old spears, and clubs.

The unity between Hutus, Twa and Tutsis began to break down. Michel Serumondo, from sector Musenyi in Gishyita, spoke of how friendships with two neighbours ended that day.

Muhirwa and Sylvestre Rwigimba were my two great friends. Their children used to visit my children and we were really close. When President Habyarimana died, everything changed.

Rwigimba was a communal policeman and the head of the cellule, and when the bourgmestre ordered the Tutsis to give up their weapons that Sunday, he gathered them up. Later Michel went to see him. One of his two wives had taken their children to her parents' home in Gishyita. He was worried about his second wife, Agnès, and their remaining children.

The evening of 10 April, I went to Rwigimba's house to ask him why they wanted to kill us. I also wanted to ask him to hide my six children because he was a friend of mine. My wife, Rachel Nyirampeta, preferred to go to her parents' house in Ngoma, Gishyita, and she left with her seven children. They all died with her during the genocide.

When I got there, he told me that it was the thieves who were trying to sabotage the Tutsis.

"I asked Rwigimba to hide my children. He replied, laughing, that he could not hide any child, but that he could hide my cows and valuable objects. I realised that our first friends had become our first enemies."

I felt angry when he told me that he could hide objects, instead of my children. He could see very well that I was hungry, but he gave me nothing to eat nor drink. Before the genocide, when I went to his house, he would welcome me with open arms, and even if he had no beer, he would go out and buy some straight away.

I was disappointed that evening. I left the house and went to hide in the bush near where I lived. I could see Rwigimba's children stealing things like chairs and clothes from my house. When I saw this I was frightened. I was afraid to stay alone in the bush, so I went to the hill with the others. All the Tutsis had come to that same hill.

In Gisovu, as in Gishyita, the local authorities demonstrated where their loyalties lay. Just two days after the President's death, Anastase Kalisa and his neighbours were visited by the bourgmestre of Gisovu, Aloys Ndimbati.

Anastase Kalisa

On Friday, 8 April, the bourgmestre of Gisovu came to Rwankuba, Bisesero cellule. He began to collect the weapons. We didn't want to give our weapons away but we had to, because the police told us that they would shoot us otherwise. Some of us eventually handed them in. Our weapons were machetes, spears and clubs. It was at this point that the Tutsis from Nyarutovu cellule in sector Bisesero, Gishyita, were attacked. We went to give them some extra support and we managed to force the interahamwe militiamen to retreat. The militiamen reorganised themselves. At about 2:00 p.m., they came back with their guns and grenades. The battle went on for a short while; in the evening they went home.

Eric Nzabihimana also watched as Ndimbati and other influential figures in Gisovu used their standing in the community to provoke violence against the Tutsis.

After Habyarimana's death, educated people like

the bourgmestre of Gisovu, Ndimbati, Alfred Musema, the director of the Gisovu tea factory, and teachers drove around everywhere in their cars, making the Hutu aware that their president had been killed by the Tutsis and that they had to start taking revenge. They also said that the Tutsis intended to exterminate the Hutus. They said this to the Hutus who had gathered in the commercial centres or on the road.

On our hill, Simon Segatarama, the councillor of Gitabura; Nzihonga, the director of a primary school and Joseph Bunozande, a teacher, really urged the Hutus of our hill to kill us.

These men enjoyed power and respect in their commune; they knew their advice would be heeded, and it was.

The Hutus immediately sharpened their machetes and they began to hunt us. At first they burned down our houses and slaughtered our cows. We fled to the hills. That was on 9 April.

The first concerted attack took place on 10 April.

On 10 April, the militiamen of Gisovu, led by Ndimbati and Musema, came to kill us with machetes, grenades and guns. They killed a large number of Tutsis.

Eric eluded the killers and made his way to Gitwa in Bisesero.

On 11 April, there was another wave of violence in Gisovu. On the 12th, Ndimbati took steps to ensure that the Hutu population were fully committed. Jean Muragizi, an employee of the tea factory in Gisovu, witnessed the manner in which he delivered his message.

On the 12th, a Tuesday, bourgmestre Ndimbati went to the market of Gakuta. He had a pistol in his hands. He asked the population to leave the market to go and kill the Tutsis. He asked the women to go and take things from the homes of Tutsis. I myself was at the market as they had not yet killed a lot of people.

The instructions were not given in vain.

After this order, the killing of Tutsis began in earnest.

Ndimbati was not alone in sowing the seeds of hatred in Gisovu. Jean recalled the contribution of the director of his factory, Alfred Musema.

I had hidden in a tea plantation in Gitabura. I saw Alfred Musema in his red Pajero with a lot of armed militiamen. They had filled up three vans which belonged to the tea factory. They were on their way to kill the Tutsis of Bisesero. It was around 15 April. That day, the Bisesero Tutsis repulsed this attack. I could see that they were strong.

Jean, his parents and other relatives headed for Bisesero because there, he said, "there were a lot of Tutsis who knew how to fight".

Alexandre Rwihimba, who was living in sector Muramba, described how the local Hutus who had been prepared to support the Tutsis in defence of their lives and their homes, deserted them when they realised the nature and scale of the opposition. The houses were burned and many Tutsis were killed. Those that survived, like Alexandre, mostly fled to the forest. He spent a week alone in hiding there. Then in the middle of the night, he took the risk of visiting a Hutu friend and neighbour, Thomas Sibomana. It was he who suggested Alexandre go to Bisesero.

He was a great friend of mine. I was carrying a machete because I thought he might kill me. When I got there, I knocked on his door. Thomas came out. He was carrying his wife's wrapover cloth. He greeted me and invited me in. He gave me food and milk to drink. He told me that the militiamen had looted our house and that many of my family were dead. He also said that the Tutsis who managed to escape had gone to Bisesero. He said that during the night he took food to the people there.

When I had finished eating, I too went to Bisesero. I made my way through the forests and had difficulty in not falling because it was night time. When I arrived there, I stayed with the people from Gisovu.

Like Thomas, there were Hutus who remained loyal to their friends, although the risks were high. Narcisse Nkusi's first thought was for the safety of his children. The family were living in sector Rwankuba in Gisovu. Narcisse had two good family friends there who were Hutu, whom he trusted would provide sanctuary for his two young sons. He then left for the hills with the rest of his family.

When I realised that the militiamen had already started to kill and to burn the houses, I looked for a way out for my children and a way to remove some of my belongings. I led my sons to my neighbours' homes. They were very close friends of mine. I took my son, Hakizimana, to Bernardin Birara's home in the cellule of Minini. He was also a very close friend of mine and we shared everything. He had even offered me a cow. Then I led Uwitonze to Paul Munyandekwe's home. He too was a good friend of the family. My father had given him a plot of land so that he could build his house.

My wife, my youngest son and myself went to seek refuge in the mountains with the others.

Recognising the turn events were taking, Augustin Ndahimana Buranga also decided to evacuate his entire family from cellule Nyarutovu to the hills.

I used to live just next to the road in Nyarutovu. A few days after the President's death, I saw militiamen, soldiers and policemen gathered together in the Muhuhuli forest. They wanted to attack our region. I was frightened because I had seen that in the sector of Mubuga, they had already begun to kill the Tutsis and to burn their houses. I told my wife, Bertilde Mukangango, and my three daughters—Uwamahoro, eight, Uwera, seven and Ingabire, a baby—that we had to quickly leave our house and go and join the other Tutsis who had gathered on the Bisesero hills.

We left all our valuable objects in the house because we thought that we would be returning to our things straight away. However, this was not the case. As soon as we left our houses, the militiamen began to loot and destroy all the houses owned by the Tutsis in Bisesero.

Léopold Ngezahayo and his family felt too frightened to remain in their home in cellule Ruronzi, sector Gitabura in Gisovu. On 8 April, they left for Bisesero sector in Gishyita, but were again forced to leave by violence. They proceeded to Kazirandimwe where they received a warm welcome from other displaced Tutsis and felt safe. But it was a precarious refuge. A week later, they were, once again, on the run.

Some policemen—Rukazanyambi, Sebahire and Seti—had come from Gishyita commune. They shot at us. They were accompanied by peasants armed with machetes and clubs. We put the women and the children together to collect stones for us to throw at the enemy. As for the men, we faced the attack, armed only with sticks and stones. We tried to defend ourselves because we had no other way of escaping. People died in the attack, especially women and children who were incapable of running.

Their next destination was Muyira hill. Léopold commented on their choice of this hill.

We wanted to link up with the Tutsis in that area who had resisted the attacks coming from Mubuga, Musenyi and Rubazo.

Damascène Ntaganira, accompanied by his wife and child of three years, deserted their home in Kibingo, Gisovu, heading for Muyira, a hill with historical significance for the family.

Our parents had survived the massacres of 1962 after taking refuges on Muyira. We went there for this reason.

Aloys Murekezi and his relatives chose Muyira for the same reason.

During the killings in 1962 and 1973, our parents also fled to this hill. From there, they succeeded in defending themselves.

In all the neighbouring communes, the violence was exploding. Tutsis were fleeing their homes. Some some went to the Catholic Parish of

Aloys Murekezi

Mubuga, others to Mugonero hospital in Ngoma or elsewhere. Innocent Ndahimana, from Ruragwe sector in Gitesi, explained how and why he went to Bisesero.

The interahamwe militia from Rutsiro launched an attack on Gitesi. The Hutus and Tutsis formed a unified front to resist these attacks. The next day, everyone realised that this was about ethnicity. As a result, the Hutus distanced themselves from the Tutsis. Tutsi houses were burned down and their cows were stolen. The following day, the Tutsis were killed over two consecutive days.

I used to be a servant for a Hutu family. The head of this family wanted to kill me but I managed to escape. I fled to Bisesero where my family were. The Tutsis there had always resisted previous attacks launched upon them.

With every assault and massacre in the communes neighbouring Bisesero, the level of fear rose. Survivors would make their way to the hill as the last outpost of hope; almost all of them had escaped massacres orchestrated by the men who were to distinguish themselves in Bisesero—Clément Kayishema, Dr Gérard Ntakuritimana and Obed Ruzindana amongst others. Some of the earliest refugees were the survivors from the 12 April massacre at the commune office of Rwamatamu; they were followed by those who fled the following massacres:

15 April: The Catholic Parish of Mubuga, Gishyita.
16 April: The Adventist Parish and Hospital of Mugonero in Ngoma, Gishyita.
17 April: The Parish of Kibuye, Gitesi.
17 April: Home St. Jean, Gitesi, Kibuye.
18 April: Gatwaro Stadium, Gitesi.
28/29April: The hill of Kizenga, Rwamatamu.

Many of the refugees who sought refuge in Bisesero had been driven out not only of their homes, but from other hills which had been their initial refuge, such as Sakinyaga and particularly Karongi, which is another very steep hill. In sector Mara in Gishyita, an attack by local killers on 9 April drove people to Karora hill, from where they would mount a brave defence. Anathalie Usabyimbabazi described how, once again, they were forced to leave and to keep running from one illusory sanctuary to another.

The assassins came in droves to kill us; most of them were people from surrounding areas. There were very few soldiers with grenades.

Our men and boys defended themselves with stones and spears against the assasins' grenades and machetes, and we women, together with the girls, would stockpile more stones to help them. In all, we numbered almost 5000, and we fought as best we could. But as there were so few of us compared to them and we were so ill-equipped, we were defeated. After our defeat, I ran away to Murangara, which is another hill, but we were followed there by those same assassins, who eventually caught up with us. That was where the lives of my two children ended. I was beaten all over with machetes, especially around the head and neck. They left me for dead, but once they had gone, I got up and made my way to the Parish of Mubuga, arriving there on Sunday, 10 April.

After the 15 April massacre at the Parish of Mubuga, Bisesero was Anathalie's next destination.

Other [survivors of Mubuga] went up to Bisesero. I too went to take cover at Bisesero in order to join the other Tutsis who were under threat.

Alphonsine Mukandirima was staying with her aunt in Gishyita when the killings began. She was eleven at the time. On 8 April, they left for Jurwe in Bisesero. But the following day, armed groups descended upon them and they ran towards Gititi. The killings continued, claiming Alphonsine's mother amongst their victims. Alphonsine and her brothers came across her body as they were fleeing and buried her. Then they hurried towards Bisesero.

We were repeatedly being attacked so we decided to join the other Tutsi refugees who were on Muyira hill in Bisesero.

Elizaphan Ndayisaba, a boy of twelve, was doing what he most loved to do—look after his family's cows—when his father found him one evening on the hill of Kagali in Bisesero.

He had come to tell me to take the cows to Muyira hill immediately. There were many frightened people gathered there. I put my cows with the other ones which were there. From that day on we stayed on that hill. We never had anything to eat during the day. There was not enough grass for the cows to eat either. Often it rained and the children shivered in the cold.

Claver Mbugufe and his family left their home in Bwishyura, Gitesi, on 13 April. They stopped in Karongi and then continued on to Bisesero. His wife, Jeanne, and his two children—three-year-old Nyirahabimana and one-year-old Musabyimana—died at Karongi on 26 April when vans brought soldiers from Kigali and militiamen from several communes of Kibuye. Even though a large number of people died, the killing continued for another three days after which Claver and fellow-survivors found their way to Bisesero.

There were a lot of refugees at Bisesero, many more than there had been at Karongi.

For the next two months, Claver would spend his time running between the slopes of Karongi, Muyira and other hills in Bisesero. Most of those who left other massacre sites for Bisesero would lose their lives there. And the refugees who abandoned Bisesero in the early days for neighbouring parishes, hospitals and hills also became victims of the genocide.

April 1994
Fighting Back

Terrified by the escalating violence, local people scrambled to the summits of the hills of Bisesero. They climbed Rubazo, Kiziba, Ngendombi, Murambi, Mutiti, Kivumu, Rurebero, Kazirandimwe, Gitwa, Uwingabo, Nyiramakware and Rwirambo hills, among others, but above all they assembled on Muyira, which was covered with forests and bushes, making it easier to find somewhere to hide.

During the 1962 and 1973 massacres, Tutsis had also fled to Muyira hill and, from there, succeeded in defending themselves. It was on this hill that most of the fighting took place in 1994; there that the refugees gave, in the words of one survivor, "every ounce of their strength" to defend their lives.

By 9 April, there were already thousands of refugees on the hills of Bisesero. Some had come with their families and livestock, confident that history would repeat itself and they would hold their ground. Others came alone, their families already killed and homes destroyed in the immediate violence which signaled the beginning of the genocide. Among them were the sick and the wounded and those distraught by grief—some had probably already lost hope. Tutsis came to Bisesero from all over the region, realising they would have to unite to survive. When they reached there, it was clear that the fight would be long and hard.

According to Uzziel Ngoboka, the first battle on the hills of Bisesero was fought on Rurebero hill on 9 April. The assailants came from Gishyita commune.

The assassins were armed with guns and grenades, and their supporters with machetes and clubs, whilst we had only stones and a few machetes to our name. We nevertheless fought, and during the first assaults we lost forty people whilst the assassins lost only seven of their own.

We were defeated on Rurebero hill and so had to withdraw to Kiziba hill.

Edmon Mugambira was also at Rurebero and then at Ngendombi, before he too reached Kiziba. He said initially they were fighting mainly peasants with traditional weapons, but as the battles continued, the assassins became more numerous and better armed.

When we reached Ngendombi, we fought again, throwing stones and spears. It was a failure for us; we moved to Kiziba where there were other Tutsis who had come from Gishyita and Bisesero who were fighting against the other killers. We supported them, but it was serious because the attackers had grenades and rifles, while we had no firearms.

Assassins of all kinds, including women and children, arrived at Kiziba blowing whistles and shouting "Tubatsembatsembe", meaning "eliminate them all", to terrify the refugees. Amiel Gafirigita's wife and some of his children were killed on Kiziba hill. He and his three remaining children, two of them injured, continued to put up a fight.

We tried to fight on the hill of Rurebero. But the situation was serious because the assassins had guns and grenades. They killed. We moved to the hill of Kiziba where we were also killed. But our children fought back because there were victims amongst the attackers. But without any doubt, there were more victims on our side. We found some guns which belonged to the aggressors who had been killed. They surrounded us in groups. We too organised our people in groups, just like them. They killed us. It was during this period that my wife was killed. My children also died during this period. I held out, but with difficulty because I was very tired.

The refugees ran to Muyira hill, where a group of them had begun a determined effort to hold the assassins at bay. Efesto had gone to Muyira at the outset of the genocide. Most of the refugees who were there at this time had either come from Bisesero, or from other sectors of Gishyita. As well as Tutsis, there were a number of Hutus and Twa, equally frightened by the growing insecurity. Efesto explained how, in the midst of despair, the refugees began to work together for their survival.

We gathered together on the hill. People were starting to panic. They couldn't eat from fear. Me and other young people like Nzigira, Gatwaza and Habimana went up to the other young people who were afraid and tried to raise their spirits. Two older people, Karamaga and Birara, were giving encouragement to prepare the people for battle against the militiamen. The children and women started to look for stones to collect. We put them in our bags. For the first few days, everyone warmed themselves at night by the fire. Often, however, it rained and the people shivered in the cold.

Nteziryayo's father had led his family and their cows to Muyira hill. Still a young boy aged nine, Nteziryayo tried to find reasons for their hunger, homelessness, despair, and the succession of brutal attacks. His father could give him no answers. The only motivation guiding the refugees now was the struggle for

Muyira hill in Bisesero where most of the fighting took place.

Claver Mushimiyima aged 17

life and even Nteziryayo had a part to play in it.

I kept on asking my father why we were suffering like that, why we couldn't find any food and why we had no place to stay when we still had our houses. I also asked him why people had begun to hunt us down and why people were being killed whereas before they had died a natural death. Why had the death of Habyarimana, someone who I had never seen before in my life, sparked off the killings of innocent people? My father did not reply to these questions. I always used to ask these questions at the end of each day on the hill.

When many people had assembled on the hill, all the women and children would have to go and collect stones to prepare for battle. We covered all the hills of Bisesero, looking for stones. We then gathered all these stones in one place, Muyira.

Léoncie Nyiramugwera went to the top of Gitwa hill with friends and family. She and the other women went in search of stones while the men tried to hold back the killers. Worn down by the endless violence, they finally concluded they would have a greater chance of survival if they were to gather with other Tutsis on a single hilltop, Muyira.

We suffered a lot on this hill. We had to stay outside which was hard as we were used to being in houses. People began to suffer from diarrhoea. There was very heavy rain as it was April, the rainy season. Added to all these problems was a sense of panic that we would be killed by the militia.

It was on Muyira that the refugees developed a strategy which would allow them to survive the month of April. Claver Mushimiyimana gave an outline of their plans.

We decided that all the men and boys would fight, fearless of the noise of the grenades and guns. Should anyone be killed, then everyone else would move forward and mix with the assassins. The women and girls would gather stones to enable the men and boys to get hold of them easily, as our arms were very important. This is how we fought the next morning.

Siméon Karamaga was at the heart of the effort to devise a defence strategy. The refugees had only traditional arms—spears, machetes, swords, knives and nail-studded clubs known as massues—as a shield against guns and grenades. The first step was to elect leaders.

We decided that we should all stay on just one hill, so we left with our children and the most important of our goods, our cows. There were too many of us on this particular hill, Muyira. We decided to choose some people who would be able to lead us. We wanted to choose someone who was not afraid and who would be able to spur us on, someone who also had experience when it came to battle. We therefore appointed Aminadabu Birara as commander. He was a wise man, the same age as me. He laid out a plan for us to follow so that we would be able to repel the militia. Birara was amongst the Abasesero who had taken part in the battle of 1959. Unfortunately, he was killed towards the end of the genocide in Bisesero. I was appointed his deputy and I was in charge of my own sections.

In the event of battle, the refugees were required to act with tremendous courage, by running down the hill and mingling with their enemy, using a tactic known as *Mwiuange sha*, which means "go and merge."

The militia were always dressed in white when they launched an attack. When we saw them coming, I would go in front of everybody and ask them to lie down. The militia would approach us, shooting as they advanced. When they saw that we were all lying down, they would come up to us. I would ask the Abasesero to get up and go amongst the militia. In this way they would not be able to throw grenades nor could they shoot us with their guns because there was a risk that they would kill their own people.

Our commander Birara would stay behind everyone to keep an eye out for those who were afraid. He would hit anyone who refused to advance. Women and children were also obliged to bring stones and clubs. Our commander would try and hide the Abasesero corpses during the fighting so that the others would not suddenly become frightened.

Edmon felt that even as they prepared their defence, the refugees knew that death was inevitable.

Our preparation was like a suicide attempt. How could we prepare ourselves to fight against someone who has a rifle when we had nothing?

He gave details of the way the refugees positioned themselves on the hillside, to protect the most vulnerable.

The men who knew how to fight rated each person's capability. They grouped together the strong youths and the strong men, in the first rank, in the middle of the hill; the girls and women were collecting and piling up the stones in the second rank; and the old people were with the cows at the summit of the hill. Those of us who were at the front formed a line so that when the killers were shooting at us, the victims would be less numerous. We also lay down on the ground when they had not yet reached us. We did not waste stones, we had to throw stones when we were sure that we could tell exactly where the enemy was aiming.

As they faced a daily succession of attacks, the refugees developed a routine for managing the battles with the militia and soldiers, as well as the fight against hunger and the elements. Although their number was ever-increasing, they remained united, as Siméon recalled. This was the fundamental factor in their ability to fend off their killers.

Often we managed to repel the enemy quite far back. I liked to be in front of the others. I would sometimes have to tell the Abasesero to retreat if I saw that we were becoming scattered or that we might fall into the enemy zone.

There were some young people amongst us who were there to help direct the others during the battles. The young people we chose to do this were Nzigira, Birara's son, who is now dead; Aron Gakoko, who is alive; Efesto Habiyambere, who is also still alive and Habimana, now dead.

Each time we fought a battle, we would meet on Muyira hill to sum up the day's events. In the evenings we would gather together and allocate new tasks to one another. We needed a lot of strength to work, so we would slaughter the healthy cows, drink the milk and then eat the meat. This gave us back our strength.

One group was in charge of the cooking whilst another group would watch out for the enemy so that they could not creep up on us unawares. Other people were in charge of burying our people who had been killed. We also constantly restocked our supply of stones.

It rained all the time and we did not get a lot of sleep but we still managed to remain positive because we saw how well we were defending ourselves against the militia, despite the fact that we had no guns. Instead we used our clubs. A militiamen who received a blow from this died immediately.

But, as Siméon emphasised, above all the refugees advanced into the battle because they had no alternative, "nowhere to run". Eric paid tribute to their leaders and spoke of the bonds that held the refugees together.

We were attacked frequently, but in the early days, there were not so many deaths and we had set up a very good system to defend ourselves. We knew very well that we had no refuge since our authorities and our Hutu neighbours wanted to kill us. We therefore decided to unite our strength in order to fight, even though we only had machetes and spears.

The older generation of Abasesero had instilled the fighting spirit in their children, as Sylvère Gatwaza's testimony shows. Then aged 24, Sylvère had made a commitment to fight early on, when he and his friends chased a neighbour's killer at home in their cellule of Ngabo in Gishyita. After this, they searched for weapons, and once at Muyira, asked for instruction on how best to use them.

We asked the older people to teach us how to fight. Every day the militiamen arrived in cars which belonged to Obed Ruzindana and the bourgmestres of Gisovu and Gishyita in order to kill us. Nevertheless, during the month of April, they were disappointed because we killed a lot of militiamen.

Uzziel was one of the refugees who used the tactic of mingling, on Sunday 10 April.

The Kinyarwanda expression Mwiuange sha *basically describes the tactic of mixing with the assassins as they approach, thus removing their ability to shoot at us; this then allows us to use machetes just as they do. The assassins began to realise that, in this manner, they too were*

Sylvère Gatwaza, a 27-year-old farmer

suffering heavy losses. They fled in order to return the next day, Monday, which proved to be a repeat of Sunday. At night, we would bury our dead and treat the wounded.

David Kayijaho identified two of the organisers of the militia who arrived that Monday.

On Monday 11 April, the interahamwe militia who were in Ruzindana and Mika's car, invaded us. We fought them until we realised that we had lost a large number of people. We then fled into the bush. The militia continued their massacre by hunting us in the bush. People did not stop dying. Two brothers of mine fell victim to the massacres. My mother, who was blind, did not leave the house, and it was burnt down with her still inside it.

Bernard Kayumba was at the Parish of Mubuga when most of the refugees sheltering there died on 15 April. He went to Bisesero where he found the same killers as at Mubuga—Sikubwabo, Mika and Muhirwa—and others. He named the other men who made killing at Bisesero part of their "work."

The organisers of the massacres at Bisesero were Eliezer Niyitegeka, the minister of information; Clément Kayishema, the préfet of Kibuye; Charles Sikubwabo, the bourgmestre of Gishyita; Aloys Ndimbati, the bourgmestre of Gisovu; Obed Ruzindana, a businessman; Alfred Musema, the director of the tea factory in Gisovu; and the councillors Mika Muhimana, Muhirwa and Vincent Rutaganira.

Josué Rubambana from Nganzo in sector Gishyita went to the hill of Runyangingo in Bisesero after his wife and young daughter were killed on 16 April in Mugonero. He remained immobile under a pile of corpses, leading the militia to believe that he too had died. But he had not seen the last of the men who planned and carried out the massacre at Mugonero.

The same génocidaires—Dr Gérard, Obed Ruzindana, Clément Kayishema and Charles Sikubwabo—used to come every day to kill us. I also saw Musema, the director of the Gisovu tea factory at Bisesero. The vans of the Gisovu tea factory used to transport génocidaires.

But we too, we organised ourselves and we killed a lot of militiamen and soldiers. We used stones and clubs.

The overnight transformation of local government officials, policemen and soldiers into executioners was a sight which most refugees found difficult to believe. Anathalie Usabyimbabazi expressed her sense of shock.

We could not believe that our local policeman, armed with his gun, would shoot on people armed only with stones. In the end he was killed at the hands of those so poorly equipped compared to our well-armed attackers.

Pascal Mudenge, from Musenyi in Gishyita, fought off the assailants at Rurebero on Monday. They came back with soldiers, guns and grenades, and the refugees ran to Muyira.

The next day, Charles Sikubwabo, the bourgmestre of the commune of Gishyita, led a great massacre. We resisted and the enemy retreated back to the hill of Gitwa. We only had stones, which the women and children had collected, clubs and very few machetes to use. We fought without respite. We had no other choice but to fight. The bourgmestre went to ask the préfet of Kibuye for further reinforcements. He told him that Bisesero had been taken over by the Inyenzi and that they had put up their flag.

Almost everyone had a part to play in the defence. Léoncie emphasised the importance of the women in the fighting.

The militia would come towards us shooting and our men would chase them away with spears and machetes. We women and girls would run behind the men carrying stones in wrapping cloths. We were very fast when carrying these stones; there were some girls who were very brave and fought more than the men.

The old and the young shouldered the suffering equally. Nteziryayo, then aged nine, recalled their collective experiences.

The women and children fled. The militiamen ran after us to try to kill us. When they caught up with an old man or a child who could not run, the militiamen would just kill him or her immediately with his machete. Another group of militiamen went to destroy our houses and gather our crops from our fields. They also stole our cows.

Every day the militiamen came over to kill us. Each time I ran like some sort of animal. When we ran like that we had no idea of the whereabouts of our mothers or fathers. I had to eat the twigs from the trees. I saw the corpses of the members of my family on the hills. Sometimes when I was running, I would stumble upon someone who had been hit by a machete but who was still breathing. I felt terrible if anyone asked me for water which I could not find.

Caritas Nyirakanyana, aged eight, joined in the effort to survive.

I was with the children and the old people who used to gather the stones to facilitate our struggles to defend ourselves. But when it was time to flee, we ran with the others. Those who got tired were killed by the assassins. The hills which we fought on were Rurebero, Kiziba, but most of the time on Muyira. I was lucky. Because I was small, when I became tired the men carried me on their back while running.

Our leaders told us that when we mingled with the assassins, they could not shoot us but would use machetes and massues. Since we also had these weapons, there were deaths on both sides. That is why when the assassins approached us, we used the same method. But we were the ones

David Kayijaho, a 32-year-old farmer

who lost a lot of people, to the point that our men and young people were almost wiped out.

Emmanuel Sinigenga, then only eleven, also showed great courage.

The killers came in large numbers; they threw grenades and shot from a distance. We decided to approach them because we had the habit of mingling with them in such a way that they could not shoot at us on account of the short distance between us. On those occasions, they used machetes like us. In such situations, they ran quickly. They did not want to die even though they were killers.

There can hardly have been a more testing experience for any young person or child. Memories of those months will never leave them. As young as he was, Antoine Ngiruwonsanga, aged thirteen in 1994, knew that the refugees were only allowed to retreat from battle when the order had been given for all to run. He spoke of the pain he lived through as he continued to fight.

It was terrible to lift a stone in your hands which were constantly bleeding. When you threw it it didn't even go further than ten meters, because we had no strength.

Despite her age—seven years—Uwayisenga made her contribution to the refugees' defence.

There were people who used to ask us to collect stones. We gathered them up. The men used these stones to chase away the militiamen.

However bravely they struggled, lives would be lost. With the first attack upon the refugees, came the first deaths. Catherine Kamayenge, aged 76, had gone to Muyira with her husband, Marcel Gasamunyiga, her daughters—Berthilde Mukagasana and Ancilla Uwimana, and their children. Her husband was killed soon after their arrival.

It began to rain at the time and we were shivering a lot. The cows mooed and the children began to cry. From that day on, we spent our lives in the bush.

The next day, the interahamwe started to attack us. They were led by our councillor, Muhirwa and a policeman, Rwigimba. My husband was the first to die because he was the one who was guarding the cows when the militiamen came to steal them. My husband was hit on the head with a stone and he died immediately. We did not have too many problems burying him because it was still at the beginning of the genocide and things had not become too serious.

Even though the génocidaires were attacking us, we still tried to organise ourselves. The men carried spears and machetes to try and defend us. The women and girls had the responsibility of collecting stones so that they could push back the attackers. We therefore had to spend the whole of each day collecting these stones. My old age did not exempt me from the agony of collecting stones.

But some of the refugees had serious wounds by the time they reached Bisesero. They could do nothing to advance the collective battles. One of them is Thamari Nyiranturo, then aged 57. Herself an Adventist, and the widow of an Adventist pastor, Thamari took refuge at the Adventist Parish of Mugonero. She was hit on the head with the butt of a gun during the massacre of 16 April and "took the path to Bisesero".

The militiamen came to kill in Bisesero too. As I didn't have the strength to run or to pick up stones, I went into the bush. I stayed there since I could no longer walk. The wound in my head was infected. For nearly three months of the genocide, I was in the bush without moving, without eating. Flies came and fed on my wounds; I didn't have the strength to drive them away. The rain fell on me.

Intense suffering and loss marked the everyday experience of the refugees in Bisesero. Valence Nsengiyumva was just eight at the time, but he will never forget witnessing the murder of his mother. His parents had taken him and his brothers to Bisesero when the killings began.

The assassins came to kill us at Bisesero, despite the fact that we had done nothing to them. My parents and brothers joined our neighbours to go and fight the assassins, but they had guns and grenades and greatly outnumbered us. They shot at us. Seeing very many of our people lying dead, we fled. I ran away with my parents. But after a few days, my mother became tired and the assassins caught up with us and killed her with their machetes. They beat me too about my body and especially around my head, which is why I carry these scars on my face.

"I laid where I fell. At night I managed to sit up and I could even hear my father's voice. But he had no idea where I had fallen and been left for dead".

In the end, I managed to climb up to the position where he was and found him with my two brothers.

When the assassins attacked our people once

more, I remained with the old who did not have the strength to fight, behind the others. I found it difficult to run because of my injuries, and that is why the assassins caught up with me again and hit me with their machetes. In the end, my older brothers hid me in a place unknown to the assassins, and would come to see me during the night; the assassins would pass close by me during the day, but they never once found me.

Starving the refugees out was a central line of attack; Augustin described how women and children ensured the success of this strategy.

Even women and children from Bisesero killed. They were also the ones who took our crops from our fields. I personally saw women killing my elder brother's two children. My brother was called Charles Munyaburanga.

Children, as well as adults, were unprepared for the speed with which friends turned into enemies. Uwayisenga, aged seven, was puzzled as to why her father insisted that they leave their home in sector Rwankuba for Bisesero.

When we arrived on this hill, I heard people saying that a certain Habyarimana had died and for that, it was necessary to hunt down the Tutsis. I asked my mother if we too were Tutsis, and she told me 'yes'. We remained on this hill trembling. We couldn't sleep. The small children were crying. There were too many of us.

When the militiamen came, we immediately dispersed; children became separated from their mothers while fleeing.

Uwayisenga was alone when she came face-to-face with a militiaman who had once been a friend.

One day the militia came to attack us. When I saw them, I ran. There was one militiaman who saw me running. He came up behind me to kill me. He was a strong man and he caught me. I no longer had the strength to run because I was hungry and tired. When the militiaman caught up with me, I was astonished because I realised that he was my friend. His name was Hazigama and he was from Rwankuba. Before the genocide began, Hazigama used to come to our house everyday. He farmed my father's fields and he received a salary. He received his salary on time and we never had any problems.

Despite the fact that he worked for my father, I had a lot of respect for him. When he finished work, he used to come to the house and I often gave him water so that he could wash himself. My mother gave him food. We used to play with him and he was like a brother to us even though we were not from the same family.

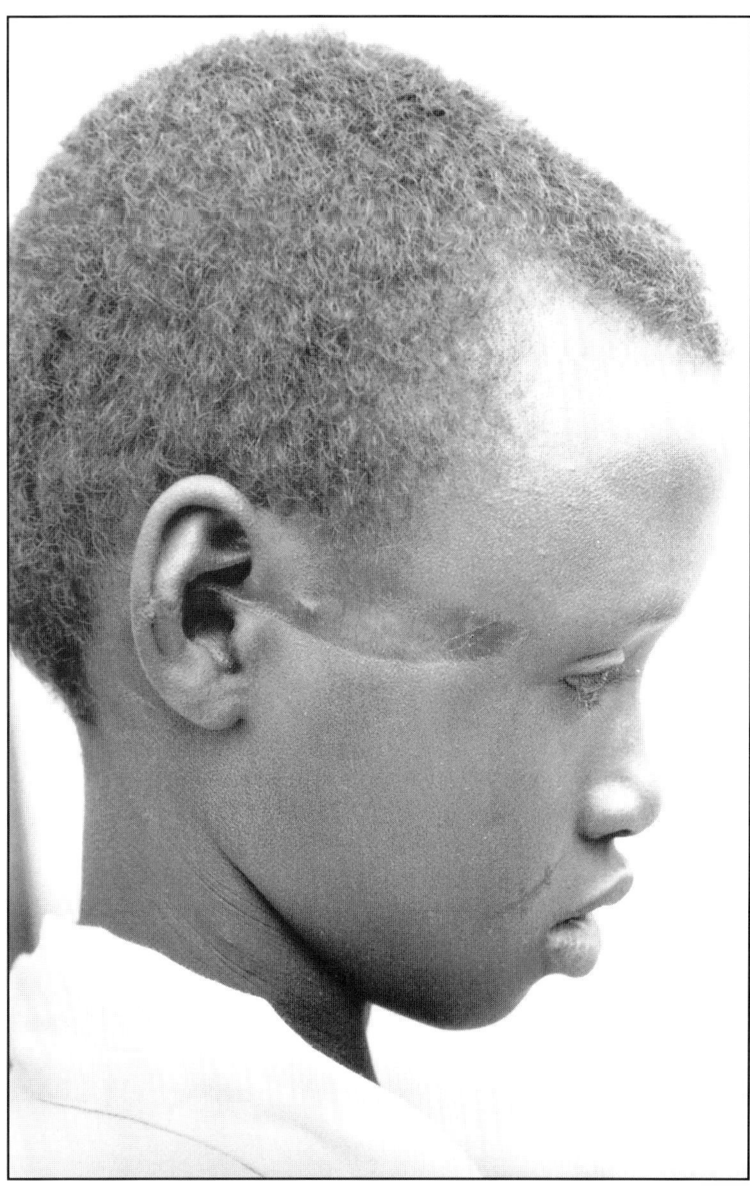

Valence Nsengiyumva, aged twelve

With the innocence of childhood, Uwayisenga turned to logic to make sense of a world beyond her comprehension.

Hazigama was just about to kill me; I asked him why he wanted to do this when I had done nothing to hurt him. I begged him to take pity on me. He said nothing but just hit me on the head with a machete. He had bits of wood in his hand which he stuck into my face. When he thought I was dead, he left. I lost a lot of blood. I was like a corpse. There were wounds all over my body. I was stretched out on the grass. There were corpses next to me. I couldn't think any more.

Uwayisenga is probably only alive today because, unlike many other children, she was found by her mother. After she had nursed her wounds with water and comforted her, Uwayisenga's mother hid her in the bush.

I stayed there since I couldn't run anymore. I smelt terrible because of the wounds which were not being taken care of. I no longer even had the

Uwayisenga, aged eleven, scarred by machete cuts

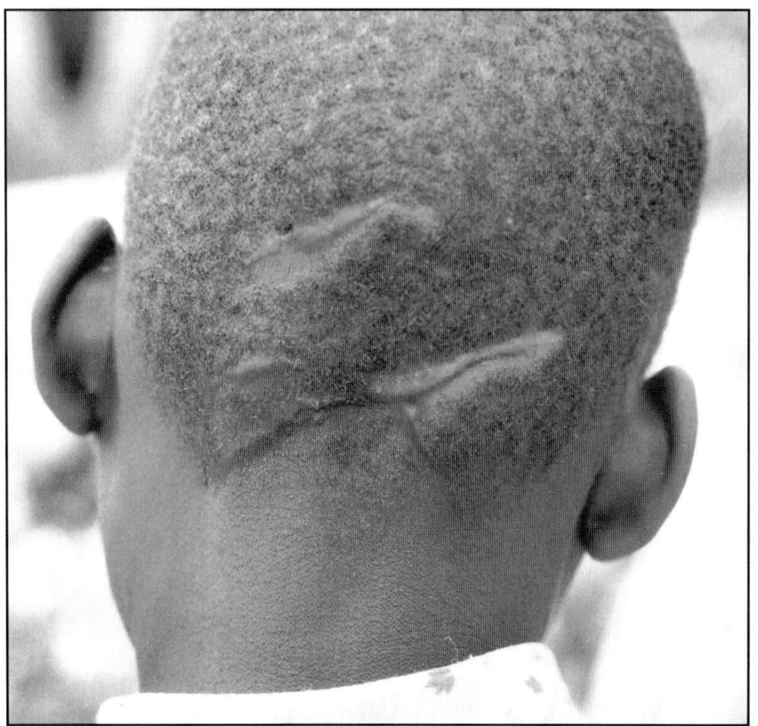

strength to fight off flies and other insects. I found some freshness when rain fell on me. As I was surrounded by corpses, the militia were not interested in me as they thought that I too was dead. I remained there, like a corpse, until the arrival of French soldiers.

The battles usually began at around 9:00 a.m. and lasted until evening. The bourgmestre of Gishyita, Charles Sikubwabo, and the bourgmestre of Gisovu, Aloys Ndimbati, were among the leaders. Most of the assailants knew one or many of their intended victims—they included former friends and neighbours. The refugees killed many of their opponents, including communal policemen and soldiers, taking their guns. Augustin Ndahimana Buranga recognised many of the attackers immediately.

For the first few days, the attacks were launched by the bourgmestre of our commune, Charles Sikubwabo; the councillor of sector Gishyita, Mika; the councillor of sector Musenyi, Muhirwa; the councillor of sector Mubuga, Vincent Rutaganira and many other powerful militiamen. Obed Ruzindana came afterwards. We were also well-organised; we went to fetch stones, spears and swords so that we could defend ourselves. We put up a strong fight during the month of April and at the beginning of May. We managed to kill a lot of militiamen, soldiers and police.

"We knew the militiamen who attacked us at the beginning. They used to be our neighbours. They would often call out our names and tell us not to run so that they could kill us more easily".

In the evenings, when they left, each family gathered somewhere on the hill to decide on a way to find some food. My family and I preferred to meet in Kazirandimwe, where my wife came from. Very early in the morning, we would go back to Muyira to be with the others.

On certain days, the militia did not appear; Léoncie explained why.

On Tuesdays and Wednesdays, the Abashi from

Idjwi in Zaire went to the markets to buy what the militia had looted from the Tutsi houses. On Tuesday the market was held in Gitonde, in Gishyita commune, and on Wednesday the market was held in Mugonero. On those days only a small number of people attacked us and we obtained some security. This was because lots of the militia had gone to market.

However, the strength of the opposition increased with the visible contribution of Obed Ruzindana. Ruzindana was a businessman in Kigali but a native of Gisovu, and a powerful figure in the area. He was involved in the killings from the outset. On 10 April, Jean-Damascène Nsanzimfura was standing at the top of Rurebero hill and saw Ruzindana's lorry delivering machetes.

The lorry stopped at Obed's and Obed himself distributed the machetes among the population. The businessmen of Mugonero and other educated Tutsis were killed immediately. The Tutsis who escaped the massacres in Mugonero fled straight to Bisesero and told us all about Obed.

Ruzindana soon became a regular participant in the killings at Bisesero. Efesto Habiyambere spoke of the onslaught orchestrated by Ruzindana.

The militiamen launched attacks every day. They arrived in Obed Ruzindana's vehicles which were in fact trucks used to transport tea from Gisovu. When they arrived they were singing. They were wearing white clothes and grass on their heads. When I saw them, I would immediately take my spear and club and put the bag of stones around my neck and I would ask the others to follow me. Nzigira would take another group and we would follow the orders that Birara and Karamaga had given us.

When the militiamen attacked, we would lie down at first. This was because they were throwing grenades. Afterwards, we would mingle with them and fight. When they saw that about two militiamen were dead, they would immediately retreat. Someone would be looking to see if the stones were all gone and then they would ask the women and children to quickly get more. If anyone from our group retreated out of fear, Birara or Karamaga would immediately hit them with their clubs.

In the evening, when the militiamen had gone home, we would get together again so that those who were still alive should know that they had to carry on fighting until the very end. When my mother was still alive, she used to come and beg me not to go in front of the others when a battle took place. She wanted to prevent me from doing this because I was the only boy in a family of girls. I was the only son she had. For the first time she was afraid that I would die. Not once did I listen to my mother's advice. I always went to the front. During the whole of the month of April, we were attacked, but each time we were the victorious ones because we managed to kill many militiamen, police and soldiers. We also took their weapons, such as guns.

Léoncie also said that the militia were transported by Ruzindana, adding that she had discovered he was also paying them.

They used to come in a blue lorry which belonged to Obed Ruzindana. I recognised this lorry because, before the genocide, my husband and I were clients of Obed Ruzindana. He often used to bring beans, sorghum, soap, salt, etc. We would buy these things to put in our shop. When Obed had finished selling these goods, before returning to Kigali, he used to go to Gisovu commune to have some tea. I therefore knew him very well.

As I was carrying the stones to fight I saw Obed Ruzindana with a gun in his hand. I distinguished him from the other militiamen straight away as I

Léoncie Nyiramugwera a 56-year-old trader

Uzziel Ngoga, aged 25

knew him well.

Pascal Mudenge said that Ruzindana came with "three busloads and three Daihatsu vehicles of interahamwe and ex-FAR soldiers". The killers were now better organised, well-armed and—with the prospect of material rewards—inspired by a genocidal frenzy. Yet still the determination of the refugees prevented them from outright success. Indeed on one occasion, the refugees came close to eliminating Ruzindana himself; Uzziel was among the group of fighters.

On 12 April, a vehicle owned by Obed Ruzindana came. It was full of soldiers and followed by very many farmers chanting war cries. Our intention was to mix with them as they approached us. Ruzindana parked his vehicle to let the armed soldiers descend, and the soldiers then began firing at us. We got down on our hands and knees and began crawling, but that didn't prevent some of us from getting killed. However, as they came close up, we once more managed to mix with the enemy and we began to close in on Ruzindana. Ruzindana fired at us, but we were too many to stop, and so he ran. We gave chase, and he dropped his Kalashnikov, deciding instead to use his hand gun to fire on us even as he ran. When he got back to his vehicle, he and a number of others drove off, back to where they came from.

Following a series of defeats, the attackers recognised the importance of sowing division in the ranks of the refugees. They exerted pressure upon the Hutus and Twa of Bisesero, who had initially fought alongside the Tutsis, to switch sides. Claver Mushimiyimana remembered how the majority of them left around 20 April.

We lost many lives that day, but we had beaten them. That's when they decided to come at night to visit Bisesero's Hutus and Twa to encourage them to leave us Tutsis, telling them we were the real enemy in their midst. Most of the Hutus and Twa left us in the middle of the night, leaving us feeling deceived and virtually alone in Bisesero. Those of us who remained were left to reorganise our positions and strategy, to fill the gaps left by those of our neighbours who had left.

The Fighting Intensifies

Throughout the first weeks of April, Tutsis had arrived in Bisesero, fleeing massacres and searches in the surrounding communes, and swelling the ranks of the fighters. Although many lives were lost, there were usually new recruits to replace them. The number of refugees at this time is thought to have been approaching 50,000. However, towards the end of April, the refugees were significantly weakened. The hardship of life on the hill meant that they were invariably hungry, thirsty or tired, and often sick. Catherine explained how the génocidaires ensured that their opposition was worn down.

They continued to kill the people, to steal the cows and to gather the crops so that we would die of hunger. It was done in such a way that to get food, we would have to buy it. What we did manage to buy came from young people who risked their lives fetching it from the mountains at night. At the time, an ear of sorghum cost thirty francs, a stem of sorghum cost twenty francs.

The desertion of their Hutu and Twa allies was a major setback for the refugees. By converting some of them to the ideology of genocide, the organisers gained a source of inside information, prompting them to change their military tactics. Uzziel spoke of the consequences.

The assassins began coming during the night to spread propaganda in the homes of the Hutus and the Twa, convincing them that the problem was not with them, but was instead encompassed by a single word, Tutsi. Around the 20th and 25th of April, the Hutus and the Twa left to join the genocidal killers in Mubuga, leaving us on our own. We felt as though we had been gravely deceived, with our neighbours switching sides like that. Worse still, they knew of our secret, our tactics of mixing with the assassins, and they made this known to the genocidal killers.

As a result, the assassins changed their tactics, and placed a heavy gun on top of a hill in order to fire on us from a distance. Again we were forced to withdraw, this time to Muyira hill, but they managed to encircle us with some of their people on Rubazo hill, another group on Mutiti hill, a third at Kazirandimwe, and a final group who came up from Mubuga. All of these hills surrounded the hill we were on, and so we too changed position to allow us to defend ourselves as a single unit, splitting ourselves into four groups, just like the assassins. Our women and girls formed a fifth group to assist us by collecting stones for us to throw at the assailants. So each group of assassins would encounter one of our groups, and whenever men in our groups fell, we would send reinforcements to their aid. However, we lost very many of our own during this time.

Michel was one of those wounded that day in a grenade attack which killed five others.

On 25 April, militiamen arrived in cars. They were dressed in white. They shot at us and we ran away. They hit the children and women who could not run with their machetes. I was running with a group and a militiaman was chasing us. He threw a grenade at us. Five people died outright. Their legs, arms and head became detached from their bodies. The shrapnel from the grenade explosion hit my right leg and I fell down immediately. The militiamen who were coming up behind us took no notice of me, thinking that I was dead because I was covered in blood. From where I was lying, I could hear militiamen complaining and asking why Obed Ruzindana was so late in giving the order to go back to receive the reward that he had promised for them. They were congratulating themselves for having killed so many Tutsis.

In the evening, when the militiamen had gone home, the refugees started to bury the bodies. My wife came to see me and she tried to heal my wounds with cow's butter. I could not run so I stayed in the bush. I could see everything from there.

Also hiding because of her injuries, Alphonsine Mukandirima found that the bush had its own dangers.

I discovered that I had gangrene on my foot. I could no longer run. Since my brothers had been killed, I had to hide in the bush all alone. I bandaged my leg and ran behind the old people during the attacks.

We were also persecuted by the Twa who hunted us down in the bush with their dogs. They used machetes and spears which they would throw in the bush to see if we were there.

The surviving refugees sank deeper and deeper into utter despair; many of their companions had died, particularly women and children, and others were badly wounded. Now the dead could only be given hasty burials, lacking in ceremony. And yet, as Alphonsine commented, the refugees somehow found the strength to take on the génocidaires.

They beat us, forcing us to disperse and leave behind many dead. At night we managed to regroup and reorganise, allowing for the fact that there were very few of us left. We felt at a loss, unable to bury our dead as we had done previously. We decided to keep fighting these assassins; we kept this up for several days, after

Ku Nama hill, where the militia parked their vehicles before the daily killings.

which the assassins went away for a few days.

Didas Hitimana named the leading figures among the killers.

I used to see Gérard Ntakuritimana often. He liked to wear white shorts and a white shirt. Other leading génocidaires also came, like Obed Ruzindana, the préfet, Kayishema, soldiers as well as all the militia. I don't know Musema, but many times at Bisesero I saw the vehicle of the Gisovu tea factory, full of militiamen. They killed a lot of Tutsis in Bisesero, torturing them. All the hills were covered with corpses.

It seemed that the génocidaires would achieve their aim. Eric described how they supervised the massacres.

Every day, I saw Obed Ruzindana; Ndimbati; the préfet, Kayishema, and Musema with their cars which were transporting the militiamen. They liked to stop at a place called Ku Cyapa, watching how their militiamen were killing us. The génocidaires wanted to neutralise us with gunshots and grenades.

Before she arrived in Bisesero, Anathalie had sought protection on the hill of Murangara. Instead, her two children were killed there and she was beaten with a machete, especially on her head and neck. In pain and weak from her wounds, Anathalie could only try to hide behind other refugees during the fighting. She too left Bisesero for a short time, only to be driven back there by fear.

As the days dragged on, I became very tired. When I reached the point where I felt I was about to die, I went to the home of a Hutu whose wife I knew well. She was called Rose, and she hid me for a while, but soon the neighbours suspected that I was hiding in my friend's home. When they discovered me there, I tried to run away from them but they gave chase and it was only through sheer luck that I put a lot of ground between them and me. I finally rejoined the others who I found were suffering the same problems as myself. At night, the assassins would return home, only to come back and continue the fight the next morning. We would also use the night-time to reorganise and plan the next day's tactics.

Claver Mbugufe also tried to escape the fighting.

When I saw that things were complicated in Bisesero, I went back to the mountain of Karongi during the night, together with a small group. We spent some days there. Then the militia came to search Karongi. So we returned to Bisesero. We had to look for something to eat at night. But we had to be very careful not to leave any marks. Otherwise, if villagers saw our footsteps in the plantations, they would report that refugees were nearby. Then searches would be organised. That is why we had to change our hideouts very frequently.

Some of those wounded in Bisesero and in other massacres, as well as old people, women and children, tried to shield themselves from the violence, and to take shelter from the rain and the cold, in an Adventist church located in Ku Murambi, situated between sector Ngoma and sector Bisesero in Gishyita. This part of Gishyita was populated principally by Tutsis, making it an obvious target for the génocidaires.

Didas Hitimana was one of the Adventists who used to frequent the church in Murambi. At the beginning of the genocide, he had taken his wife, Catherine Mukantaganda, his son, Aimable Musabyimana, and his brother, Claver Kayibanda, together with his wife and three children, to the Adventist Parish of Mugonero. He himself returned to Kazirandimwe to look after his cows. His family were all killed in Mugonero on 16 April. He and other survivors from this massacre ran to the hill of Gitwa in Bisesero.

One day in April, I saw the pastor, Elizaphan Ntakuritimana, with a lot of militiamen in his Hilux van, coming to this church in Ku Murambi. There were a lot of wounded people, as well as the old, women and children who had spent the night in this church.

When Elizaphan Ntakuritimana arrived with the militia, they massacred all these Tutsis who were in the church, which they then destroyed. They put the iron sheets in Elizaphan's car, then they left, saying they had just destroyed the church of the Tutsis. I was close to the church.

Elizaphan Ntakuritimana, the father of Dr Gérard Ntakuritimana, was president of the Adventists in Kibuye. Vincent Usabyimfura, the current councillor of sector Ngoma, was also hiding nearby. An Adventist, he knew Elizaphan Ntakuritimana well, which is why and his family believed they would be safe in the church of Mugonero. Instead, most of them lost their lives there on 16 April in a massacre in which Elizaphan, working closely with his son, played a central role. Vincent left at midnight and made his way to Gitwa hill.

Gitwa was close to the Adventist church of Ku Murambi. After the departure of the killers, women, children and wounded people used to go to spend the night in this church. They used to join us again on the hills at about 9:00 a.m.

Towards the end of April, very early in the

morning, I saw Elizaphan Ntakuritimana, with his car full of militiamen. He was driving. They went to the church of Ku Murambi. They killed all the wounded people, all the women and all the children who had not joined us. Afterwards, they destroyed the church and took away the iron sheets in Ntakuritimana's car.

"I strongly condemn Elizaphan Ntakuritimana. He was a pastor. Before the genocide, he taught us about loving God and loving one's neighbour. But then he participated in the genocide, becoming a real killer".

Even when the battles at Bisesero were at their most fierce, and the chances of survival looked negligible, the refugees held on because there was nowhere else to run to. By the end of April there was no safe place left for Tutsis in Kibuye. The majority of the Tutsi population in the region had been slaughtered in churches, hospitals, stadiums and commune offices where they had taken refuge, or in their homes.

April was the rainy season. It was cold and wet on the hills of Bisesero, which were often covered in fog. The refugees were hungry and they could do little to heal their festering wounds, beyond cleaning them with rainwater. Families became dispersed by fear and panic, stumbling upon each other's corpses, or finding one another under the most difficult of circumstances. Immaculée Mukamuzia said one day of fighting came to be like another, except that the number of corpses increased steadily.

At first we were able to bury our dead, but as time went on, they became more and more numerous, and eventually we had to give up. The conditions under which we lived caused us to lose count of the days and lose track of the date. At one point during the fighting, some of the assassins even began breaking our cooking pots which held what little food we had. During the following days, even if we found things to eat, we had no means of preparing our food.

As May arrived, there looked to be little prospect of survival. Uzziel lost most of his family around this time.

I cannot remember the exact dates when my mother, brothers and sisters were finally killed. In all, seven of my family were killed, and I remained with my younger brother and my father. A few days later, I discovered my other younger brother, seven at that time, who had been beaten with machetes around the head.

At night, the killers would return home, allowing the refugees a brief respite. This was the time when they would organise and lay out their plans

for the next day. This was also their only opportunity to hunt for food. Alexandre Rwihimba was fortunate to have the help of an old friend.

At around 8:00 p.m., we would return to Gisovu to look for food in the fields. I used to go to Thomas Sibomana's house to ask him for food and I used to give him money to buy beans and salt from the market. Then I would come back to collect the items of food. Sibomana was really a very good friend of mine. He told me which people had stolen my belongings.

Towards the end of April, I went to his house and talked a lot with him. He had taken part in the meetings held by the authorities and he also listened to the news on the radio. Looking for something to raise my spirits, I asked him whether he had heard if peace was on the horizon. Sibomana looked very sad and said 'Don't even think about peace. Aloys Ndimbati, the

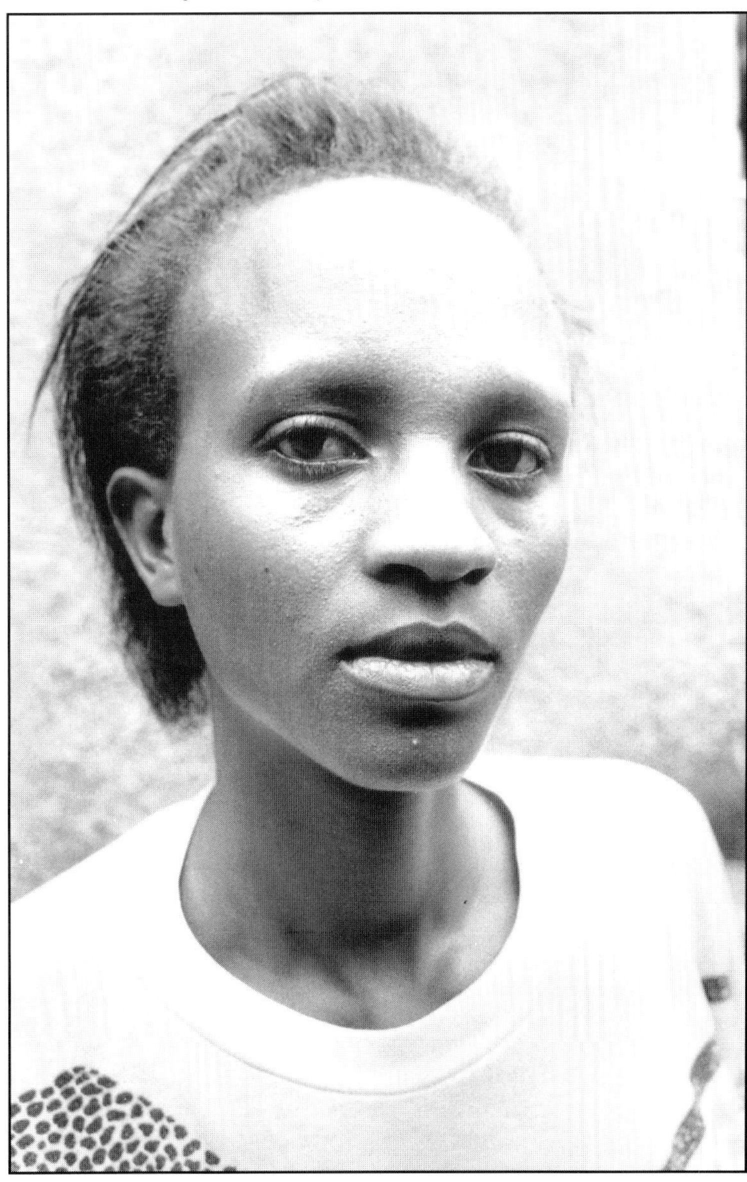

Immaculée Mukamuzia

Alexandre Rwihimba

bourgmestre of Gisovu, has given his car to Jonathan Ruremesha so that he can go and call Yusufu in Cyangugu. The object is to bring Yusufu and his militiamen to Kibuye to help exterminate the Tutsis from Bisesero who have a very strong defence. So now you see that you are going to be killed'. Faustin Mugenga, a teacher in Gisovu, confirmed this after the genocide. He said: 'If the bourgmestre had not told Ruremesha to go and call Yusufu and his militiamen from Cyangugu, not many of you would have been killed because you were very strong and the militiamen from Kibuye were worn out'.

When Sibomana had told me that, I was afraid. I went back to Bisesero. For a few days we were not the object of any attacks. Previously, we had been attacked every day.

Gaspard Gashabizi had only just arrived to join his parents and other close relatives on the hill of Kivumu in Bisesero, when a massive attack took place. Gaspard spoke of Dr Gérard Ntakuritimana's presence among the assassins. He recognised him from the 16 April massacre at the church and hospital of Mugonero; he had helped to orchestrate and implement the slaughter in his own hospital.

At about 9:00 a.m. I saw Dr Gérard in his van, with many militiamen. Dr Gérard was dressed in white trousers and a white shirt. The militiamen began to massacre the Tutsi.

Among Dr Gérard's victims were several members of Gaspard's immediate family.

Gérard had a rifle. He came to where I was with my family. He shot at us. He immediately killed my father, Anastase Mbuguje; my little sister, Colette Nyirantagorama; my older brother, Mathias Murekezi who was a shopkeeper and Dusabe, my father's other wife. I was hit by a rifle in the thigh and on my hand. After they had killed a lot of people, the militiamen returned home.

Although many lives were lost that day, the refugees put up a successful defence. When three Tutsis were killed by a grenade, the refugees retaliated, killing the lieutenant who had thrown it. Later they discovered the extent of Ruzindana's involvement in the plot to eliminate them. Uzziel described the confrontation.

A group of young men went for the lieutenant who came from Gisenyi. He had fired on them, but was unable to stop one of them from striking him on the neck with a machete. The lieutenant resisted this attack, continuing to shoot, but another threw a spear at him, causing him to weaken. A third chopped at his arm with a machete, causing him to throw down the gun. We grabbed the gun and chased after a guard from the Gisovu commune office who also had a gun. We killed the guard, taking his gun. We got the upper hand and beat off even the local hoards who had been slaying us with their machetes.

The lieutenant had a sheet of paper which he attempted to tear up before dying. We asked him what was written on the paper, and he showed us a part of it which specified the week for the annihilation of the Bisesero Tutsis. The sheet also showed the amount in francs of the reward for doing this. At the bottom of the sheet was written c/o Obed Ruzindana, but unfortunately the man who had kept this part of the sheet of paper was killed during the days that followed.

Although this paper was lost with the murder of the refugee who had taken it, many of the other refugees remember the incident. Aloys Murekezi gave the names of some of those killed.

He had killed Gérard Ruhanga, Rugombamishari's son. He had also killed Gatsimbanyi. We were so angry by this time that we pounced on our enemies and succeeded in killing the lieutenant. We first kidnapped him and took away his gun. We checked his pockets and found a piece of paper. There was a message which said that he had been assigned to kill all the Tutsis from Gishyita, Gisovu and Rwamatamu and that in return he would receive a financial reward once he had completed this task. We then killed two policemen from the commune of Gisovu, one of whom was called Sebahire and the other was called Rukazamyambi. We tore their weapons off them, two guns. The other person we managed to kill was Nsabimana, the driver of an organisation; we took his gun off him as well. He had just killed Martin Ntamakemwa, Bugingo's son.

Maurice gave details of the attack upon the lieutenant and the tactics the refugees used to survive.

Around the end of April, I began to see Obed Ruzindana. He used to come in a white van full of soldiers armed with guns. Obed had one too. Each time they attacked they would surround us and we would have to find a way to escape by breaking out of their circle. Each time we passed next to Obed, he would fire at us.

During this period, we fought against an ex-FAR lieutenant. We were surrounded in the usual way and we tried to get out of the circle. This took place in Bibande, in a banana plantation which belonged to someone called Nkiriyaho. The battle lasted a long time. There was a lieutenant with a pistol who was shooting a lot. One of our people, Ntagozera, hit him on the head. The soldier lost consciousness and immediately lost control of his bladder. His pistol fell to the ground. We thought he was dead. However, this was not the case as he managed to kick Jean Rutabana. We immediately finished him off with machetes. Nzigira, our colleague, was dealing with the other four accomplices and we eventually killed them. We found the lieutenant's identity card. He was from Gisenyi, commune Gaseke.

There were bee hives in this banana plantation. The owner was a beekeeper. We used the hives to chase away the attackers by tipping them over so that the bees would sting them.

According to Claver Mushimiyimana, the refugees had overcome their assailants once more.

Another group, of which I was a member, not only fought off the attack by a Gisovu guard, but also managed to kill the guard. Despite losing many of our own people, we won the battle that day.

But, as Jean Muragizi noted, hunger and cold had made them very weak.

The militia came every day. As the days progressed, the génocidaires killed a lot of Tutsis because they were using grenades and guns. Because of hunger, we no longer had much strength. In addition, we were trembling on account of the rain. Women, children and the old were the first to die. But we too, we killed some militia and policemen of Gisovu like Sebahire and Rukazamyambi.

According to Jean, the murder of Sebahire infuriated the Minister of Information in the interim government, Eliezer Niyitegeka, a native of Gisovu who lived close to Jean. He had come to Kibuye to lend weight to the campaign against Bisesero.

Eliezer Niyitegeka came to take revenge because Sebahire was his great friend. I used to see Niyitegeka together with Obed Ruzindana, Musema, Ndimbati, etc...

In early May, many of the refugees began to think that the fighting had come to an end. Efesto said: "We thought that peace had been re-established and we started to farm our fields and to bury the dead." Maurice had reached a similar conclusion.

We began to bury the bodies. We also started to go back to our activities as survivors, like working on the fields. We thought that the genocide was over.

Uzziel thought it may have been an offensive by the refugees which brought the conflict to a temporary halt.

The encounters with the killers resulted in a number of deaths amongst them, and so they retreated from us. We went almost a week without being attacked.

But as events were to prove, the suspension in attacks was a period of preparation, allowing the génocidaires to gather reinforcements. Their most brutal and successful massacre was yet to come.

The Onslaught of 13 May

Agnès Mukamurigo

Friday 13 May marked the beginning of the end for the refugees in Bisesero. Every survivor remembered it as the worst moment in the collective struggle; the assault that revealed the massive resources available to the génocidaires and their resolve to eliminate every Tutsi in the region. Alongside local militia, a substantial number of soldiers and Presidential Guard, there were reinforcements from some of the most experienced killers in Rwanda. Militia came from Bugarama in Cyangugu, as well as Gisenyi, Ruhengeri and Gikongoro. The leaders were all armed with guns. They included Clément Kayishema, Alfred Musema, Obed Ruzindana, Charles Sikubwabo, Aloys Ndimbati, Dr Gérard Ntakuritimana, a medical doctor in Ngoma, and John Yusufu Munyakazi, a farmer from Bugarama, Cyangugu, and an MRND stalwart.[2]

By mid-May, these men were veterans of killing operations, with extensive experience in the organisation and execution of huge massacres in which tens of thousands of Tutsis had perished—at the stadium of Gitesi, the commune office of Rwamatamu, at the Parishes of Shangi, Mibilizi, Kibuye, Ngoma, the hillside of Kizenga, and countless other killing sites.

On 13 May, the slaughter began at about 9:00 a.m. and continued until 4:00 p.m. It was relentless. Léoncie said the refugees retaliated against the gunfire of the militia, but their attempts to throw stones were futile: "The soldiers and militia were picking up the stones we were throwing and throwing them back at us. Stones and bullets were falling on us like rain. After a few minutes we saw the corpses of children, women and old people".

To distinguish themselves from the "enemy," the organisers wore white shirts, and instructed their fighters to wear leaves in their hair. Some were in some sort of military uniform, while others wore MRND shirts. The number and array of weapons available to the killers made it impossible for the refugees to mount an effective resistance. Inevitably, the assault destroyed both their capability and the confidence they needed to continue the struggle.

Jean-Damascène Nsanzimfura described the arrival of the troops of the genocide.

On 13 May, the soldiers and militiamen came in eight buses, vans and lorries that were being used for building the road between Kibuye and Gitarama, and in a lot of other vehicles owned by soldiers and the authorities. Other people came on foot, wielding machetes; they were singing and whistling and beating drums. That day, I saw the préfet of Kibuye, Clément Kayishema; Eliezer Niyitegeka, Obed Ruzindana, the bourgmestres of Gishyita and Gisovu. They all stayed at the primary school in Bisesero to watch their soldiers and militiamen killing us. Virtually all the women and children were killed that day.

Siméon emphasised that the women and children were most vulnerable. Tragically, his own family was among those killed that day.

A large number of militiamen and soldiers from Gitarama, Gisenyi and practically the whole country arrived in buses and trucks. They surrounded us and shot at us persistently. Many women and children were killed that day since many were unable to run. My wife, Marthe Nyirahategeka, and my seven children as well as my grandchildren were killed that day.

The militiamen were always dressed in white and they wore green plants on their heads. They were like madmen. That day they managed to kill many of us. The hills were covered in dead bodies.

At the end of the horrific events of that Wednesday, the list of the dead must have seemed endless. Ndayisaba also lost his entire family.

They surrounded us and then began to throw grenades at us. Then they made their advance. The soldiers shot bullets at us and the militiamen finished the Tutsi people off with machetes. They killed practically all the women and children that day. My family was also killed. They were:

My mother, Everienne Nyirabukezi;
My older brother, Francisco Ngendahimana, his wife and children;
My younger sisters, Mukamuhirwa and Mukagatares, students and Uwankwera;
My younger brothers, Cyriaque Rugwizangoga, a schoolboy, and Sibomana, a baby.

Some refugees continued to try to mount a defence. Claver Mbugufe was one of those who showed unflinching bravery.

We spent the entire day running up and down. We tried to concentrate our defence in one area in order to break their stranglehold. We did everything possible to kill any one of them who stood in our way. Sometimes, we even managed to wrest guns from soldiers and policemen. We killed many of these aggressors.

2 For further information about the leaders of the massacre, see the following publications by African Rights: *Rwanda: Death, Despair and Defiance*, August 1995; *John Yusufu Munyakazi: The Killer behind the Refugee,* Witness to Genocide, Issue 6, June 1997.

Ndayisaba, aged 34

Efesto described how he came to survive the massacre.

There was no longer any point in throwing stones now. We had to create a path amongst the militiamen so as to avoid being caught. Our men all attacked one particular group of militiamen who were consequently frightened and they opened up the path for us. We ran to hide in the bush.

Léoncie eluded the killers by using this opening. She heard sounds of the continuing violence from her hiding place in the bush.

In the bush I heard gunfire and the noise of children screaming as they were being killed. I also heard militia passing by the bush where I was hiding. They were saying: 'Yusufu really helped us a lot. Thanks to his militia we've been able to exterminate a large number of Tutsis'. Another militiaman said: 'I can see that we've still got bullets left in our guns. Did you know that Yusufu and Obed said that we were not allowed to return with any bullets left? They'll tell us off and say that we haven't done anything even though we've killed a lot of people. We have to fire into the air and bushes and finish off the bullets so that those two don't give us a hard time'. After giving this advice, the militia fired lots of bullets, even into the bush where I was hiding, but I didn't come out as I knew what their objective was.

These militia were wearing red and white clothes. They also had grass on their heads. Some of them were speaking the Igikiea dialect spoken by people from the region in the north of the country.

Edson Turikunkiko was hiding in the bush when he overheard the attackers.

I heard them say that the soldiers had come from different préfectures and that they knew how to 'work', meaning kill the Tutsis.

They launched attacks on the outskirts so that we became completely surrounded. One massacre, 13 May, was particularly violent; many women and children were killed. The people who managed to survive were those who could run. We sought refuge in the bush; but the killers still continued to hunt us down.

Ndayisaba managed to escape.

That day, 13 May, we were unable to defend ourselves. There were too many militiamen who were heavily armed. Everyone had to look for a way to escape. I ran away from the militiamen who were behind me. Unfortunately, I ran up to where the bourgmestre, Charles Sikubwabo, and Obed Ruzindana were, together with other important militiamen. They were shouting to the other militiamen to kill more people. They were wearing white clothes. When they saw me running up, they told them to kill me. Sikubwabo was carrying a gun in his hand. He shot me in the right shoulder. I carried on running although I was bleeding profusely. I hid in the bush.

During the day I would hide in the bush and at night, I would leave to go and look for grass to help heal my wound. I remained where I was with no food to eat.

"All I could see were corpses and wounded people".

Innocent said that, faced with the might of the militia surrounding them, the refugees reached a collective decision to run.

On 13 May, we were unable to retaliate. We gathered together at Muyira. We decided that our

Edson Turikunkiko, a 22-year-old farmer from sector Bisesero in Gishyita

tactic would be to run and hide in the bush. I fled towards a bush. That evening, I felt ill and I hid in a tree. Three groups of attackers passed right next to the tree without seeing me. It was only when the fourth group passed by that they found me. They told me to get down but I refused. I was hit on the head and shoulder with a stone so I got down and ran into the forest. They couldn't find me. My father and brothers were dead by this time.

Vianney Uwimana's testimony illustrates the organised nature of the massacre.

On 13 May, at about 9:00 a.m., we were all gathered on Muyira. We saw a large number of militiamen and soldiers coming in buses and trucks. As soon as they got out of their vehicles, they proceeded to attack us. They whole of the surrounding population came along, armed with all sorts of weapons such as guns, large bamboo sticks, machetes, swords etc. We did not recognise them. The militiamen who attacked us before 13 May were our neighbours.

I was with a boy called Simon who came from the commune of Rwamatamu. He had come to Bisesero to escape the massacres of Kizenga. When he saw how the militiamen were killing the Tutsis, he told me that they were Yusufu's militiamen because they had done exactly the same thing in Kizenga. They cut their heads or feet and hands.

There were too many heavily-armed militiamen and we had nothing to repulse the attacks with. Our spears and stones had no effect, so each person just had to find a way to escape.

A group of Abasesero gathered together and tried to find a weak side in the militiamen. They broke through to get to a path which was an escape route to the bushes. This is how I managed to escape. However, all the women, girls and children were killed. I could see corpses everywhere on the hills. That evening we all met up, but none of us could speak. We were extremely sad.

The accounts of the massacre of 13 May are agonising. The refugees had sustained themselves over the period of a month in the face of hardship, loss and constant conflict, only to be massacred in their tens of thousands in the most brutal ways possible. Augustin described how the events of 13 May left him bereft of his wife and children.

On 13 May, I was in Kazirandimwe with my wife, children and mother, Adèle Nyiramahe. We had been hanging around there because the militiamen had not come for a few days. We therefore thought that the militiamen had stopped the attacks.

At about 9:00 a.m., I saw the Tutsis who were at the primary school of Gitwa, running. I also heard gunfire. The militiamen had surrounded us and they were shouting a lot. They had arrived in a great number of cars. We trembled when we saw all this. I went behind my family and together we ran to Muyira. My wife could not run because she was pregnant and my children were small. Due to the bullets that were coming from all directions, we dispersed. As I was running, I fell in a ditch and above me was a big rock. I stayed there, trembling with fear. I could hear people crying as they died.

In the evening, when the militiamen had gone, I left the ditch. I couldn't find the way because there were bodies everywhere. The militiamen had killed that day in a very unusual way. They either cut off someone's head or their feet and hands. After having taken off their clothes, they would then abandon them. Women and girls were killed in a barbaric way. The killers stabbed their vaginas with sharpened bamboo sticks. That day, more than 20,000 people were killed.

Before 13 May, when the militiamen hit someone with a machete they did it without aiming anywhere particular. When the militiamen killed a woman or girl, they did not stab them in the vagina with a bamboo stick.

On 13 May, I looked tirelessly for the bodies of my people.

The refugees would die in mounting numbers as the catastrophe unfolded. Elizaphan Ndayisaba was twelve; he discovered that Muyira had become a graveyard, and that the bodies included those of his immediate family.

The little children started to cry. My mother put Nyirakanyana on her back and my older brother did the same with Mbonimpaye. We then ran in different directions. Many people were killed that day. When the militiamen had gone home, someone came to tell me that my whole family had been killed. When I heard this, I went to every hill to try and find the bodies of my family. I went everywhere. I saw people who had been hit by machetes, talking to each other. One person was saying to another: 'Are you dead yet?'

I carried on looking until I came across my mother's body and my little sister who was on her back. They were both dead. My older brother was next to my mother and on his back was Mbonimaye. My older brother was still breathing but the child on his back was dead. The dogs were coming to eat the corpses.

"I watched how my mother, who had nursed me, was going to be eaten by the dogs. I felt sad. She was lying there without any clothes on".

I went to look for my paternal uncle, Zacharie Hategeka, to help bury my mother. We went to look for some small hoes to dig the grave. Some people had brought their hoes with them when they had left their homes.

We could only dig a small grave. We hardly had any strength left because we had spent many days running and had had no food. We then buried her. Ndagijumana, my older brother, was still alive so we left him. Eventually he died too but I did not bury him.

The militiamen carried on killing. I ran and hid in the bush. All my clothes were torn. I could no longer wash and my skin was like an animal's.

Emmanuel Gahigiro, a 33-year-old farmer from sector Bisesero in Gishyita

Emmanuel Gahigiro spoke of the total devastation left behind by the génocidaires.

Many women and children died that day. My wife, Mukamuhizi and one of my two children died on 13 May.

All the hills were covered in bodies. I ran to escape and I hid in a bush. As I was running that day, I saw Obed Ruzindana, the préfet Kayishema, Ndimbati and Sikubwabo, the bourgmestres from the communes of Gisovu and Gishyita. I had known all of them before the genocide. I didn't have a chance to see many other people because I was running.

From that day on, there was no reprieve. We were attacked every single day. We spent the nights in the bushes next to corpses and we ate nothing.

Narcisse's wife and mother were killed on 13 May and he was badly wounded. He searched, in vain, for the remains of his family.

"The entire hill was strewn with naked corpses."

When the genocidal criminals had gone, I started to look amongst the bodies in the belief that I would be able to recognise my family. However, it was impossible because of all the blood covering the bodies. I stayed in the bush alone. There was nothing but corpses surrounding me and there was a terrible odour. Dogs, crows and insects came to devour the decomposing bodies.

I realised that I was going to die, so I went to a Hutu friend's house. His name was Zéphanie Munyakayanza and he was from Muyira. He welcomed me into his home and made me some food to eat. He heated up some water so that he could treat my wounds. I realised that I could create a lot of problems for him because they were already starting to search the Hutu houses. I chose to go back to the same bush and stay there. The militiamen were combing [the bushes] constantly but God kept me from their grasp.

Eric lost his mother on 13 May.

Because of our resistance, the génocidaires organised a terrible massacre on 13 May. That day, I saw many buses which were transporting the militia and the soldiers, as well as the lorries of the Gisovu tea factory. Many people with machetes also came on foot. They encircled us on the hill of Muyira. Grenades and bullets fell on us like rainfall. My mother, Yurida Nyiranshongore, was killed when she was in the midst of handing stones to me for our defence. Many women and children were killed because they were unable to run. That day, we realised that it was impossible to resist and each person looked for a way to flee.

After the killers had left, the survivors' first thoughts were for their loved ones, the living as well as the dead. Eric looked for his mother's corpse.

She was with many other corpses. As it was impossible to bury each person, we put them into a communal grave. Other corpses were left exposed on the hills.

Sylvère Gatwaza pointed out that the refugees were already exhausted and hungry, when the killers took their cows and their food supplies.

The militiamen had gathered all our crops from our fields. They had also broken our utensils which we needed for cooking. That day, they managed to separate us in such a way that it made it easier for them to kill us. The hills were covered with bodies. From that moment onwards, I decided to hide in the bush. All my brothers and sisters were dead.

I stayed in hiding until the French soldiers arrived.

Having lost most of his relatives on Kivumu hill, Gaspard asked another refugee to help him reach Muyira hill, where his wife and children had gone. They went there at night. The killings in Kivumu had been led by Dr Gérard. For the second time, Dr Gérard was involved in murdering members of Gaspard's family.

On 13 May, Dr Gérard came back. He was with Obed Ruzindana and Yusufu. They killed using rifles, grenades and machetes. My wife, Marcianne Nteziryayo, was killed with a machete, while my child, Pascal Mutuyeyezu, one year old, was killed on his mother's back.

I was in a bush; fifteen militiamen with rifles came. I had a sword in my hand. A militiaman approached me; straightaway I cut off his ear with my sword swinging around in all directions. The militiamen said that they would come back and kill me another day.

Alexandre said he was on a nearby hill and witnessed how the Tutsis on Muyira hill were wiped out. He described how the group of refugees he was with also died under a cascade of grenades and machete blows which lasted for six hours. He managed to hide in the bush, only coming out to bury the dead. The cruelty of the killers was imprinted on the bodies of their victims.

In the evening, all the survivors of this massacre gathered together; we went round to look at all the bodies that were lying around. We began to put them in a large pit which was already there. This pit had been dug to make bricks for the construction of a primary school in Bisesero.

We wept as we collected the corpses. Some of them were women who had died with their children on their backs. With some we only saw their head or legs. Some of the dead no longer had any eyes. We suffered as we put the bodies into the pit; whilst the militia were drinking, singing and eating our provisions which they had stolen from our houses.

When we had finished putting all the bodies into the grave, we put earth over the top. We realised that we would not survive if we stayed in Bisesero. So a few others and I decided to leave for Burundi. We went to the fields to look for provisions and we found maniocs and bananas. I took my spear and a young boy who I was with took a gun that we had taken from a militiaman. The gun only had five bullets in it. Twenty-nine of us left, each holding a machete or a spear. Some girls and children accompanied us too. I was also with my younger brother who had just finished the Grand Seminary.

Like many others who sought to leave Bisesero, Alexandre was forced to return, six days later, in the recognition that there was no way out of Kibuye. According to Eric, who was also one of the group of refugees who tried to escape to Burundi, 25 of them were killed at a roadblock in the forest of Nyungwe. When they returned to Bisesero, they found that the situation had become even worse.

Many people had now died in Bisesero. We could see bodies everywhere. All the survivors gathered together on just one hill. At night I went back to Gisovu to fetch some food. One time I lay down in the bush, just behind a military roadblock, so that I could follow their conversation. They were saying 'Yusufu's militia have killed a lot of people in Bisesero'. Others added 'they also ate a lot of meat in Mugonero. Any Hutu from Kibuye who finds a cow must give it to Yusufu's militiamen as a reward'. I went back to Bisesero so that the militiamen would not find me.

Nathan Gatashya had come to Bisesero following a massacre at Mugonero hospital on 16 April. His family had survived Mugonero, only to be killed at Bisesero on 13 May.

My beautiful wife, Erina Nyirahabimana, died, like the rest of my family: my brothers and sisters, my cousins, aunts and uncles...etc. I did not have any children.

We tried to defend ourselves, using spears, stones and swords. The mountain was covered with dead bodies. I was in a hole. Dr Gérard used to come back with these militia; and sometimes he cut off the arms and legs of the Tutsis, and then left.

An injury to his back while he was running away, saved Chadrac from certain death. After the massacre the survivors tended each others' wounds.

I lay still where I had fallen and nobody found me. In the evening, I went to look for the others who had survived. I found them in a house which had been destroyed and which had no roof. We spent the night there. Those who were still in good health looked after me by using traditional medicines and warm water. They did the same for those who were wounded. We collected water in broken jugs.

Mukahigiro and her children were one of the earliest arrivals at Muyira.

Despite the fact that life was hard, we bore our sufferance and did not lose our will to live.

The events of 13 May tested Mukahigiro's stamina to breaking point.

On 13 May, many soldiers and militiamen arrived. They surrounded us and began a large-scale massacre. Many women and children died that day. I hid in a bush; fortunately I managed to escape death. I saw how the militiamen had killed the people, so I took my two children and went to the edge of Lake Kivu to kill myself.

Before she acted on her impulse, Mukahigiro spotted two men who had found a boat to take them to Idjwi Island, and joined them.

Bernard Kayumba found it difficult to describe the sheer scale of the assault.

The single largest massacre took place on 13 May. It really was massive. It seemed as if the whole of the surrounding population, from a large number of communes, had come to kill us. They had even come from Cyangugu and Gisenyi. There were a lot of buses and other types of vehicles which had brought the interahamwe. The cars of the Gisovu tea factory were also there. They shot and shot at us. We scattered in all directions. Many people died. It was no longer possible to keep up our resistance.

"Dr Gérard was telling these génocidaires to kill everybody—the children, the young people, the old and not to have pity for the pregnant women".

The killers began to lob grenades at us; others used machetes. That day, everyone in my family was killed. The hill was full of corpses.

Bernard was fortunate in finding a bush where he could hide. From there, he watched Musema decide the fate of a pregnant woman.

On the 13th, I saw Musema take Gorette Mukangoga; she was pregnant. Musema cut her open with a sword, saying that he wanted 'to see the stomach of a Tutsi woman'. He was cold-blooded about the whole thing. It was appaling. I saw what he was doing quite clearly; I was hiding close to where Musema had parked his red car. I continued to see him in Bisesero after that, always shooting at us.

Thirteen-year-old Jeanne d'Arc Rwabirembo, from sector Musenyi in Gishyita, was also at Muyira on 13 May.

I saw Dr Gérard, Charles Sikubwabo, the

bourgmestre of Gishyita and Obed Ruzindana. Their cars were transporting soldiers and militiamen. The militia had put white bands and leaves on their heads. Dr Gérard was dressed in white shorts and a white shirt. He had a loudspeaker in his hands.

Elizaphan Ntakuritimana, the father of Dr Gérard and the president of Seventh Day Adventists in Kibuye, made his contribution to the success of the genocide in Bisesero. After his wife, three young children, parents, brother and three sisters died in Mugonero on 16 April, Edison Kayihura, a farmer and Adventist who knew and had worked for Elizaphan, joined the refugees in Bisesero, on Muyira hill.

The militiamen came every day. Elizaphan Ntakuritimana also came to kill us at Bisesero. I saw him on 13 May together with his son, Gérard. Elizaphan came in his car, a white Hilux, while Gérard was in the car that belonged to Mugonero hospital. I passed Elizaphan while running. He had a gun. Obed Ruzindana and the préfet, Kayishema, were all there on the 13th. That day, they killed a lot of Tutsis, especially women and children. These génocidaires put leaves on their head. They came back on the 14th to comb the area. I hid in a bush and by chance escaped.

Saying the refugees had decided to "die fighting", Vincent Usabyimfura, the current councillor of sector Ngoma, described how the well-planned massacre of 13 May crippled the refugees' chances of resistance and survival.

A lot of militiamen came on 13 May, with many cars. They killed a huge number of people. Self-defence was impossible. Everywhere, there were corpses; everyone looked for a hideout.

One of the many people who could not find a hiding place and who died is Vincent's father, Athanase Mushimiyimana.

The many parents who lost their children on 13 May live with terrible memories of their childrens' last moments at Bisesero, the violent separation and their inability to save their children from a horrific death. Agnès Mukamurigo and her husband, Michel Serumondo, who also escaped, lost six of their seven children that day.

There were not more than forty women survivors after this massacre. Many women and children fell prey to the attack because they could not run as fast as the men. The killers would pounce on the women and children when they got tired and would kill them with a machete.

I was with my seven children during the massacre but six of them died as a result of it. Three of my children died on the spot. The other two died the next day. The one that I was carrying on my back was hit by machetes on the 13th and died three days later. Only one of my children, Adrien Harelimana, is left. He is sixteen years old and is disabled. Even though some women had the strength to save themselves, many of them were killed because they didn't want to leave their children, who were crying after them. When my children died, I ran with the men. I carried on hiding and did not lose courage.

Bernard Kayumba arrived in Bisesero after escaping the 15 April massacre at the Parish of Mubuga.

Anastase Gasagara and his wife, Emerithe Mukansamaza, had six children. All of them were killed on 13 May.

My children were with me at the time. I began to run. But then I heard my children saying, tearfully: 'Papa, Papa, are you going to abandon us?' I went back to them. I put the two little ones on my back and shoulders. The others stayed on the ground. They were able to run on their own; nevertheless they were killed by the militiamen.

"What haunts me is that my children might have died thinking that I had abandoned them. But I just didn't have any way of hiding them. All six of my children were killed."

When the militiamen had gone home, Anastase discovered his wife.

She was lying on the ground; she had been cut by machetes. Her clothes had been taken off her. She looked at me as if to say goodbye. I began to cry. I went to get some leaves from the trees to place on her body because she was completely naked. I went to fetch her some water to drink. It was all dirty; but we didn't have anything to draw the water out of the well with. I had to use leaves from trees to give her the water; the alternative was to use objects that the militiamen had broken and left behind. She managed to regain a bit of strength from the water that I gave her, although she had lost a lot of blood.

Since the militiamen were launching attacks everyday, they once again hit her with a machete but she didn't die. Instead she carried on suffering. When the militiamen hit her with their machetes for a third time, she died.

Catherine spent the days after the massacre searching for the corpses of her daughters.

We felt totally demoralised, so much so that each person just looked for a way to save himself. That day the elderly, the women and the children were killed, unable to run for their lives. We could see bodies on the hills. There were people who were almost dead and babies feeding from the breasts of their dead mothers. My son, my daughter's child and myself went to hide in the bush. Each evening we came together as usual, to see if we were still all alive. That day we waited in vain for my daughters; my son helped me search for them among the corpses, to check whether they were dead.

Two days after their death, we found them in a place called Runyangingo. We didn't have any hoes to dig a grave, so we just put them on the grass. Then we returned to the bush.

Following the massacre, the hills of Bisesero were almost deserted. Some of the survivors gathered at Gaheno; Léoncie among them. Together they wept many tears of mourning for an entire community of people; the corpses of their friends and families lay beside them, now too numerous to bury. The will to survive which had driven the refugees' struggle for over a month, was all but destroyed in the massacre of 13 May.

That evening the militia went home. I heard the voice of someone who was very sad, saying: 'All of you who are still alive, come out of your hiding places. The militia have left'. I came out and went to Gaheno, the place where all the survivors were grouping together. I had to jump over lots of corpses.

When I got there I saw many wounded people who were asking us for water, and children who were crying beside their dead mothers. We spent the night crying.

The survivors dispersed looking for hiding places; Nasson Ngoga was among them.

The remaining survivors fled towards the forest and to the bush. During the days which followed, the interahamwe and locals tried to find us in the forest to kill us. Sometimes, when there were only a few attackers, we defended ourselves and managed to force them to retreat. This went on until the end of June.

As many as 20,000-25,000 people are estimated to have been killed on 13 May. The hills of Bisesero were covered with their naked and mutilated bodies. The testimonies of survivors deliver a vision of hell on earth; they must have felt that nothing could equal the suffering which this day had brought. But even as they searched for the bodies of their loved ones, and began to absorb the extent of the human catastrophe, the killers were preparing to return.

Despair and Danger 14 May

The génocidaires allowed the survivors no respite, launching an attack almost as soon as it was light. Although the assault of 14 May is said to have been as cruel as the preceding one, with a large number of dead, the survivors mostly remembered the day as the one on which they found the corpses of their loved ones. It is impossible to imagine how they must have felt as they stumbled over the remains of their families, some of them virtually unrecognisable, their bodies a testament to the anguish they had endured. Their memories of this day evoke an overwhelming sense of sorrow.

Early on the morning of 14 May, Augustin was searching the hills for the bodies of his wife and children and helping to draw together the remaining survivors, when the killers arrived.

We were rounding up the children who were crying next to the bodies of their mothers, when we noticed that the militiamen were coming back. We left the children and ran. I remember one woman, the wife of someone called Ignace, Berchimas Mbayi's son. She was suffering a lot because her feet had been cut.

At that point I ran and hid in my father's banana plantation which was close to the road in Nyarutovu cellule. The militiamen continued to massacre all the Tutsis who had escaped the day before. In the evening they went home, either in cars or on foot, taking with them our cows they had taken from Bisesero.

As the militiamen were leading the cows away, I heard them saying 'Yusufu's militiamen have taken a lot of cows compared to us'. The others replied 'If they've taken a lot of cows, that's because they deserve it. If they hadn't come to help us how would we have exterminated the Tutsis who were there? They have taught us a lot about how to kill the Tutsis'.

As they were talking and discussing, they suddenly saw a large bush which was next to me. They said 'Are there any Tutsis hidden here?' They searched the bush and found two Tutsis hiding there. One of them was Gakwandi from the cellule of Karama, sector Musenyi. They were seriously beaten and then they were forced to move the cows along with clubs. These Tutsis never came back.

That night and every night which followed it, for many days, Augustin continued the search for his family. Nothing could have prepared him for what he would find.

I wanted to bury them because the dogs and crows had already started devouring the corpses. I hid by day, and looked by night. The fourth night I came across my daughter's dress. I began to look at the other bodies nearby. I saw a woman with no feet. Her head was torn away from her body and she was lying with her child who was also dead. I looked closely and I realised that it was my wife. I looked at her legs. The child still had its clothes on and I recognised it. I immediately went to fetch my late wife's uncle so that he could help me with the burial. Together, we put a bit of earth on top of the bodies. We had no more energy left to dig a grave.

Augustin Ndahimana Buranga aged 41, from Bisesero in Gishyita

Efesto also searched long and hard, but he never found the bodies of his children.

On 14 May, they came back to comb through everything.

"We could no longer see any grass. Instead, we saw corpses".

Efesto Habiyambere

There were women with children on their backs who were dead. The killers had undressed the bodies. It was a terrible sight.

As I was walking at night, I fell over my mother's body. I asked the survivors to help me bury her. I don't know where the bodies of my children and the other members of my family are exposed.

The refugees knew they could not bury all the victims. But they were determined to do what they could. Léoncie described the fate of those who ventured out early on the morning of the 14th.

A group went to bury some of the people. As they were digging the graves, the militia encircled them and killed them immediately.

From that time on, we lost any hope of living. Whenever we saw a person, people would say: 'He's going to kill us.' I tried to encourage the people I saw by advising them to carry on fighting until the arrival of the RPF soldiers. The militia still kept coming to finish off their work. Birara, who died towards the end of the genocide in Bisesero, gathered people together and made them carrying on fighting.

Vianney found the bodies of his family. He began to bury them, but was unable to continue what he had started.

On 14 May, the same militiamen returned. We were in the process of looking around for a way to bury the old people, when I caught sight of them. I ran and hid in a bush again. As I was running, I heard orders which said 'You, Yusufu's interahamwe, this way. Ruzindana's interahamwe, go that way. Musema's interahamwe, go that way'. I could hear victims crying. They were mostly children.

The killers left in the evening. I went in search of my family members. I had been told that they were dead. I carried on looking and on the 15th, I saw their bodies. They were piled up in the Runyangingo stream. My mother, Cécile Mukamuhinde, my father, Patrice Rwabukwisi, my sisters—Xavérine Murekatete, Anisie Mukamurenzi and Mukamutesi—were all dead. My three nephews were also there.

I started to take them out of the stream. I took my mother out first. She was naked. I put her body at the side of the stream. Then I took my sister out. When I saw what a state their bodies were in, I panicked. I ran and left them there. I had wanted to take them out of the stream to bury them so that the dogs would not eat them. Unfortunately this is precisely what happened.

According to Maurice Sakufi, the wives of militiamen had stolen the clothes from the bodies of the dead.

At night we looked for water to drink and went through the fields to look for potatoes or bananas. However, the wives of the militiamen, who came with their husbands at the time of the attacks, had already gathered all the food. The role of these women was to gather crops from the fields and to take the clothes off the dead bodies.

The killings continued and the number of corpses increased. The assailants of 14 May also included militia from different communes. Jean-Damascène described how they identified themselves.

14 May was a Saturday and the soldiers, militiamen and their leaders came back to hunt us down.

The militia donned a kind of uniform. They wore short-sleeved shirts and put leaves in their hair: the Gisovu militiamen wore tea leaves in their hair, the Gishyita militiamen wore banana leaves and the Mugonero militia wore pea leaves so they could recognise each other.

Aloys Murekezi escaped the massacre, but was pursued by determined interahamwe.

The day after the massacre of 13 May, there was another attack. We fled towards Gitesi, battling against the interahamwe who kept on stopping us. I was hit on the arm with a stone. We did not return to Muyira because the whole hill was covered with corpses. Interahamwe vehicles followed us all the way to Gitesi, near Karongi, and they shot at us. They made us go back to Bisesero. There were very few survivors from this massacre. All the women, children, young girls and old people died as a result of this massacre. We carried on running like this until the end of June.

One of the men who returned on the 14th to supervise the clean-up was Elizaphan Ntakuritimana. Vincent Usabyimfura, an Adventist, recognised his car.

I saw Elizaphan Ntakuritimana's car, a white Hilux. These two days, 13 and 14 May, they killed in a special manner. They cut off the legs and the arms and then left the victims. Before, when they hit with machetes, they did not aim at a specific part of the body. The crows and dogs came to devour the corpses.

Aware of the determination of the killers, Eric remained in his hideout in the bush.

The génocidaires came back on the 14th to undertake a combing operation. From that moment, I stayed in the bush. I no longer moved. I ate the grass.

Nteziryayo witnessed the murder of his mother. He doesn't know what date it was, but he remembers it happened following a large scale massacre. It seems likely it was around this time.

The militiamen came shooting as usual. I ran with my mother. She was very tired but she carried on running. One militiaman tried to shoot us and she was hit by the bullets. She fell down straight away. The militiaman approached her and finished her off by hitting her with a machete. I hid in the bush and watched. She was hit on the head and the legs. A lot of blood was flowing from her body. After my mother's death, I wanted them to kill me. But I managed to keep on hiding.

For the whole of the genocide, I lived in the bush. We shivered in the rain and no-one took pity on me. I couldn't sleep and we couldn't wash either. My clothes were in shreds. I was lucky not to be killed by the genocidal killers for so many were already dead. All the hills in Bisesero were covered with bodies.

The Relentless Slaughter

For the rest of May the refugees suffered attack upon attack, with many of the most important killers returning at intervals to assess whether the militia were completing the task they had been set. Survivors remembered massacres on 20, 21, 25, 30 May. They also spoke of the loss of their families, attempts to bury them, hunger, thirst, heavy rainfall, cold weather, fear and a general sense of despair. While the interahamwe had been promised rewards for eliminating all the refugees at Bisesero, the refugees had no such incentive to keep up their resistance. It increasingly looked as if death was inevitable and the regular and ferocious massacres which continued throughout May and June were confirmation that the battle would be in vain.

It was left to the leaders of the refugees to encourage the rest to fight back, but they were equally vulnerable, as Efesto explained.

The militiamen continued to come, although there were not as many of them as there were during the attack of 13 May. Despite there being only a small group of us left, now that practically all the people were dead, we carried on fighting. Nzigira gave us much courage but unfortunately he was killed.

Nzigira and I were together the day he was killed. The militiamen were throwing stones and saying 'These are the people who are preventing us from receiving our reward from Obed Ruzindana. We have to find a way to kill them'. Nzigira was then hit on the foot with a stone. He began to limp. I helped him withdraw because I could see that it was impossible to carry on the fight. As we were walking back, a soldier saw us and shot at us. Nzigira was hit and he fell. The militiamen came to finish him off with a machete. I was shot in the knee but I was still able to walk. I went and hid in a bush. The militiamen who saw me going into the bush set light to it to kill me. I escaped from the smoke and went to hide elsewhere.

I remained in Bisesero, with all the bodies around me. I couldn't find anything to eat or drink. I was very thin and my hair was dirty. My skin was all scaly because I hadn't been able to wash myself for two months.

Some of the refugees had given up all hope of survival towards the end of May. For them, Maurice said, the only remaining concern was to make sure that their death was quick.

Anastase Gasagara

Around 20 May, militiamen came in Toyota vans. We were exhausted by this time and we had no energy left to run. The people who were caught were hit with machetes by the militiamen. We decided to run over to where the leaders of the militiamen were, the place called Ku Nama, so that we would be shot rather than be killed by a machete.

That day all of us ran towards Ku Nama. The militiamen increased their fire because they realised that we wanted to attack their leaders. About eighty people died instantly. I ran with my machete in my hand until I got to Ku Nama. I saw Yusufu, carrying a gun, in the shooting position. He was wearing a hat that Muslims wear and a boubou. He was standing in front of a yellow truck and beside him were other militiamen including Obed and Mika.

Just at that point, I heard Birara's voice telling us to retreat. He saw that many of us were being killed. I retreated and hid in the bush. I was very fortunate not to die that day because I had been surrounded by bullets.

Vianney's hideout was discovered on 21 May.

Vianney Uwimana

I ran and the militiamen shot me in the right foot. I ran a long way and managed to hide in another

bush. The militiamen were afraid to come in and so they set fire to the bush. I was lucky, because the fire did not reach where I was. I could not walk so I stayed in the bush for a long time. During the day I saw the militiamen coming to kill us. I had put a lot of grass on me as camouflage. At night, the dogs fought with each other when they came to eat the corpses. I stayed where I was without any medical care and without eating. I was afraid of being killed.

Elizaphan Kajuga lost his wife, Adèle Mukangakwaya, and his two children—a baby and Gaspard Nsengimana, a fourth year pupil at primary school—during the killings around the middle of May.

It was on a Saturday at around 9:00 a.m. They parked their vehicles at a place called Ku Nama. Afterwards they surrounded us and began to throw grenades at us. They were also shooting their guns and fighting with their machetes. They neutralised us, so much so that we could no longer put up a resistance.

Each person looked for a way to escape. The women and children, who no longer had the strength to run, were killed instantly. All the hills of Bisesero were strewn with bodies.

Elizaphan spent the days that followed running and hiding in the bush.

Everyday the militiamen came. My clothes were torn and my feet were swollen. I had nothing to eat. In the evening, when the militiamen went back home, I would go along the hills looking for water from the streams.

"All the streams of Bisesero were filled with bodies. The water had become red. I became used to seeing bodies the whole time so I no longer felt sick."

I drank the water despite the fact that I saw the bodies of my own family members in the water. I couldn't do anything about it. There were only a few of us still alive. Many of us were ill and had been hit by machetes. Despite all the problems we had, the people, who still had some strength left, continued to fight. As we were fighting, we thought that the RPF soldiers would eventually arrive to free us.

Daphrose, fourteen, had hoped to find a sanctuary in Bisesero.

I was happy when we got to Bisesero; I thought that we had arrived somewhere safe. However, it was quite the contrary to what I had thought. Every single day the militia attacked us. They were heavily armed. The Tutsis gathered on one hill and looked for stones and clubs.

The militia had leaves on their heads and were dressed in white. They would attack us at about 9:00 a.m. and go home at around 4:30 p.m. The first militiamen would arrive, shooting their guns and the Abasesero would go amongst them with their clubs and fight. The women and children would carry stones and the others would hide in the bushes. The children were crying, calling out for their mothers. If a militiaman came up to a child, he would kill him immediately with a sword or machete. The militiamen gathered all the provisions and took away the cows. We couldn't find anything to eat on the hill. The water from the streams of Bisesero had turned red from the blood of the bodies. It was therefore impossible to find any water to drink.

When the militiamen left, I wandered around the whole hill, looking at the corpses, but there were too many to bury. I saw dead women with their children on their backs who were also dead. The bodies were bloated. The rain fell on us all and dogs came to eat the corpses. We really tried to overcome all the problems which stood in our way. My brother, Niyitegeka, was killed but I didn't manage to find his body.

"Given the situation which confronted us in Bisesero, it would have been an option to gather together and ask the militia to come and kill us to end our suffering. However, we decided to carry on fighting until the end".

Obed Ruzindana remained a key figure among the attackers. His determination to ensure that every single refugee was killed was such that he tried to trap them with lies; Jean-Damascène gave an example.

They continued to hunt us down. When the militia realised they could not kill us all, councillor Mika of Gishyita sector; the bourgmestre of Gishyita, Charles Sikubwabo; Obed Ruzindana and a police officer came. They came in a khaki Hilux driven by the bourgmestre. When they got close to us, they stopped and we immediately ran. Obed called somebody by the name of Rusanganwa; I was hiding close by. Rusanganwa went up to him, because he could see they had not come as militiamen.

Obed said to him: 'Do you know who I am?' Rusanganwa answered that he knew very well who he was, that he was Obed Ruzindana. He said he was not Ruzindana, that he was from Kigali and had come to guarantee the safety of the Tutsis who had fled to Bisesero. Then he asked Rusanganwa how many of us were left.

Obed sent Rusanganwa to tell the rest of us that the war was over and that we should go to the primary school in Bisesero, where we would be given clothes, food and medical treatment and where we would be safe. Then they left. After they had gone, we went up to Rusanganwa to ask him what Obed had said. He told us what I have just told you.

We decided not to go to the school, but we sent two of our wounded to test the situation.

The following day their suspicions were confirmed. Ruzindana returned with lorries, but they were filled with soldiers, not supplies. They began by killing the two injured people who had been sent to the school, before they turned their firepower on the refugees. Among the many occasions in which Ruzindana participated in the campaigns in Bisesero, Jean-Damascène remembered this as one of the most vicious.

Jean Munyangeyo also remembered the constant presence of Ruzindana at Bisesero, including the visit disguised as a humanitarian initiative.

One day, Ruzindana came with his interahamwe militiamen. He sent us a message, saying that he was bringing medicine for the wounded. He wanted to assemble us together in order to kill all of us. We did not, however, respond to his invitation because we had discovered his objective.

Claver Mushimiyimana said that the refugees were prepared for the battle.

Our representative told us everything that was said, causing us to get ourselves organised for what we suspected was to come. Both lorries and ONATRACOM buses [public buses] came, but the lorries were filled with soldiers armed with guns and grenades.

By this time, the deteriorating mental and physical state of most of the refugees meant that they were fighting almost out of instinct and fear, regardless of what they could hope to achieve.

The militia attacked us virtually every day, but they had become discouraged because the food they had stolen from Tutsi homes had run out. Those of us who remained were like animals. We had already killed some policemen and militia, as well as an army officer, so the militiamen who were attacking us were afraid.

To give these murderers an incentive, Obed paid them to kill us.

Ruzindana continued to orchestrate the violence throughout May, according to Alexandre.

There was another day, a Wednesday morning at the end of May [the 25th], when an attack was launched by Obed Ruzindana, whom I knew because he frequently came to Gisovu, and Dan Ngerageze [assistant bourgmestre of Gishyita] with about 500 militiamen. We were not afraid in the face of this attack because there were very few of them in relation to other attacks.

My older brother, Ignace Kayinamura, went to hide with his three children in the bush. The bush was near the road. When the militiamen came, they searched through the bush. They discovered

Jean Munyangeyo

my brother and took him and his three children to Obed and Dan. I could see them because I was near them.

A refugee called Assiel Kabanda fled near where Obed was. He heard Obed telling his militiamen not to kill Ignace but to drive him to Mugonero market to torture him. Dan said that it would be better to kill him straight away. He was killed together with his children. When the killers had left, Assiel buried their bodies. He told me about this before his own death.

Obed Ruzindana's father, Elie Murakaza, also played an important role in the killings. Murakaza, a former bourgmestre of Gisovu, was also a businessman. He was a regular visitor to Bisesero, coming in his black Mercedes Benz. Because of a car accident, he was on crutches. But that did not dampen his enthusiasm for encouraging and giving advice to his son's militia. He also gave them orders—to drive the cows they stole from dead and dying Tutsis for sale at the market of Mugonero. Jean-Damascène summed up the importance of this father and son team.

When I was a child, the people of my region talked a lot about Obed Ruzindana and his father, Murakaza, because they were big businessmen in the region. They owned lorries that transported tea from Gisovu to Kigali. As a result, I have seen Ruzindana around ever since I was a child.

Just as Obed and his father were the first in our region to become rich, so they also became prime movers of the genocide in our region.

Maurice said he has also known Elie Murakaza since he was young and he identified him at Bisesero in May.

During the genocide, Murakaza came to Bisesero. He was accompanying his son, Ruzindana. In May, I saw him in Birembo (Bisesero) in front of his Benz car. There were armed soldiers all around him who were guarding him because he could not defend himself alone. I saw Murakaza that day as I was running to fight the interahamwe.

Another day, I saw Murakaza in the place called Ku Cyapa in Bisesero. That day I was running again and I passed Murakaza who was giving orders to militiamen to drive away the cows that he had looted. He asked them to take them to Mugonero. Since the genocide had begun, he had opened a cattle market there to sell the cows that he had found in Bisesero. One cow cost 15,000 francs. The Zairians came to buy the cows and then they would use boats to take the cows over to Zaire.

Murakaza and his son, Obed, killed a young girl called Mariboli. She was Ndengeyinka's child, who himself was from Bisesero. This girl had hidden in the bush. The militiamen saw her and took her to Obed. When the militiamen came to attack us, this girl came and showed them where we were hiding. The girl used to come in Obed's car or alternatively in his father's car. After the genocide, we did not see this girl again, which meant that she was killed.

Obed and his father, were the leaders of the militia because in the evening before leaving Bisesero, the militiamen would argue and say: 'We will take the cows that we have stolen to Murakaza to sell them to the Zairians.' Others would say: 'We will also take them to Gitesi or Rutsiro'. However, I saw the cows being taken to Mugonero to Murakaza.

Murakaza was a genocidal killer, like his son.

It was also clear that Yusufu remained in a position of control. Léoncie heard his name mentioned by militiamen.

Another attack which I cannot forget took place on 25 May. Again, the militia came in lots of cars. I was in Kazirandimwe near Muyira. They shot at us. The militia who arrived where I was were really panicking and saying: 'Where are we going to return to if we don't find Ndamage, who Ruzindana and Yusufu asked us to kill'?

Ndamage was a trader. He was the son of Bisangwe and a native of Gisovu commune. I heard militia everywhere asking if he had been found. He was finally killed.

As usual, I hid in a bush. Lots of militia were milling around near me. I heard some of them saying: 'Work quickly. When are we going to get to Gatare?'[in Cyangugu] Another of them said: 'They can see that the Tutsis from Bisesero are finished. Our work is finished'. Other militiamen said: 'It's time to go back. Where shall we go today to have some beer'? They replied: 'When we get back we can go to Ngoma or Mugonero'

That evening, we met up together, but we were only a small group because the others were dead. I couldn't find my husband. The next day, I heard that he had been killed. His younger brother and other people who were still alive helped me look for his body. When we found him he had a small hoe in his hand. He had been struck on the back with a machete and received bullets to the head. He was still wearing his clothes. Other bodies no longer had their clothes on. We buried him. By this time I was completely exhausted.

In a later attack, Léoncie was caught by the militia.

I went and hid in a bush in Uwingabo. I no longer had the strength to run. The militia discovered a child who ran away crying. He came into my bush. The militia were looking for him and found me as well.

Three militiamen came and shouted when they

saw me. I told them that I would give them money if they didn't call for the others to come. As soon as I mentioned money they started searching me. They took off the wrap-over cloth I was wearing and found the 50,000 Rwandese francs that I had. I was left with a little yellow skirt and a red blouse. After they had taken my money, they hit me on the head with machetes. When they left they thought I was dead. I had spent about two months running even though I was old. I didn't eat and I saw corpses exposed all over the hills. When I was hit with the machetes, I didn't resist and passed out straight away.

When the militia left, the Tutsis who were still alive went round all the hills looking at the corpses and the injured. That evening as they were walking round, they picked me up and took me to Gaheno where a man called Mudacumura lived. This was the place where the injured were gathered.

When I arrived there, they began seeing to my wounds with warm water and special healing herbs. Very early in the morning, before the attacks, they would put us injured people in the bushes and put grass on top of us to hide us. Here we suffered even more.

We stayed in this situation until the French soldiers arrived towards the end of June.

Obed Ruzindana was perhaps the most regular attendant of the slaughter, but he was one of several leading génocidaires involved. Another frequent participant was the director of the Gisovu tea factory, Alfred Musema. Anastase Mushimiyimana heard how he convinced some of the militiamen to join in the killings.

There were those who came from commune Gisovu, under the leadership of the director of the Gisovu tea factory, Musema. He directed the militiamen to Bisesero, telling them that the Inyenzi at Bisesero wanted to go and destroy the factory, which was the reason why they should wipe them out.

Aron was with the refugees on Muyira hill; his wife was killed there. He remembered the killings of May as frequent and lethal, and led by Ruzindana and Dr Gérard.

Every day Obed Ruzindana and Gérard would come to kill us with many soldiers and militiamen. They came dressed in white, white shirt or white hat, so as not to be confused with the Tutsis. You'd think they were pupils in uniform. We tried to resist them for three months with stones and spears. But the militia killed more than forty thousand people including my wife, Erina. We stayed at Bisesero until the arrival of the French. There were about a 1000 of us, including 600 who had become disabled from the grenades and from being beaten with machetes.

Aron Gakoko

Jean Nzabihimana had escaped the 16 April massacre in Mugonero, led by Dr Gérard. At Bisesero, he again confronted Dr Gérard.

Gérard came on a regular basis accompanied by Habimana, a motorcycle repairer, and other assassins and military men. The first two came in a white Toyota van. He usually wore white shorts. He himself shot my brother in-law Samuel, a trader. His wife was also killed by Gérard and even their youngest child, Victor Byiringiro, a pupil in primary school. He also killed Seth Bayiringire, son of my elder brother, twenty-three years old and in his final year at CERAI.

Léopold recalled one massacre in which the principal génocidaires led the way.

A large number of people came. They were led by the bourgmestre of Gishyita, Ndimbati; the director of the tea factory in Gisovu, Musema and Ruzindana, Murakaza's son. FAR soldiers, interahamwe militia and peasants armed with clubs and machetes took part in the massacre. We fled into the bush. Those who stayed behind were stabbed with machetes. We dispersed; each person looked for refuge in the bush. Our

Jean Nzabihimana

adversaries went home at night; as a result, we would assemble at that time to find out who had been killed.

During the days which followed we developed a system which involved pouncing on smaller groups of assassins at a run. This was a means of finding a route out, as we were surrounded by killers. We continued to run. Our goal was to tire them out since, as candidates for death, we knew that we were running for our lives.

Bellina Nirerere arrived at the hospital in Mugonero just as the massacre in which her family perished—and which Obed Ruzindana helped to direct—was about to get underway. She then made her way to Murambi in Bisesero and found that she had not escaped Ruzindana.

Obed arrived; there were some soldiers with him. They disarmed the Tutsis, taking their spears and machetes away from them. They told us that the war was over. The women, children and old people who could not run assembled in one place on the orders of Obed. He informed them that they would be protected there. Instead, they were killed. I was afraid, so I left for Bisesero.

Jérôme Bayingana[3] lived in the cellule of Kanyinya, sector Ngoma in Gishyita and was also at the hospital on 16 April.

Myself and other young survivors of this massacre went to Bisesero. Dr Gérard and Obed Ruzindana came again, to look for us. They had trucks filled with militiamen. These men came well armed and shouting. We tried to defend ourselves using stones and spears. With these weapons we killed a lieutenant and some policemen. After the death of these soldiers, Dr Gérard, Ruzindana, and some other militiamen and soldiers came in the morning, shouting loudly that they were coming to take revenge upon us and that they would kill us all. They began to shoot at us and threw grenades. Lots of people were killed.

Eliezer Niyitegeka took time off from his ministerial responsibilities to play a direct role in the killings. Jean Muragizi knew him from Gisovu, and watched him in action in Bisesero.

I was coming out of a bush in Cyamaraba. The militia were leaving to go home; it was about 3:00 p.m. I saw Eliezer Niyitegeka calling out to the militia to come back and kill, saying that it was not time to leave.

The struggle against the militia was increasingly hopeless. Uzziel pointed out that although they had captured weapons in earlier battles, they did not have the ability to use them. These guns were buried after the bullets ran out.

Towards the end of May, we had almost fourteen guns, but no cartridges for them. The assassins redoubled their efforts and we lost very many people—although they too suffered, their losses were fewer. During the attacks, we heard the assassins say "Yusufu's group, come and get your dead" whilst others would say "Mika's people, don't forget your dead". There were other group leaders too, such as a councillor called Munyantwale from one of the sectors in Gishyita commune, the former bourgmestre of Gishyita, Charles Karasankima, and a local policeman called Rwigimba, who has since returned to Rwanda [see below].

Obed Ruzindana shot me towards the end of May, and I was hit in my leg which still bears the scars. After being shot, I found I could do nothing but hide behind others in my group.

The refugees never abandoned the hope that the RPF would arrive in Kibuye before it was too late. Eric had a radio and was buoyed by the news in early June that Gitarama had fallen to the RPF. He decided, once again, to leave Bisesero and to seek sanctuary elsewhere. He and five companions left for Gitarama.

When we arrived in Gasenyi in Kibuye, the students and teachers of Gasenyi primary school saw us; they ran after us in order to kill us. They shouted a lot. We ran back to Bisesero.

---

3 Jérôme has died since this testimony was taken.

Pascal Mudenge also tried to reach Gitarama.

We realised that there were really very few people left from our area; so we decided to head towards the bush to find refuge. However, the hunt for us continued and when they discovered our refuge, all we could do was to run to save ourselves whilst they chased us.

One day, we decided to head for Gitarama. We had heard that this préfecture had fallen into the hands of the RPF. When we arrived in Karongi, in the commune of Gitesi, we ran into further attacks and were forced to return to Bisesero.

June 1994
Nearing the End

By June, Justin Mudacumura said, the refugees were continuing to fight without caring about the risks. They had nothing left to lose.

Towards the beginning of June, we had about fifteen guns belonging to assassins we had killed. When we were fighting, our objective was to kill someone who had a gun or a grenade, even if it meant losing a lot of people on our side. It was in this context that we were able to kill soldiers and interahamwe, including a lieutenant from Gisenyi who had killed a lot of our people. The killers used to come a lot towards the end of June, because buses and vehicles belonging to the authorities used to come to see how the Tutsis of Bisesero were continuing to resist. Because we had nothing to save, we fought, aware of our predicament. This is why the French found so few people still alive.

Emmanuel Sinigenga, aged eleven at that time, told of the mood among the refugees in the final month of the killings.

There came a time when the cruel people killed so many of us that we fled the place. We dispersed in different directions. During the night, those left on our side reorganised themselves again. The men and the young people used to encourage the people that in a few days, the RPF would provide us with reinforcements. The women and girls who were tired stayed where they were and the assassins killed them. During the last days in June, before the arrival of the French, there were more killers on each occasion. They came with a lot of energy. But our energy was weakening more and more. There were so few of us left to fight, but we continued to resist.

It was clear that the militia's energy was sustained by material incentives. Jean-Damascène witnessed Obed paying off the militia.

On 3 June, I was hiding in a bush when Obed brought the soldiers and militia to massacre us. They stopped hunting Tutsis at 3:00 p.m. and Obed called them all together in Nyarutovu cellule. The soldiers formed one group and the militia formed another. Then Obed gave them some money. Once they had been given their money, they went home.

In another massacre on 8 June, Jean-Damascène had one more lesson in the sheer brutality of the leaders of the genocide.

The soldiers arrived, together with Kayishema, Eliezer Niyitegeka, Obed Ruzindana, Dr Gérard and many militiamen. The leaders went to the primary school to witness the massacres. They had brought beer and goats' meat to make brochettes. Since there was a major massacre that day, we were running around all over the place, wielding our spears. And, as we ran, we accidentally came upon the great perpetrators of genocide—Obed, Niyitegeka, etc.

We got there just as they were in the middle of eating and drinking. When they saw us, they shot at us, and we carried on fighting. They left their food and beer and got into their cars. We threw stones at the cars, breaking their windscreens. They drove off towards Gisovu and councillor Mika was shooting at us as he left.

After that, they came back to hunt us down, cellule by cellule, scouring every nook and cranny.

Mu Yoboro, a stone on the hill of Gitwa, used by the militiamen for sharpening machetes.

Bernard Kayumba was hiding nearby when Charles Sikubwabo sealed the fate of two businessmen from his commune, one of them Jean-Damascène's father.

Justin Mudacumura

Jean-Damascène Nsanzimfura

In June, I witnessed Charles Sikubwabo kill the businessman, Assiel Kabanda. He shot him, then asked his militiamen to cut off the victim's head. As Kabanda was someone they looked for everywhere, he said he wanted to show the head to the préfet, Kayishema, and so receive his reward.

Sikubwabo also killed Innocent Muganga, the father of my friend, Jean-Damascène Nsanzimfura.

When Sikubwabo was not murdering Tutsis, he, like other génocidaires, was making a profit from the genocide, looting the homes of Tutsis and selling the iron sheets on Idjwi Island.

In the days that followed, Ruzindana found and killed many other Tutsis, men, women and children. He took a small child, who had also survived the killings, and gave him clothes and food, then persuaded him to reveal the hiding places of the other refugees. Jean Damascène confirmed his account.

The boy showed Ruzindana where Assiel Kabanda's eight children were hidden—Kabanda was a businessman in Gishyita; they had cut off his head and taken it to one of his shops, telling him to get on with his business. The children were hidden in a hole. Obed and his militiamen shot them.

I was hiding close to a road. Obed drove past me. He was with councillor Mika. They spotted a stand of trees. They stopped the car and looked underneath the trees. They found a man and a child and killed them both. Then Obed and Mika drove off again.

Augustin gave more evidence of the central role Ruzindana played in the killings.

I was too weak to fight against the militiamen, so I immediately went to hide in a bush. One day I hid in a bush in a place called Mu Yoboro. There was a large stone there that the militiamen used for sharpening their machetes. The stone is still there today. At the time, when I was in the bush, the militiamen came to sharpen their machetes. The important militiamen were walking around and looking at the corpses. Then Obed Ruzindana came up and told the militiamen to sharpen their machetes and hurry up. He also told them that they would have to work night and day to be able to exterminate all the Tutsis before the French soldiers arrived. He ordered them to burn all the bushes.

Obed left after giving out all these orders. As there were no more bushes to hide behind, I had to lie down and put bodies on top of me. When the militiamen attacked, they did not touch the rotten bodies to find us. There was a terrible odour. It was impossible to breathe underneath the corpses. The insects which came to eat the bodies, stung me.

Claver Habarugira also commented on Ruzindana's pivotal role.

They came in white clothes. They looked as though they were pupils in uniform. Obed Ruzindana and the two councillors, Mika and Muhirwa, were at the forefront. They were the ones who gave the orders to begin the attack. The militiamen would shoot at us with their guns and throw grenades. We used our stones and clubs to repel them. In the fighting we managed to catch several militiamen. They told us that they were working in order to be rewarded by Obed Ruzindana. The militiamen succeeded in killing a lot of Tutsis, including my wife and children.

The militia were a constant presence in the hills and forests of Bisesero, where they knew the refugees were hiding. Emmanuel Gahigiro was attacked on 11 June.

I was hiding from the militiamen in the forest of Nyiramukwaya. A man called Bizimungu, an ex-FAR from Karama, sector Musenyi in Gishyita, saw me and ran after me. He shot me and I was hit by a bullet in the thigh. I fell down immediately. I could no longer walk. Some survivors put me in a bush and put grass on top of me to hide me. I did not move. It rained on me and I felt just like a corpse. My wounds were infected and rotting. I stayed there until the French soldiers arrived.

Maurice was wounded at the end of May and could hardly walk. He was helpless to prevent an attack upon his wife and child, which took place in June. His life has been permanently scarred by the memory of the cruelty he witnessed that day.

That day in June, the militiamen searched through practically all the bushes. At the time, my wife and child were still alive. They were hiding a short distance from where I was. A militiaman called Sebikoba from our commune discovered my wife. She was carrying our child on her back.

The militiaman hit my wife with a machete and then he put a wide bamboo stick into her vagina. He pushed it in so far that it went right to her stomach. The child that she was carrying on her back fell to the ground. The child wandered off saying 'mummy, daddy'. He had not yet learned to speak properly. The militiamen saw the child and killed him, saying 'We mustn't let a child of Sakufi's live'.

That evening, when the militiamen had gone home, I went to see the bodies of my wife and child. When I arrived at the place where she lay, I found myself trembling. She was still breathing. I removed the bamboo stick from her body. When I had taken it out, my wife's neck cracked and she died instantly.

I went to fetch a hoe and I buried her there and then. I didn't have anything to remind me of her. She didn't have any clothes left and I had no photos of her. Fortunately, I saw the traditional sling my wife used to use for carrying our child on her back. It was next to their bodies. I picked up the sling and I still have it now.

At the end of her tether, Jeanne d'Arc Mukamana, thirteen, decided to risk travelling to Gikongoro, in the hope of reaching Burundi. She left together with three other refugees, one of them a woman from Gikongoro who was their guide.

When we got to the forest of Nyungwe, we saw a roadblock manned by militiamen. Every one ran off, each in a different direction. From then on, I was on my own. I couldn't find my way back. And yet, without this woman, I couldn't make it to Burundi. I decided to go back to Kibuye. I was alone in the bush. I had nothing to eat. My clothes were unwashed. I was like an animal.

Maurice Sakufi

After three days, Jeanne made it back to Gisovu.

I saw a pit in which the bodies and corpses of Tutsis had been thrown. Some were still alive. The children were crying, calling for their mothers. I got into this graveyard in order to hide because the militia were combing the bushes. The militia brought other bodies and threw them on top of me.

Despite the danger, Jeanne decided to go back to Gikongoro; the alternative was a prolonged stay in the pit.

I crawled out during the night and walked all night. Fortunately, I found two Tutsi women and three children and we continued on together. The two women died of hunger along the way. I stayed with the three children. When we arrived in Nyungwe forest, we found the woman from Gikongoro who had previously shown me the way. The children left to look for something to eat and were killed.

At this point, Jeanne heard on a radio that belonged to her companion that the interim government had been defeated by the RPF. She decided to remain in Rwanda.

Steadily the militia were eliminating every refugee on the hills of Bisesero. They hunted them down, finding them in bushes and in holes. It was as if the resistance of the refugees had reinforced their determination to kill them. Even though many militiamen had been killed and injured in the battles in Bisesero, their leaders used every means to ensure that they continued the slaughter. Yusufu regularly came to supervise; Maurice saw him in June, along with Dr Gérard.

Yusufu was wearing a cap. He was with Doctor Gérard Ntakirutimana. I knew the doctor because his father was a friend of ours and he had given my father a cow. The doctor was looking after the wounded militiamen. Yusufu had a gun at the time. This was in Kamina and I saw them as I was going to hide in a bush.

We remained where we were, suffering. Two of our main people, Nzigira and Birara, had been killed. They were the ones who had organised us.

During an attack around this time, Léoncie hid in the bushes. She overheard a conversation between a militiaman and the préfet of Kibuye, Clément Kayishema.

The militia came again. I went to hide in a bush near the road. We liked hiding near the road as the militia didn't think that anyone would go there. Next to this bush were the cars of the militia leaders. I heard someone saying: 'Mr préfet, do you think that any Tutsis will escape today?' Laughing, he replied: 'There really is a very good game going on here. It's best to come every day to witness it'. He also added that the bourgmestre of Gishyita commune had worked harder than the bourgmestre of Gisovu commune. When the militia had finished killing, they went back to their cars and left.

Claver Mbugufe confirmed that the préfet had been involved in the killings.

Clément Kayishema, the préfet of Kibuye, took part in the attacks against both Karongi and Bisesero. He used to come and ask the militia how far they had got with the 'work'. I heard him with my own ears when I was hiding in the forest of Nyamwishywa at Karongi.

With enemies so high up the local administration, the refugees were fighting against all the odds. The bodies of the dead were decaying on the hillside—animals and birds came to feed upon them, as the survivors watched. Siméon was among those who urged the refugees not to give in to the génocidaires, even though the militia returned daily to complete the slaughter.

A small number of us hid in a hole. It was difficult to organise ourselves and we were hungry since we had had nothing at all to eat. Even so, in the evening we all met on the hill to try and raise the young peoples' spirits so that they could carry on running and fighting. We had suffered a lot. At night we saw dogs and other animals who came to devour the bodies. During the day crows would come with the militiamen to come and eat the bodies as well.

No one took pity upon us. The militiamen returned to Bisesero every single day to kill us. The militia begged us not to run so far. If they killed us easily they would be rewarded by Obed Ruzindana.

The refugees were determined to make a fight for life; but the conditions they had to endure brought them to the edge of collapse. With his wife and four children dead, Claver Habarugira had little to hold on to.

We had nothing to eat. We slept in the bush amongst the rotting bodies. We were dying of thirst and were obliged to drink water from the stream which had bodies in it. I saw dogs which

The dense vegetation on the hills of Bisesero, which provided cover for the few remaining refugees.

came to eat the corpses and crows which came to pick their eyes out.

Catherine's words are a powerful insight into the sense of futility among the refugees in Bisesero in June.

I did not have any strength left and I could no longer eat. I had no more clothes. I was like an old animal. I saw the dogs devouring the corpses.

I hid in the bush until the French soldiers arrived.

A Moment of Hope The Arrival of French Soldiers

By the end of June, around 2,000 refugees were alive. They were hiding in holes and in the bush. They were exhausted, starving, wounded and sick. They were living in the shadow of fear. Towards the end of June, one of the refugees heard on the radio that French forces would be arriving in Cyangugu, Kibuye and Gikongoro as part of Opération Turquoise. On 26 June, they saw French reconnaissance troops passing by. Realising they represented their only remaining hope of survival, some of the refugees came out of hiding to tell them of the plight of the Tutsis in Bisesero. But this placed them in immediate danger, as Siméon explained.

We all emerged from our hiding place. Eric, who could speak French, explained who we were. The French took photos of us. The militia were there with them, carrying their weapons. The soldiers then left and said that they would be returning. When the French had gone, the militia came back to kill. They killed a lot of us that day because many people had come out of their hiding places when they had seen the French soldiers.

Eric was the person who sought to convince the French soldiers about their plight. They had come in four cars. He was hiding by the road when he first noticed their vehicles. At that hour, after 5:00 p.m., the killers had normally gone home, but he was still fearful that further torments were in store for them.

When these cars arrived close to me, I saw that they were not ex-FAR, but white people. When I saw them, I came out of the bush in order to wave the cars down. The people who were in the first two cars refused to stop even though they could see very well that I was shouting to them for help. When I saw that, I went to the middle of road to stop the other two cars. I spoke in French, but they refused to listen to what I was saying as they were with Twagirayesu, a teacher who was saying that we were not threatened. He said that we were the cause of the insecurity in the region. He accused us of having killed many people. There were Hutus who lived on the hill of Rubazo in Bisesero who had been obliged to leave their houses because they thought that the Tutsis of Bisesero could kill them. As a result, Twagirayesu was telling the French that it was only Hutus who felt threatened.

Eric looked for ways to persuade the French soldiers.

As I could see that these French men were really listening to this teacher, I called out the Tutsis who were in the bushes. I even showed them the Tutsis who had received machete blows and who had been shot. I also showed them the corpses which were there. After that, the French listened to me. The other French soldiers who had already left returned. The soldiers looked at us and asked us to continue hiding. They told us that they would come back in three days.

Augustin also witnessed Twagirayesu's efforts to dissuade the French from assisting the refugeees.

The soldiers arrived at about 5:00 p.m. They were with Twagirayesu who was a teacher and who was explaining to them that at Bisesero everyone was safe. This teacher was also a militiaman but fortunately we found Eric, a Tutsi from Bisesero, who could speak French. He explained everything to the soldiers and then we brought over corpses

Eric Nzabahimana

and the wounded to show the soldiers how much we had suffered.

The French left and four days later, they returned.

In the days before the French soldiers' return, at least 1,000 refugees were murdered, half the number that had survived. It was clearly not possible for a few soldiers to take the decision, there and then, to evacuate 2,000 people, many of them badly wounded. But the encounter, in full view of the assassins who knew the soldiers intended to return, left the refugees vulnerable. Jérôme explained what happened after their departure.

Eric, a survivor from Bisesero, had the courage to approach them. These French people asked him to look for other Tutsis. They said that they had come to save us. Later they went back to the préfecture. Before they left, Eric had called all the Tutsis, even those who were in the pits. They left us exposed and then went away. Immediately after their departure Dr. Gérard came with his militiamen; they wiped out many of the people who had been hidden before the arrival of the French.

One of the people that Eric encouraged to come forward is Vincent Kayigema, eight at the time. After he and his family had been forced out of their home in Kigarama, Gishyita, he hid in a pit located in the forest of Nyiramakware. He remained there until Operation Turquoise brought French soldiers to Kibuye. He recalled the day he emerged from this pit.

The day French soldiers arrived, we were called out. We saw cars with flags; all the Tutsis in hiding came out. The French assembled us on a hill. The militiamen, with their machetes, were on the other side. After we had been gathered together, the French left straightaway. The militia came. They killed more than half the Tutsis who were there. Fortunately, I escaped.

The decision of the French soldiers to leave 2000 terrified people—begging for their help—was inexcusable. Rwanda is a small country; the soldiers had vehicles, communication equipment and most important of all. they had arms. Having been informed of the gravity of the situation, it is difficult to understand why they did not leave some soldiers to protect the refugees while they sought reinforcements, or indeed to imagine why it took them three days to return.

Claver Munyandinda confirmed that the delay cost many lives.

French soldiers came to see us on or about the 26th of June. We were about 2,000 survivors then. They asked us certain questions to find out how we lived. We explained everything to them. They told us to continue hiding. They said they would come back on the 30th to protect us. They left. After their departure, and in this interval of four days, the attacks of the militia multiplied to such an extent that when the French came back on the 30th, there were barely nine hundred of us left. They gathered us together in one place, gave us biscuits and medical care to the wounded. The militia continued to come after that but they were not able to attack us.

Jérôme pointed out that it was left to a journalist to inform the soldiers of what had happened.

Immediately after their departure, Dr. Gérard came with his militiamen; they wiped out all the people who had been hidden before the arrival of the French.

A journalist arrived to take photos of the bodies which were on the mountain. He saw the militiamen killing these Tutsi people. He returned to the préfecture to call the French to come. The French came and stayed with us. There were about 1000 of us left out of the 50,000 Tutsis who had been in Bisesero.

When they returned, the French troops brought clothes, beans and biscuits. Nathan described how they encouraged the frightened Tutsis to come out of their hiding places once more.

The French used drums to call the Tutsi who were in the bush and holes. The Tutsi who were hidden also saw the planes of the French soldiers, which were transporting the sick people, and they came out.

The soldiers encouraged the refugees to assemble on one hill. There they sang a hymn to God, "Lord let me come to your side", Nyemerera Ngendana na we Myami. The battle against the génocidaires had ended, but their suffering would continue.

The injured and the sick were taken to hospital in Goma; Emmanuel Gahigiro was among them.

My wound was very deep so I was driven to Goma in Zaire. There I was hospitalised. When I recovered, I went in UNHCR cars to Kigali and then we moved on to Gitarama where other survivors from Bisesero were.

The survivors were at breaking point when the French troops arrived. Anathalie Usabyimbabazi had remained in the forest for two months, her wounds untreated, living on raw potatoes, surrounded by dogs who were devouring corpses. She was in such a state at the end of June that the French soldiers refused to take her, saying she was a "madwoman." But eventually they were persuaded by bystanders who told them that "she had been normal before the genocide".

The French soldiers took the remaining refugees to Rwirambo, a hill in Gisovu, for three weeks. So close to Bisesero, the threat of violence remained ever present. The survivors felt they were not safe as long as the men who nearly annihilated them were at liberty; they looked to the French troops to tackle the problem.

Anastase Kalisa, 22, used to work at the Gisovu tea factory as a casual labourer. He highlighted the role of Alfred Musema, the director of the tea factory, in the attacks against the refugees in Bisesero, and the failure of the French to acknowledge it.

I saw Musema at least four times at Bisesero. He brought the factory vehicles, full of interahamwe. He turned up twice at Bisesero after the French arrived. He told the French soldiers that 'There was no need to protect these Tutsis because the country was safe'. We saw this as another sign of his criminality. I was there when he came the second time. Everybody screamed and told the French that he should not be allowed to come into the camp. Despite our shouts that he was a killer, the French let him go.

As indicated elsewhere in this report, Musema was one of the key instigators of the killings. Jérôme also remembered seeing Musema in his car during several attacks.

Alfred Musema, the director of the tea factory of Gisovu came to Bisesero on numerous occasions in his red Pajero. After the French came, he always used to come to beg the French to hand us over to the militia.

In common with other survivors from Bisesero, Jean Muragizi, a mason in Gisovu, criticised the refusal of French soldiers to arrest Musema.

Musema worked hand in hand with the bourgmestre of Gisovu, Aloys Ndimbati, the councillor of the sector Gitabura, Simon Segatarama, and the juge president du canton, Jean Marie-Vianney Sibomana. These three were among those leading the attacks against Bisesero. These three also played an important role in enlisting the help of Yusufu of Bugarama. Musema used to transport interahamwe to Bisesero.

The last time I saw Musema was after the arrival of French soldiers. Musema came and survivors told the French that this man was a killer, that he had really finished people off. The French asked people to testify and then they let him go.

Emile Kayinamura was also critical of the French.

The French protected us, but they did nothing to punish the interahamwe who had killed us. On the contrary, these assassins had many conversations with the French.

Eric described Musema's strategy to ensure that there would be no survivors to give evidence about Bisesero.

He told these soldiers to leave and not to protect the people who were the cause of insecurity in the region. He was in a red Pajero. The survivors who saw Musema wanted to attack him, but the French calmed the situation and Musema left.

After three weeks, more differences emerged between the French soldiers and the survivors. They spoke to Eric about the future of the Bisesero survivors.

The French asked me if we wanted to remain with them or if we wanted to join the RPF soldiers. I consulted the other survivors and we said we preferred to go to the RPF zone.

The attitude of the French soldiers immediately changed.

The French became angry. They refused to give us any more food.

Philimon Nshimiyimana also noted the negative reaction of the French soldiers when the refugees made their preference clear.

After three weeks, we expressed our wish to join Kivumu, the zone controlled by the RPF soldiers. This decision provoked the anger of the French soldiers, so much so that they stopped giving us food.

The French soldiers transferred most of the refugees to the zone controlled by the soldiers of the RPF in commune Kivumu, Kibuye; some were also taken to the camp of Nyarushishi in Cyangugu to join survivors from Cyangugu.

Chadrac remembers the moment the French troops returned, the protection they offered initially and the bitterness which developed later.

The wounded were taken to hospital and those who remained were given food to eat and soap to wash with. Because of the bad conditions, our legs had swollen and we had difficulty in walking.

Three weeks later, we were taken to the RPF

Philimon Nshimiyimana

zone at Nyange [Kivumu] as we had requested.

When the French soldiers realised that we did not wish to remain with them, they became angry and stopped giving us food.

Léoncie was also aware of the tension with the French soldiers.

A few days after their arrival, the French asked us if we wanted to stay with them or if we wanted to go to the RPF soldiers' zone. Everyone chose to go into the RPF zone. From that time on they were angry and cut back all they had been giving us to eat. After they had driven us to the RPF zone in Kivumu commune, the RPF soldiers took us to Kabgayi.

Maurice said the French asked the refugees if there were any Inkotanyi [members of the RPF] among them; then they were asked for their opinion about the RPF.

They asked us who we liked more, the French or the Inkotanyi. Of course we replied in their favour. When we said that we wanted to join the Inkotanyi, they would refuse biscuits for the whole day. It was a punishment. Journalists from RFI obliged us to sing for them.

The refugees spent a week in Kivumu, under the protection of the RPF, then were taken by them to Kabgayi in Gitarama.

Chadrac Muvundandinda

The Principal Organisers of the Genocide in Bisesero: A Brief Update

All the key organisers of the genocide in Bisesero fled Rwanda in July 1994. With rare exceptions, they remain outside the country. Nevertheless, most of them have been indicted by the United Nations Criminal Tribunal for Rwanda. Those who have been indicted include:

Eliezer Niyitegeka, Minister of Information in the interim government:	Remains at large.
Clément Kayishema préfet of Kibuye:	Was arrested in Zambia and is currently in custody at the Tribunal's Detention Facility in Arusha, Tanzania.
Charles Sikubwabo, bourgmestre of Gishyita:	Remains at large.
Aloys Ndimbati, bourgmestre of Gisovu:	Also remains at liberty.
Alfred Musema, director of the tea factory in Gisovu:	Was arrested in Switzerland on 11 February 1995 and transferred to Arusha on 20 May 1997.
Obed Ruzindana, a businessman:	Was arrested in Nairobi in September 1996 and shortly afterwards transferred to Arusha.
Elizaphan Ntakuritimana, an Adventist pastor and president of the Adventists in Kibuye:	Was arrested in Texas, USA, released in December 1997 and has been re-arrested. He remains in detention in Texas pending attempts to ensure his extradition to Arusha.
Dr Gérard Ntakuritimana, a medical doctor, and the son of Elizapahan Ntakuritimana:	Was arrested in Côte d'Ivoire on 6 November 1996 and is currently awaiting trial in Arusha.
Mika Muhimana, councillor of Gishyita sector, Gishyita:	Remains at liberty.
Vincent Rutaganira, councillor of sector Mubuga, Gishyita:	Remains at large.

Other génocidaires who played a prominent role in Bisesero, and who remain outside the country, have, so far, eluded justice. They have not been indicted by the International Tribunal or arrested in the countries where they are thought to be living. The most important of the men in this category is John Yusufu Munyakazi, one of the men who contributed the most to the genocide of 1994. Rwigimba, a communal policeman in Gishyita and Ezéchiel Muhirwa, returned to Rwanda with the influx of refugees in November 1996 and were subsequently arrested.

The Survivors Living With The Legacy of Bisesero

The main subject of this report is the collective struggle mounted by the refugees in Bisesero—their unity and courage, as well as their shared sense of anguish and loss. But it is important that the way in which the experiences of Bisesero and of the 1994 genocide marked the lives of each individual is not forgotten.

Throughout April, May and June 1994, the refugees at Bisesero fought every minute of every day for survival. When they were not giving all their energy to the battles against the militia, they were struggling against the cold and rain to find food, water, stones, a place to hide, or to bury their dead. They lived through daily agony, but they refused to give in to the genocide.

For the very few who did survive, another kind of fight began almost as soon as the genocide ended. The family, friends, homes, possessions or possibilities they had before 1994, were largely destroyed. Many were either sick or wounded and all were emotionally scarred. Survivors of all ages had to begin their lives again in July 1994—most had been left with nothing, beyond the companionship or support of other survivors. The massacres at Bisesero have devastated their lives. It is impossible to imagine, let alone to measure, the loss and hardship they have endured. The struggle of the refugees at Bisesero continues.

Soon after the genocide was brought to an end in July 1994, many of the survivors of Bisesero began to go back home. Like the others, Narcisse Nkusi found there was nothing to return to, nothing to return for. His home had been demolished and, like his companions, Narcisse had to shelter in former bars and shops in the centre of the village, away from his land which was his only source of food and income. He is surrounded by constant reminders of all he has lost, most importantly his wife and three young children.

I feel saddened by the bones on the various hills that were gathered just five metres from my house. Before the genocide, each time I left my house, I would see many cows on the hills, and children playing on the hills too. Now all I see are bushes which shelter wild animals and bones in practically every corner of the village.

Almost an entire future generation was slaughtered in 1994. The murder of so many of the children of Bisesero is one of the greatest tragedies of what took place there. Michel Serumondo survived with one of his two wives, Agnès Mukamurigo, but they will never recover from the loss of the rest of the family—another wife and thirteen children.

When we come home and don't see the children next to us, we cry. We have both lost our appetites. A dead body was something which was greatly respected before the genocide. When they were buried, people came to say goodbye for the last time. Afterwards, the neighbours and friends came to visit the bereaved family. Now we see the

Survivors of the killings in Bisesero, with some of the bones they have collected for burial.

Narcisse Nkusi

Michel Serumondo

skulls of Tutsis everywhere we go. We don't have the means to pick them all up and bury them. What I find shocking is that the militiamen crush any bones that are in their way, which shows how little they respect the person. These are the militiamen who have not yet been arrested.

Even the simplest chores have become difficult, and are one more occasion to mourn the death of their children.

My wife is old. She was hit with clubs during the genocide so now she is disabled. Nevertheless, she is the one who draws the water from the well, who fetches the wood from the forests and who completes various household tasks. I have to farm and look after the cows I found after the genocide. It used to be my children who looked after the cows during the genocide. Now I have to run behind the cows. This causes me a lot of pain since my right leg isn't totally healed.

In addition to her six children, Agnès has lost most of her female friends.

When we went back to Gishyita, I felt very depressed because I realised that I was the only woman survivor left from my hill.

"I felt very alone and I still feel this way today."

At the age of 61, Thamari Nyiranturo spends most of her time in bed, in tears. Over a period of 35 years, she has lost all her family— her parents, siblings, husband, daughter and grandchildren—in the massacres that have punctuated her life. Her only son fled Rwanda for fear of being killed and died abroad in an accident. Her daughter and four grandchildren were killed in 1994.

I don't know what I am still doing in this world. I have never seen my parents. I became a widow when I was still young, my son is dead and my daughter Louise and her children died during the genocide. I have done no wrong in this world; people were being killed simply for being Tutsi.

I don't know if there will be someone left to bury me the day I die. Otherwise, I will be like my children and my husband whom I never buried. Their bones are left exposed in the street. I have a wound at the bottom of my heart.

Catherine is alone at a time in her life when she should have been surrounded by children and grandchildren.

Before the genocide, I had a husband who I lived with. He was very caring towards me. I also had seven children, boys and girls. Six of them died during the genocide along with their children, husbands and wives. They were:
Thaddée Rutabendura, who died along with his four children;
Anastasie Mukamutesi, who died her three children;
Marie Mukandoli, who died with her six children;
Bernadette Nyiranjara, who died with her four children;
Berthilde Mukagansana, who died with her three children;
Ancilla Uwimana, who died with her three children.

I used to live like a queen amongst my children. We had three large houses and several stables for the cows. We even had a place to put the goats. I did not work at all; I didn't even sow or reap the crops. My work just consisted of serving the food to my children and checking to see if the calves were being well-looked after. When the evening meal was over, we used to sing and dance, especially when a marriage took place. I had a happy heart.

Now I spend the days alone. My only son who I

Catherine Kamayenge

stay with, teaches in a school and only comes back home in the evening. The only child left of my daughter who was killed, comes home late in the evening as well from school. I have to try and prepare something to appease the hunger of my son and the young boy as they return from school shattered.

I am unable to draw water from the well so I have to go and beg here and there in the neighbourhood so that I can have some food to prepare. I find it difficult to sleep. At night, I often wake up to see if the day is dawning. I'm sure my insomnia is because of the terrible memories of the events.

At the age of 76, Catherine, who has lost everything, has to sleep on a mat next to the front door, without a blanket. She suffers from regular bouts of malaria and bronchitis and never has any money to pay for treatment.

Catherine now lives in the commercial centre of Gishyita, returning home fills her with misery.

"I have a large wound deep in my heart."

When I go back to Bisesero, seeing the bones of people who have not been buried immediately reminds me of my family and my neighbours with whom we lived peacefully. I feel disturbed at once when I see them. When I see where my house used to be, I feel like committing suicide. Yet my faith in God holds me back.

Catherine's thoughts of suicide are shared by other survivors. With his wife and six children among the victims, Anastase Gasagara asks himself why he is still alive, with so little to live for. He returned to Gishyita in September 1994. After staying with other survivors near the commune office in what he called a camp, he decided to return to his hill to farm.

At the camp we talked and shared everything from food to suffering. At least I could talk and laugh there. However, when I returned home, I began to wonder why I had not been killed during the genocide. I saw how they had completely destroyed my beautiful house. I cried a lot that day. I remembered how my children used to play in the yard of the house before the genocide began. I looked where my room and the stables for the cows had once been. I wanted to kill myself. I couldn't see the point of living anymore.

Determined not to return to the camp, Anastase began to build a small hut, with the help of other survivors who remained together until each person or family had their own dwelling.

When I went to my hut I had nothing but a bed cover. Every night I lay awake, thinking about how they had killed the Tutsis in Bisesero. Each time I went to fetch wood from the forest, I only saw people's skulls. Instead of pursuing my search for wood, I would return home immediately. Before the genocide, only the children used to fetch wood. It was shameful for a man to do it.

I had to look high and low in the fields to find

Stanislas Ruhamuliza

food. Even if I was lucky enough to find something, I still didn't have a pan to cook it in. I had to go and beg my neighbours for one. It was degrading to go and have to beg for something from the families of the people who had looted our houses and killed our families.

Even if I did manage to prepare some food, I lacked the appetite to then eat it. Instead, I would think of how I used to eat with my wife and children. I asked myself why I needed to eat when the bodies of my family were still lying outside on the hill.

Stanislas Ruhamuliza was a cattle breeder in Bisesero. After his sons had grown up and had their own herds, there was insufficient land for pasture and for his sons to build homes. In 1990, Stanislas decided to emigrate to Uvira in Zaire. He sold all his cows in order to purchase land in Zaire, and took his wife, three daughters and a son there with him. He left three sons and a daughter in Bisesero. When the genocide began, Stanislas had settled down in Uvira and was preparing for his remaining children to join him in Zaire.

Following the killings, Stanislas sold his fields and cows and returned to Bisesero looking for news of his family. Nothing could have prepared Stanislas for what he found there. When he arrived, he discovered that his four children and eight grandchildren had been killed.

Everything I saw around me made me feel anxious. I wondered whether this was really the Bisesero I had known. I felt as though I was dreaming. It used to be full of cows and was the home of many Tutsis. All I could see were skulls and the debris from the houses which had been destroyed.

"Whenever I saw a skull, I began to cry. I imagined that it was perhaps the skull of one of my children. It is terrible living in Bisesero after the genocide."

Stanislas cannot accept the death of his children.

How can I forget how much I worked for the survival of my children before the genocide? I had to leave so that they would have a future. But now they have killed them and my children have not fulfilled my dreams. I bitterly regret having left my children in Rwanda.

I do not know how to feel good about life. I can see that for the whole of my future life I will be unhappy.

As he reflects on his ruined life, Narcisse's thoughts are of the children who could have brightened his future.

My children could have been a comfort for me. But the ones I took to my so-called friends were all killed. They had extended families, and I do not understand why they could not hide the younger children who were the same age as their own children. They readily agreed to hide objects rather than people.

Justin Mudacumura also lost his family. He expressed his loneliness in profound terms.

The genocide of April 1994 marked me in a way that I can never forget: I lost my wife and six children.

"I remain alone, like a tree without branches."

Justin's words are echoed by Azelle Nyirahabimana. Her husband and three children "were killed by neighbours, using machetes and hoes". In the same attack, Azelle was cut with machetes, and left for dead. She received no medical treatment and her wounds became infected. She now suffers from pain in the chest, neck, and back, and from constant headaches. Above all she suffers from the loss of her loved ones.

The pain that is in my head gets worse when I remember the death of my children and their father. I remarried, but the distress is still there. I won't be satisfied even if they work miracles for me. The things that we lost mean nothing to me: cows, goats. The house was destroyed; all that is gone for me. I am like a tree which has neither roots nor branches. I don't even have a life; I have no hope for my life. I am in despair.

Anathalie Usabyimbabazi lost her husband, Ferdinand Ntagara; her three children; her parents; two brothers, killed with their families; and three sisters, killed with their families in Kibuye.

I live alone in the house. I am always thinking about my children and my husband.

Everyone who loved Anathalie has been killed; finding the resources to look after herself is no easy matter.

My health has suffered under the blows of machetes and massues I received during the April 1994 genocide. I have no money to pay for any healthcare, or to buy any posessions. Everything we had was stolen, and all our houses were destroyed. I have no work which pays me a wage as I was not fortunate enough to receive an education. I am stuck, without a future. I am sorry that I have remained in this world.

The eerie silence in his house and dreams about his family prevent Innocent Ndahimana from sleep. His parents, four brothers and his sister died in Bisesero, where they lived as farmers. He also lost numerous nephews, nieces and in-laws. Only one brother survived.

I live alone in this house. Before the genocide I had a large family. At night, all alone in the house, I find it impossible to sleep. When I do manage to get to sleep, I just dream about the members of my family who died during the genocide. After such dreams I can't get back to sleep.

She grew up surrounded by siblings, but Bellina Nirerere no longer has a family to call her own.

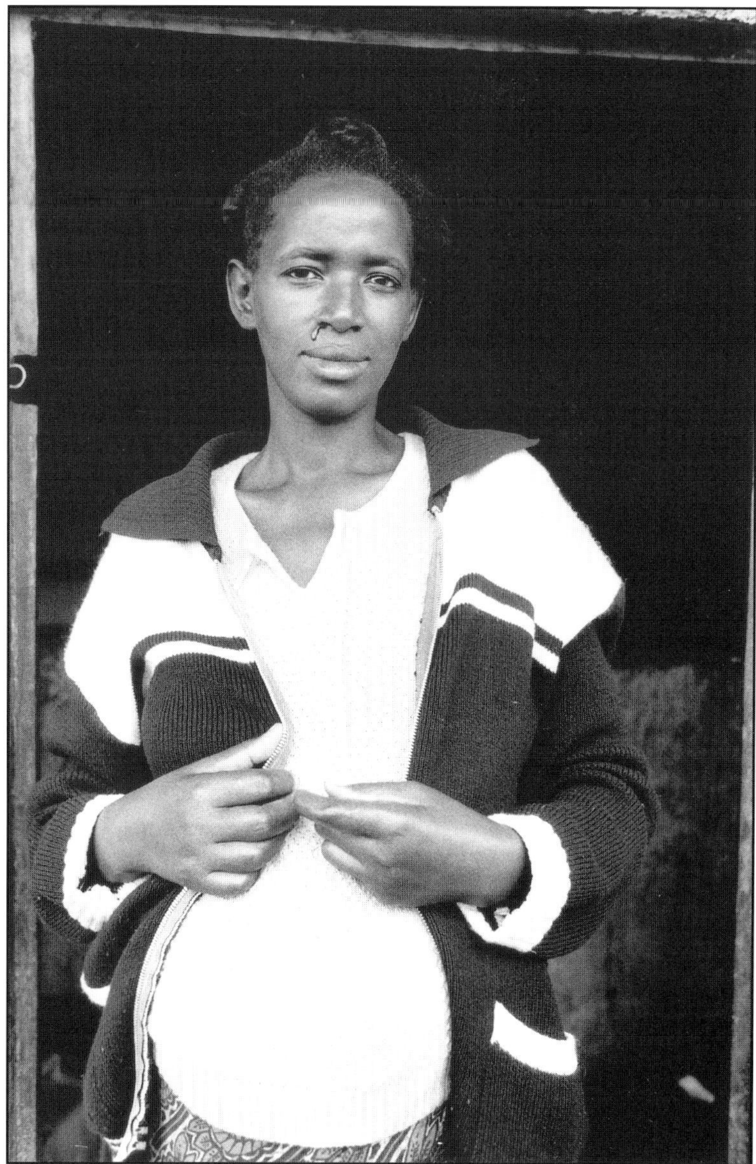

Every single member of my family is dead. My life is in the hands of God.

Azelle Nyirahabimana

For Edson Turikunkiko, 23, home has become an empty house.

I am all alone because my mother and seven brothers all died. Our house was completely destroyed, so I had to rebuild it. It is difficult because I have to live there on my own. Because I feel so lonely, I often think about those I have lost. I came from a large family and before all I had to do was to look after the cows. However, all the cows have been stolen and being alone means that I now have to do all the domestic chores.

Bisesero is one of the rare massacres of 1994 of which most of the survivors are male. On the open hillside, the men, especially men in their prime, had the advantage of speed over women and children. As a result, Bisesero has proportionally a large number of male survivors; most of them are widowers. Pascal Mudenge is one of them.

Pascal Mudenge

My wife and I were married for only two months and now she is dead because of the genocide.

The disappearance of their larger families heightens their sense of isolation.

I am all alone. My mother and her nine children are also dead. There are so many other victims of the genocide from my family.

Pascal needs his strength to continue his life as a farmer, but he has experienced difficulties.

I was hit on the head and shoulders with a massue. Now, I have difficulty in carrying heavy objects on my head. I also have trouble carrying out tasks which require a lot of strength.

Chadrac Muvunandinda spoke for many other widowers in Bisesero.

I am full of grief because of the deaths of my children and my wife. I am alone.

The situation for the few children who lived through the killings at Bisesero is equally painful. Education represents the only hope for the future of Rwanda's child survivors, and they themselves see it as their best chance in the battle for recovery. But many in Bisesero have abandoned school. Nteziryayo, alias "Matoroshi", has decided to become a cattle breeder. He is thirteen years old. Before Habyarimana's death, he was in his first year of school in Gako, sector Rwankuba.

I was very good at my lessons. Whenever we had exams I would come second or third in a class of more than forty students. Children of my age preferred to look after their cows, instead of doing their studies, but I preferred to study a lot. My mother, Erina Nyiransabimana, encouraged me to go to school too. Every morning, very early, she would give me some milk and food so that I had enough energy to study. In the evenings, I would come home and study. I did no other work apart from that, because my father and older brother looked after the cows.

Nteziryayo's love of school is a now a distant memory. When he returned to Bisesero, he was looking forward to life at school. Once there, he was made to feel like "a stranger", humiliated by his apparent poverty and battered by loneliness and fear.

"I know that studying is very good, but I no longer have the will to carry on with my studies. In class, I was unable to speak; I felt like a dumb person".

Now, I look after nineteen cows; I spend all day in

the pasture with the cows with a club in my hand. The club is called umushabarara and it is very solid. I feel very happy when I see that my cows have eaten fresh grass and have drunk clean water. In the evenings, I sing to my cows.

But when night falls, memories intrude.

At night I think about the genocide and my mother's death comes back to my mind. I still wonder why the genocide took place. They killed all the children, the mothers, the old and the young people.

Daphrose Mukankundiye used to dream of going to university. But now, at the age of eighteen, she has, instead, become a young housewife in Bisesero. Her family consisted of ten people; now only Daphrose is alive. She went to Bisesero with her brother, Niyitegeka, where he was killed. Her parents—Selemani Nkundamaria and Eugènie Mukakabera—and six siblings were murdered in their home in Bahare, Gitesi.

Before the genocide, I was a well-off child. I was in the fourth year of primary school in Nyarugati, Gitesi. I intended to complete primary school, then move on to secondary school and continue on to university. I thought I would be able to find a good job after finishing all my studies. Now, I have abandoned my studies.

When her guardian suggested she get married, there was little discussion. But the circumstances in which her marriage took place were far removed from her memories of previous weddings.

I accepted because I had no choice. A boy from Bisesero brought round some beers and he also delivered a cow. I was then driven to his home. Before, when a girl was going to get married, she usually bought plates, cups, clothes, cases, etc... There was usually a ceremony on the day. However, I received none of these things; nor did I have a ceremony. I left like a thief who wanted to hide. I was ashamed of my marriage because I was still very young. I will probably soon get pregnant and there will be no-one to help me. My husband is also a survivor of the genocide.

The militiamen's families, who are my neighbours, are quite aware that I have got married. Instead of coming to help me make a home, they make fun of me by saying "This girl is just a girl and she's got married. Other girls her age are still at school, but instead she goes in search of a husband!" They do not realise that I left school because of them. They killed my parents who could have helped me with my schooling.

Elizaphan Ndayisaba, sixteen, lost all his family—his parents, two brothers and three sisters. He has returned to Bisesero, to live with his uncle, Hategeka, who is also alone, and he helps him to farm. Before the genocide he used to look after his father's cows; he had begged his father to be allowed to leave school to tend the cows. He remembers it as a happy time, so remote from the difficulties he now faces.

Some survivors have managed to reclaim what they lost during the genocide. Others have found their cows. I don't know where to go to get anything back. Before the genocide, my father had a lot of cows and other things which were worth something. My uncle doesn't have the time to help me. I am alone so I can't cultivate my father's fields. All that is left now are are bushes.

I can't get to sleep anymore at night because this is the only time I have to reflect. I wonder why I ever left school. Before the genocide, I used to think that in leaving school my father would give me a lot of cows and would build me a house etc... Now all these projects will come to nothing.

Before the genocide, I used to get into bed with my brothers and before going to sleep, we would

Elizaphan Ndayisaba

chat and play together. Now when I go to bed I think about the genocide. When I close my eyes I see all the bodies that were at Bisesero, especially the one of my mother with the child on her back.

"I have become disheartened. Nothing seems to give me back my courage. I don't know what my future will be anymore".

The children who are here and who are my age, don't want to come and play with me anymore. The survivors who trust me are at the orphanage. I don't want to go to the orphanage because I don't want to go to school. I am forced to live with old people.

Other children my age, who still have their parents, wear new clothes on special days, for example at Christmas, and when they go to mass. However, I am left feeling sad and I look at my clothes which are all worn. I wonder why they killed my parents and the other Tutsis who gave me things. The clothes that I wear today are ones that I found at the orphanage. They are all torn now but I can't find any others. I have to walk barefoot because I can't find any shoes, although I used to have some before the genocide. I can't even find any soap to wash myself or my clothes. I am really very poor.

I wonder what we have done to have to suffer like this for the rest of our lives. I haven't been able to answer this question.

Alphonsine, fifteen, is also missing her brothers and her parents.

I lived with my parents and brothers before the genocide. I felt good when I chatted with my brothers and my parents gave me everything I needed. Now, I am alone and no-one cares about me.

I remember the life I used to lead before and I feel great sorrow. I think about all the members of my family who are now dead. To ease my distress, I usually find a place where I can be alone to cry.

I am disabled and have become ill. I don't have any money to get treatment. So ultimately I am all alone.

Uwayisenga is now eleven. Her father, Ezéchias Nsengamihigo, and four of her five siblings were killed. Her mother and one sister survived. In Bisesero, they found her paternal uncle whose wife and children had been killed. In time, Uwayisenga's mother and her uncle married and
she had a new baby brother, Ndimurwango. But her future was blighted by her injuries.

It was in April 1994 that I began to suffer. I couldn't do anything because of the injuries I received from the machete. I even had to leave school because I was ill and had nowhere to study. Before the genocide, I had been in the first year of primary school in Gako. I followed the lessons very well. Nevertheless, I was happy to see my mother taking care of me and I looked after the baby.

When I go to bed, I immediately think about how the genocide was carried out in Bisesero. My head hurts all the time. Before the genocide, I used to eat and sleep without any problems. I didn't have to think about my future because my parents looked after me, my brothers and my sisters.

Her mother died in February 1997 and Uwayisenga has became a mother to her baby brother.

Now I am like an old mother. I wonder how my mother's baby will grow up. When he cries, I cry too. Other orphans from the genocide have been put in the orphanage of Nyamisaba in Gitesi. I cannot abandon my father's fields to go to an orphanage. All I want to do is to live here in Bisesero and to look after the cows and the baby.

"I don't want to go back to school because I can't see the point of studying."

The permanent sense of mortal danger is another link to the genocide.

When I farm or look after the cows on the hills, I shake from fear. Someone told me that the person who hit me with the machete is hiding in the area. I am scared that he will kill me. I don't feel comfortable. I don't play anymore because all the children of my age are dead.

Vincent Kayigema's parents, three brothers and two sisters were killed. In addition to missing their parents and siblings, children also feel the absence of their friends. Vincent, eleven, spoke of the companions he lost, along with his childhood.

During the night, I always think about the children, neighbours of my age, with whom I used to play football and who are now dead, even they were innocent.

Eric Nzabihimana used to be a teacher, but the cruelties he suffered at the hands of fellow-teachers and of students has killed his desire to teach.

I abandoned the profession. I remembered very well how students ran after me during the genocide, wanting to kill me, when I wanted to go to Gitarama.

Fear still dominates the lives of survivors. Siméon described how they returned to Bisesero and tried to "start life over again", building huts, as all around them lay the remains of their families. He speaks of a community shattered by the genocide and continually marginalised. And he tells of the renewed threat to their existence.

On our way to fetch wood, we could see our own children's skulls. We have tried to accept that our life will be difficult without our children or wives, but what hurts us deeply, is that the militiamen still want to kill us, even now. We are unable to sleep. The militiamen have killed some survivors who had been with us during the genocide. They were hit over the head by machetes, just like in April 1994.

"Before the genocide, the Abasesero was full of strong men. The few men who remain today will die of sorrow".

We have lost all faith in life. We cannot forsee the future of Bisesero. We are beginning to rebuild houses but if the houses are finished, we will need wives to have children with so that we can carry on the name of Abasesero. We need this so that we will be able be protected.

For the most part, the survivors have had to try to rebuild their lives without help from others. One local initiative by survivors, for survivors, has provided some support. Sylvère Gatwaza is involved in an association called 'Abadaharana' of Bisesero. Through this survivors have been able to assist each other.

We now have cabbages, peas and potatoes growing. With the money that we will receive by selling these products, we are going to be able to start a business. Someone called Claver Buzizi, from Bisesero, and who works in Butare for a church organisation, has built us a house for doing business. If any survivor has a problem, we will help him by giving him some money.

Another association is in the process of building us one hundred houses on the hill of Gisoro, in the cellule of Gitwa in the Bisesero sector.

Perhaps by getting together, we will be able to do something.

However, many survivors are still affected by the injuries they received in 1994. Anastase Kalisa went back to Bisesero to rebuild his home, but his shoulder was injured by a massue and he often becomes ill. His wife was also ill and in hospital at the time of the interview.

Edouard Nduwamungu

Before the genocide, my family had been a large one. I lived with my parents, brothers, nieces and nephews. Now I am all alone. We used to live off the land but all our cattle was stolen and now the fields are barren due to the lack of manure from the animals.

Edouard Nduwamungu is from Uwingabo in Gishyita. He is a farmer. His wife and children were killed in front of him at Mugonero hospital. He himself was badly wounded there by fragments of grenades. He then fled to Bisesero where again he was attacked—cut with machetes on his head and spears in his stomach. He had no medical treatment, and became badly infected. When the French arrived, Edouard was on the point of death.

Mukahigiro

Even now I am feeling the consequences. I have headaches which don't stop and infections in the scars.

From a material point of view, I used to have cows and goats, I had houses which were well equipped, but today I have neither houses, nor cows, nor goats. Nor is there any work that I can do as I am not well enough to cultivate. I won't remarry because I have no desire to do so. Although I am alone, I don't have the courage to remarry in conditions like this. I can't remarry without a house and without a means of building one, without a future for a family because I am not in good health. I am also not able to get treatment because I have neither support nor aid from outside because they killed all my acquaintances and they stole all my property.

Mukahigiro, aged 47, lost her husband before the genocide. They had several children, and she relied on her eldest son, Mutware, a teenager, and her extended family to help her. But although she and her three children survived the killings at Bisesero, and returned home to Musenyi, Gishyita, a year later, they are no longer able to support themselves.

I found my house completely destroyed; I had to go and live in Bugingo's house. Bugingo was someone from my family who was dead. His house had not been completely destroyed. I had to go and fetch some corrugated iron that had been thrown away and survivors helped me put the roof together.

I don't have enough utensils in this little house. There is just one plate. We sleep in the same room as the children. We have no mattresses so we have to make our beds out of grass.

Habineza, my child, is studying at the primary school. He doesn't have the necessary things for school: no exercise books, no pens and often the teacher throws him out of the classroom because he has not paid. My child has to come home for a few days and then he goes back to school again, without paying his school fees. He is then expelled again from class.

During the genocide, Mutware was hit a lot with clubs and stones. He is therefore unable to help me and now I have to do all the work.

My problems are too much for me. I have put all my trust in God. What shocks me is that although my children still have their mother, they are still suffering because of the poverty we live in.

When survivors fall ill, they encounter the full extent of their isolation. When Claver Habarugira, aged 36, first returned to Bisesero, he became very ill. He lost his wife, Bonifride Mukangemanyi, and four children, on Muyira hill.

I was unable to eat or sleep in my house and eventually I became ill. I had to stay in bed without any medicine. There was no-one who could drive me into the sun to warm myself up. I nearly died because I was so ill. Luckily I got better. During my illness, I thought a lot about my children and family who were all dead. My wife used to look after me whenever I was ill before the genocide. She would bring me sauces and soups. The whole family would come and see me and as a result of such encouragement, one would get better quickly.

My family's remains are left exposed on the hill and we cannot bury them.

"Before the genocide, I was surrounded by the houses of my family. All I have around me now are bushes. I regret the fact that I didn't die during the genocide.

I have put my trust in God".

Bisesero was a very well-known place. We had many cows and no-one ever succeeded in stealing our cows during attacks. There were a great many of us and there was a feeling of solidarity. Only old people are left now. We are widowers. We are nothing.

Only four people from my family survived the genocide. One is a child who is at the orphanage, another has lost his leg. I ought to look after them but I don't have the means to do it. This is why I'm so distressed.

Ndayisaba, aged 34, was in shock and deep depression when he first arrived back in Bisesero. It brought home to him the death of his mother, three brothers, two sisters and countless other relatives. Still suffering from an injury to his right shoulder, he was unable to farm and, for some time, he thought he would "die of loneliness and hunger".

All that was left of my father's house was bushes. No-one else from my family was there. The other survivors helped me rebuild a small house. I moved into a badly built house, all alone, without any materials. I had no plates, pans, chairs and food. I spent all day in bed without eating and just drinking water. I was ashamed of walking around because I had no clothes. The only ones I did have were torn and unwashed because I didn't have any soap. I also didn't have any money to buy any. I had to wash my clothes at night because I didn't have any others to wear.

My parents used to look after me before the genocide. When I went home my mother immediately used to give me food to eat. I also had brothers, sisters and friends and I always felt comfortable around them. When I was alone in the house, I used to think about all the people who were killed in a barbaric fashion. Their bodies were still exposed on the hills and sometimes I would see the dogs scratching at someone's bone. All this increased my distress.

Léoncie Nyiramugwera was fortunate enough to go to Belgium for medical treatment, thanks to the help of her son. But she has not fully recovered.

"I am always getting dizzy and I can't walk in the sun. I can't sleep at night".

Memories of the genocide at Bisesero have prevented many from returning to their homes. Maurice Sakufi is now renting a house in Kigali, where he has remarried and has another child. But he can never forget the wife and baby boy who died in Bisesero. He thinks about how before the genocide he used to breed cattle and sell the milk and how he had built a beautiful house on his farm, and he cannot feel at peace.

Claver Habarugira

I often go back to Bisesero to visit the other survivors and to see the things I lost during the genocide. Although I am still alive, I cannot sleep when I remember how the people were killed at Bisesero.

When I go back to Bisesero, I have nowhere to stay.

"I find it shocking to see all the bones lying on the hills when I return to Bisesero".

Vianney Uwimana, 28, is living and working in Kigali. He too finds it painful to visit Bisesero.

Bisesero was a place that I loved very much. There used to be a lot of people who lived in this region. Many of them were members of my family. Everywhere, I was welcomed warmly; I could eat where I wanted. Now, if I return to Bisesero, it is the bones of these people which welcome me. These skulls are exposed everywhere on the hills. I have lost all hope in life.

Augustin Buranga now works for the same company in Kigali as Vianney. He is filled with bitterness and sorrow and, at the age of 41, has given up on life.

I am all alone in the house. I have not yet remarried. I am still always thinking about my wife.

"I don't have the will to live any more now that I am alone. I feel like a corpse. The State just talks about reconciliation on the radio, instead of coming and helping us".

He has only returned to Bisesero twice. The last time was in April 1996, when he saw some of the militiamen involved in the killings, and the place where his family was killed. He immediately fell ill.

I visited the hills of Bisesero and I went to the place where I had buried the members of my family. Afterwards, I went to Nzamwita's home, who is a survivor from Bisesero, to spend the night there. That night I fell ill. Nzamwita and another survivor drove me to the health clinic in Mubuga. I was immediately hospitalised. I spent a week and a few days in bed in the clinic. Instead of getting better, my illness got worse. It was because of everything I had seen. Other people who were ill had people with them who looked after them. Lots of people came to visit them and bring them milk, juice and fruit. I was all alone. I couldn't even find anyone to say hello to me. The only visit I could expect was from Nzamwita who was also poor. When I was ill, no one offered me milk as they did for the others who were sick. No-one asked my forgiveness for what they had done to me during the genocide.

Augustin had no money to pay for his treatment and Nzamwita, also poverty-stricken, had to do so.

I saw how barbarically they killed during the genocide. The rich and poor died in the same way. I have also seen how the survivors have been treated after the genocide. Children have abandoned schools because they can't pay the school fees. I feel very disappointed with all this.

"I see no point in me being reconciled with anyone because I am no longer a person. The only thing that I have chosen to do, is to pray until the end of my life".

Preliminary Census of the Victims of Genocide in Bisesero

1. Commune Gishyita

1.1 Sector Bisesero

1.1.1 Cellule Nyarutovu

No.	Name	Age	Sex	Occupn.	Marital Status
1	Innocent Muganga	44	m	herdsman	married
2	Marianne Mukamunana	41	f	farmer	married
3	Béatrice Uzayisenga	18	f	student	single
4	Eugénie Mukangoga	16	f	student	single
5	Corneille Uwimana	14	m	student	
6	Vincent Muganga	12	m	student	
7	Chantal Uwanyirigira	9	f	student	
8	Appolinaire Semutwa	82	m	herdsman	married
9	Adèle Nyiramahe	70	f	farmer	married
10	Basile Mudenge	28	m	farmer	single
11	Gaspard Nkusi	33	m	herdsman	married
12	Catherine Mukasine	12	f	student	
13	Virginie Mukangoga	9	f	student	
14	Eric Nshimiye	6	m	student	
15	Eugène Binwangari	4	m	student	
16	Son of Nkusi	1 m	m		
17	Charles Rwamanywa	64	m	herdsman	married
18	Madeleine Mukaruziga	56	f	farmer	married
19	Casimir Musabyimana	24	m	farmer	single
20	Célestin Ndwaniye	58	m	herdsman	married
21	Léocadie Nyirabititaweho	54	f	farmer	married
22	Claver Ndahimana	26	m	herdsman	single
23	Xavéra Nyirabahutu	78	f	farmer	widow
24	Ruhumuliza	33	m	farmer	single
25	Mukabutera	41	f	farmer	divorced
26	Karamuka	58	m	herdsman	married
27	Nicodème Kabwana	62	m	farmer	married
28	Marie Nyirabuka	56	f	farmer	married
29	Eliezer Kambanda	58	m	farmer	married
30	Erina Mukankundiye	50	f	farmer	widow
31	Jean-Damascène Nteziryayo	26	m	farmer	single
32	Gatembo	40	m	herdsman	married
33	Ephrem Gasagara	57	m	herdsman	married
34	Musoni	23	m	farmer	single
35	Vianney Higiro	20	m	farmer	single
36	Ngamije	28	m	farmer	single
37	Gérémie Nturo	70	m	herdsman	married
38	Aloys Karegera	35	m	herdsman	married
39	Anastasie Mukandori	42	f	farmer	widow
40	Mukandera	65	f	farmer	married
41	Silas Kayibanda	58	m	herdsman	married
42	Emilienne Mukarugwiza	57	f	farmer	married
43	Mukamugema	50	f	farmer	married
44	Nyirarunyonga	15	f	farmer	
45	Nyirambabazi	4	f		
46	Colette Mukagasana	23	f	farmer	single
47	Mukansanga	24	f	farmer	married
48	Aron Kanamugire	27	m	farmer	single
49	Nsengayire	29	m	herdsman	married
50	Martin Kadaraza	38	m	herdsman	married
51	Azalias Ruzezwa	60	m	herdsman	married
52	Everiénne Mukakabera	40	f	farmer	widow
53	Odette Nyiramana	21	f	farmer	single
54	Emmanuel Rubunge	20	m	farmer	single
55	Primitive Uwamahoro	23	f	student	single
56	Kamabano	57	m	herdsman	married
57	Ephrem Munyantarama	56	m	herdsman	married
58	Kajeje	14	m	student	
59	Kwitegetse	20	f	farmer	single
60	Zacharie Nkeramihigo	65	m	herdsman	married
61	Kadori	38	m	herdsman	married
62	Berthilde Mukangango	33	f	farmer	married
63	Béata Mukangemanyi	20	f	farmer	single
64	Nyirahene	58	f	farmer	married
65	Béata Nyirahategeka	21	f	farmer	single
66	Mayira	18	m	farmer	single
67	Matingiri	29	m	herdsman	married
68	Alphonsine Bucyensenge	23	f	student	single
69	Drocella Mugorewindekwe	20	f	farmer	single
70	Alphonse Munyandinda	32	m	herdsman	married
71	Rugondo Ngarambe	36	m	farmer	married
72	Niyongira	5	f		
73	Thomas Kajeguhakwa	34	m	farmer	married
74	Chadrac Kamugundu	60	m	herdsman	married
75	Amon Ngarambe	30	m	herdsman	single
76	Assiel Ntagara	36	m	farmer	single
77	Berthilde	35	f	farmer	married
78	Narcisse Musabyimana	16	m	student	single
79	Senani Ntagara	16	m	student	single
80	Daphrose Mukarubayiza	20	f	farmer	single
81	Emmanuel Ndagijimana	2	m		
82	Kangabe	48	f	farmer	widow
83	Augustin Ntagara	37	m	merchant	married
84	Daughter of Kamagaza	10	f	student	
85	Thérèse Nyiramujyambere	24	f	student	single
86	Marthe Mukarugwiza	37	f	farmer	married
87	Mafene	62	m	herdsman	married
88	François Munyandagara	42	m	herdsman	married
89	Ingabire	12	f	student	
90	Munyampundu	56	m	herdsman	married
91	Marcianne Mukantaganda	43	f	farmer	married
92	Mukankanika	12	f	student	
93	Nshimiye	8	m	student	
94	Kayihura	7	m	student	
95	Uwera	5	f		
96	Dominique Gasagara	6	m		
97	Silas Nsengiyumva	13	m	student	
98	Macenderi	3	m		
99	Bikorimana	2	m		
100	Masengesho	1	m		
101	Xaverine Mukambaraga	37	f	farmer	married
102	Nyiramidiburo	9	f	student	
103	Nyirajeri	7	f	student	
104	Wife of Munyandagara	35	f	farmer	married
105	Pétronille Mukambaraga	30	f	farmer	married
106	Nyirabazungu	5	f		
107	Eugénie	3	f		
108	Rukara	1	m		
109	Shema Rudagari	32	m	farmer	single
110	Bernadette Mukamunana	45	f	farmer	married
111	Rudomoro	8	m	student	
112	Emmanuel Munyandinda	34	m	herdsman	married
113	Isabelle Mukankusi	30	f	farmer	married
114	Ndahayo	7	m	student	
115	Erina Nyirantibiri	50	f	farmer	married
116	Thabithe Nyiraruyange	52	f	farmer	married
117	Alphonsine Uwamahoro	9	f	student	
118	Jacqueline Uwera	7	f	student	
119	Ingabire	3	f		
120	Thabithe Nyinawingeri	38	f	farmer	widow
121	Gasingwa	5	m		
122	Nyirambabazi	11	f	student	
123	Munyandinda	8	f	student	
124	Cassilde, "Mme Gatembo"	30	f	farmer	married
125	Siméon Ngoga	35	m	farmer	married
126	Alphonse Ndahimana	9	m	student	
127	Immaculée Gasagara	8	f	student	
128	Catherine Mukangamije	30	f	farmer	married
129	Phénéas Ntihemuka	28	m	farmer	single
130	Nyiranzabahimana	4	f		
131	Gakwindigiri	2	m		
132	Emmanuel Munyaneza	41	m	farmer	married
133	Marie, wife of Munyaneza	38	f	farmer	married
134	Mukanka	10	f	student	
135	Nyiramakaratasi	7	f	student	
136	André Ntizingingirwa	60	m	herdsman	married
137	His wife Thérèse	35	f	farmer	married
138	Françoise	10	f	student	
139	Manzi	5	m		
140	Benjamin	3	m		
141	Colette	14	f		
142	Anastasie	34	f	farmer	married
143	Nyiranuma	15	f	student	
144	Kampire	5	f		
145	Kamana	41	m	farmer	married
146	His wife, Bernadette	34	f	farmer	married
147	Matoroshi	13	m	student	
148	Immaculée	35	f	farmer	married
149	Mukansanga	17	f	farmer	single
150	André Karama	59	m	herdsman	married
151	Vérène	30	f	farmer	married
152	Assiel Nkusi	32	m	herdsman	married
153	Rose Mukantagara	55	f	farmer	married
154	Nyiramazuru	14	f	student	
155	Vianney Butwenge	16	m	student	single
156	Madeleine	48	f	farmer	married
157	Mukangango	30	f	farmer	married
158	Mukabadege	14	f	student	
159	Mathilde	12	f	student	
160	Munyantarama	35	m	farmer	married
161	Marcianne Nyiraromba	58	f	farmer	widow

162	Théodosie	28	f	farmer	married
163	Eugénie	5	f		
164	Rubyogo	3	m		
165	Mukandinda	34	f	farmer	married
166	Jean	36	m	herdsman	married
167	Gasurugunya	14	m	student	
168	Kaduguri	12	m	student	
169	Matarahinda	10	m	student	
170	Njakazi	8	f	student	
171	Immaculée	25	f	farmer	single
172	Sendiragoye	11	m	student	
173	Macibiri Niyonsaba	13	f	student	
174	Nyirakamagaza	8	f	student	
175	Mukamurigo	7	f	student	
176	Sibomana	24	m	farmer	single
177	Dushimirimana	11	m	student	
178	Chantal Uwimana	5	f		
179	Marthe Mukankusi	58	f	farmer	widow
180	Kibwa	4	m		
181	Samuel Manzi	7	m	student	
182	Paul Karangwa	6	m		
183	Philomène Nyiranshuti	35	f	farmer	married
184	Antoine Ndagijimana	7	m	student	
185	Pierre Nzamwita	9	m	student	
186	Anésie Nyirampeta	26	f	tailor	single
187	Régine Mukasahaha	52	f	farmer	married
188	Ladislas Nibigira	66	m	herdsman	married
189	Chrésie Nyirahishamunda	32	f	farmer	married
190	Euphrasie	15	f	student	
191	Rubayiza	8	m	student	
192	Léon Karamuka	6	m		
193	Samson Kaberuka	55	m	farmer	married
194	Nyinawankusi	50	f	farmer	married
195	Aphrodis Habiyambere	37	m	herdsman	married
196	Phrolide Nyirakimuzanye	32	f	farmer	married
197	Slyvère Hakizimana	6	m		
198	Sibomana	11	m	student	
199	Madeleine Nyirakinazi	58	f	farmer	widow
200	Aloys Ntirenganya	20	m	farmer	single
201	Dominique	36	m	herdsman	married
202	Agnès Nyiragwiza	32	f	farmer	married
203	Ntaganira	7	m	student	
204	Marie Kwitegetse	4	f		
205	Déo	1	m		
206	Gérard	3	m		
207	Marie	1	f		
208	Kaduguri	10	m	student	
209	Léonard Gakuba	1	m		
210	Ephrem	42	m	herdsman	married
211	Judith Nyirashema	43	f	farmer	widow
212	Mbindigiri	15	f	student	
213	Rudomoro	12	m	student	
214	Ignace Nkeragutabara	33	m	herdsman	married
215	Esther	30	f	farmer	married
216	Ndayisaba	5	m		
217	Nyiransabimana	1	f		
218	Adéline Mukamunana	28	f	farmer	married
219	Léonille Mukamurigo	8	f	student	
220	Murenzi	2	m		
221	Patrice Nzamwita	1m	f		
222	Rukara	1	m		
223	Agnès Mukamunana	20	f	farmer	married
224	Gaudence Kandame	58	f	farmer	widow
225	Nyirahabiyambere	25	f	farmer	married
226	Nyirahabimana	2	f		
227	Daphrose Mukamugema	24	f	farmer	married
228	Mukankusi	2	f		
229	Pétronille Mukandinda	28	f	farmer	married
230	Nyirabukara	3	f		
231	Yamfashije	2	f		
232	Espérance Nyirankundiye	7	f	student	
233	Marie Nyiraneza	16	f	farmer	single
234	Marcel Ndayisaba	33	m	herdsman	married
235	Mukamuvara	28	f	farmer	married
236	Anastase	7	m	student	
237	Marie	5	f		
238	Félicitée Uwimana	15	f	student	
239	Frédianne Mukansengiyumva	17	f	student	single
240	Antoinette Mukankaka	8	f	student	
241	Fidèle Ngoga	35	m	electrician	married
242	Béata Murebwayire	2	f	student	
243	Dative	32	f	farmer	widow
244	Béatrice Nyiramwamira	8	f	student	
245	Madeleine	6	f		
246	Spéciose	3	f		
247	Alphonse	1	m		
248	Chadrac	32	m	farmer	married
249	Dative	25	f	farmer	married
250	Nyirambaragasa	9	f	student	
251	Nyirambarara	7	f	student	
252	Sibateri	26	m	farmer	single
253	Jean Baptiste Kananura	44	m	builder	married
254	Anastasie Utetiwabo	40	f	farmer	married
255	Emmanuel Niyonteze	16	m	student	single
256	Aloys Nshimiye	17	m	student	single
257	Annonciata Majyambere	11	m	student	
258	Frodouard Majyambere	11	m	student	
259	Mupenzi Muhayimana	6	m		
260	Berchmans Mbayu	69	m	herdsman	married
261	Anathalie Kabanani	55	f	farmer	married
262	Cassien Kajonge	40	m	herdsman	married
263	Joséphine Mukandekezi	34	f	farmer	married
264	Alphonsine Yamfashije	18	f	farmer	single
265	Mathias Kagemana	15	m	student	
266	Nyiranyoni	9	f	student	
267	Modeste Murwanashyaka	7	m	student	
268	Cyriaque	4	m	student	
269	Ignace Ngoga	29	m	herdsman	married
270	Spéciose	25	f	farmer	married
271	Félix	2	m		
272	Patrice Rwabukwisi	60	m	farmer	married
273	Cécile Mukamuhinde	45	f	farmer	married
274	Xaverine Murekatete	18	f	farmer	single
275	Jean Paul	9	m	student	
276	Léocadie Mukankanika	45	f	farmer	married
277	Marie Gorette	18	f	student	single
278	Angèle Nyinawindinda	15	f	student	
279	Nyiranzage	6	f		
280	Nyirankotsori	4	f		
281	Anathalie Mukagatana	40	f	farmer	married
282	Thérèse Mukamwiza	15	f	farmer	
283	Pascal Rwamurima	13	m	student	
284	Bernard	9	m	student	
285	Kagandari	6	m		
286	Béata Gakwavu	8	f		
287	Catherine Mukarugwiza	29	f	farmer	married
288	Athanase Munyurangabo	8	m	student	
289	Slyvère Nduwamungu	6	m		
290	Védaste	4	m		
291	Godelièvе Mukantagwabira	5	f		
292	Marcianne	56	f	farmer	married
293	Jason Kanamugire	41	m	builder	married
294	Bernadette Nyirajyambere	32	f	farmer	married
295	Jacqueline Musabyimana	11	f	student	
296	Gérard Ntawuyirusha	9	m	student	
297	Lycie Mukandahinyuka	6	f		
298	Daphrose Nyirabuka	48	f	farmer	widow
299	Marthe Mukabideri	29	f	farmer	single
300	Candide Mukankanika	20	f	student	single
301	Mukamurigo	10	f	student	
302	Mukakayijuka	47	f	farmer	widow
303	Benjamin Hagengimana	75	m	farmer	single
304	Nyiranzabihimana	14	f	student	
305	Félicitée Mukankezi	33	f	farmer	married
306	Jason Muhayimana	14	m	student	
307	Ousiel Munyangabe	12	m	student	
308	Thacienne Mukankusi	10	f	student	
309	Patrice	8	f	student	
310	Marceline	5	f		
311	Zibie Kabagwiza	50	f	farmer	married
312	Jean Niragire	26	m	herdsman	single
313	Martin Bugabo	13	m	student	
314	Aimé Marie Umutoni	10	f	student	
315	Samuel Kambanda	59	m	herdsman	married
316	Isabelle	19	f	farmer	single
317	Aron Kanani	11	m	student	
318	Umuhoza	9	f	student	
319	Mukamunana	16	f	student	single
320	Eugénie	7	f	student	
321	Elianne Mukangamije	52	f	farmer	married
322	Cyprien Sebigiri	57	m	farmer	married
323	Mukabera	50	f	farmer	married
324	Mukashyaka	30	f	farmer	married
325	Immaculée	10	f	student	
326	Eliezer Kamabano	60	m	herdsman	married
327	Julienne Kanyamibwa	55	f	farmer	married
328	Valérie Mukantagara	28	f	farmer	single
329	Béatrice	18	f	student	single
330	Suzanne Nyiramujyambere	80	f	farmer	widow
331	Thabéa	21	f	farmer	single
332	Mukandori	24	f	farmer	single
333	Rukara	3	m		
334	Gasana	35	m	herdsman	married
335	Alphonse	11	m	student	
336	Nyirabukara	9	f	student	
337	Nyirakaromba	65	f	farmer	widow
338	Munyangabe	32	m	herdsman	married
339	Kayumba	40	m	farmer	single
340	Marguerite	26	f	farmer	married
341	Nyirahabimana	45	f		single
342	Madeleine Kangabo	85	f	farmer	widow
343	Cyurinyana	40	f	farmer	single

344	Vérène Kamugema	55	f	farmer	widow
345	Thomas Sindayiheba	22	m	farmer	single
346	Xavéra Butorano	18	f	farmer	single
347	Biregeya Muhayimana	15	m	student	
348	Elizabeth	10	f	student	
349	Jonas	6	m		
350	Evérienne Nyirabukezi	60	f	farmer	widow
351	Mukagatare	16	f	student	single
352	François Ngendahimana	40	m	herdsman	married
353	Mukankubana	30	f	farmer	married
354	Mukamurenzi	9	f	student	
355	Cyriaque Rugwizangoga	7	m		
356	Béata	5	f		
357	Marthe	3	f		
358	Sibomana	1	m		
359	Jolie Ngendahimana	5m	f		
360	Ezéchiel Munyandamutsa	50	m	herdsman	married
361	Azelle Nyirabugingo	46	f	farmer	married
362	Assiel Habimana	23	m	farmer	single
363	Mukarusanga	13	f	student	
364	Niyonsaba	8	f	student	
365	Munyurangabo	7	m	student	
366	Mushimiyimana	4	m	student	
367	Euphrasie Mukambaraga	40	f	farmer	married
368	Mukanzihira	20	f	farmer	single
369	Mukangemanyi	18	f	student	single
370	Patrice Mukantabana	11	f	student	
371	Mukankundiye	8	f	student	
372	Dusabimana	3	m		
373	Nyirangeneye	1	f		
374	Samuel Kabanda	40	m	herdsman	married
375	Mukarubayiza	38	f	farmer	married
376	Matoroshi	13	m	student	
377	Nyirabwoneye	6	f		
378	Samson	4	m		
379	Charles	2	m		
380	Gérard Munyampundu	40	m	farmer	married
381	Dative Mukansonera	35	f	farmer	married
382	Alphonse	13	m	student	
383	Nirere	10	f	student	
384	Nyiramazuru	8	f	student	
385	Jean Paul	3	m		
386	Esdras Munyansanga	35	m	tailor	married
387	Furaha	7	f	student	
388	Ndorimana	1	m		
389	Jonas Muramira	30	m	herdsman	married
390	Elina Kankuyo	28	f	farmer	married
391	Hesron Kamusizi	76	m	farmer	widower
392	Livera Nyirazibera	70	f	farmer	widow
393	Assiel Gasagara	45	m	herdsman	married
394	Marthe Mukangemanyi	42	f	farmer	married
395	Mukarusanga	7	f	student	
396	Busugugu	35	m	herdsman	married
397	Rachel Mukamurigo	33	f	farmer	married
398	Nyirajeri	9	f	student	
399	Macibiri	9	f	student	
400	Aloys	6	m		
401	Judith Nyirashema	43	f	farmer	widow
402	Xavéra Uzamushaka	76	f	farmer	widow
403	Sophie Mukankusi	35	f	farmer	divorced
404	Nyirabukara	6	f		
405	Pascasie	28	f	farmer	married
406	Magunzu	4	m		
407	Mathias Gahamanyi	6	m		
408	Mélanie Nyiramafaranga	70	f	farmer	married
409	Euphrasie Mukashariyo	45	f	farmer	
410	Bunyenzi	14	m	student	
411	Esther	12	f	student	
412	Ntakiyimana	3	f		
413	Evérienne Mukantagara	50	f	farmer	widow
414	Xaverine Nyirantagorama	16	f	farmer	single
415	Xaveri Harerimana	18	m	farmer	single
416	Alphonse	13	m	student	
417	Jean	15	m	farmer	
418	Munyaneza Rushihe	45	m	farmer	married
419	Mukangemanyi	32	f	farmer	married
420	Debora	30	f	farmer	married
421	Mbarushimana	10	m	student	
422	Modeste	9	m	student	
423	Cyprien Gashi	80	m	herdsman	married
424	Nyirangeneye	6	f		
425	Adèle Bambara	75	f	farmer	married
426	Chrésie Mukangango	40	m	farmer	married
427	Mukamusoni	15	f	farmer	
428	Mukabutera	13	f	student	
429	Mathias Bikorimana	11	m	student	
430	Bayisenge	5	m		
431	Martin Niyomugabo	3	m		
432	Gorette Nyirajyambere	30	f	farmer	married
433	Claver	10	m	student	
434	Catherine	8	f	student	
435	Léonidas Rwanyabuto	70	m	herdsman	married
436	Athanasie Kantarama	68	f	farmer	married
437	Anastasie Mukangarambe	17	f	farmer	single
438	Mukeshimana	15	m	student	
439	Mukarukaka	11	f	student	
440	Samuel Kanyoni	80	m	herdsman	married
441	Esther Kanyanja	75	f	farmer	married
442	Mafurere	45	m	herdsman	widower
443	Havugimana Nyakazungu	20	m	farmer	single
444	Pascasie Mukamunana	40	f	farmer	married
445	Thacienne Mukamana	16	f	farmer	single
446	Hélène	12	f	student	
447	Gaspard	9	m	student	
448	Gasurira	6	m		
449	Pronie, wife of Muganga	40	f	farmer	married
450	Elie	16	m	farmer	single
451	Mukamukomeza	14	f	student	
452	Protais	12	f	student	
453	Esther	7	f	student	
454	Ngiruwonsanga	33	m	herdsman	married
455	Uwimana	14	f	student	
456	Madeleine	5	f		
457	Pauline Kamukina	80	f	farmer	widow
458	Cyprien Mutemberezi	50	m	herdsman	married
459	Zilipa Mukalibanje	30	f	farmer	married
460	Jean Kaneza	14	m	student	
461	Phénéas Nsengimana	12	m	student	
462	Sophie	10	f	student	
463	Nyirabukara	8	f	student	
464	Ingabire	5	f		
465	Bayiringire	3	m		
466	Ntabana	2	m		
467	Marcel Sentama	35	m	herdsman	married
468	Rosalie	32	f	farmer	married
469	Nyirambabazi	37	f	farmer	divorced
470	Matoroshi	13	m	student	
471	Mukasine	2	f		
472	Nzamwita Rufuku	35	m	herdsman	married
473	Dancilla Nyiragwiza	32	f	farmer	married
474	Mukashyaka	12	f	student	
475	Berthe	9	f	student	
476	Mukankomati	3	f		
477	Nyirayeze	85	f	farmer	widow
478	Vénancie Mukantagara	70	f	farmer	widow
479	Nkejuwimye	30	m	herdsman	married
480	Alivèra	28	f	farmer	married
481	Amon Nsabimana	24	m	farmer	single
482	Rose Nyirangirumwami	52	f	farmer	married
483	Rwabukwisi	65	m	herdsman	married
484	Hana	45	f	farmer	married
485	Xavèrine	14	f	farmer	
486	Elianne	12	f	farmer	
487	Hagenimana	10	m	student	
488	Nyirarukundo	8	f	student	
489	Nyirabushungwe	5	f		
490	Ayirwanda	6	m		
491	Nyirajyambere	38	f	farmer	married

1.1.2 Cellule Jurwe

No.	Name	Age	Sex	Occupn.	Marital Status
1	Furere	47	m	herdsman	married
2	Marguerite Nyiramataza	45	f	farmer	married
3	Alphonsine Mukangango	14	f	student	
4	Angélique	10	f	student	
5	Xavérine Nyiracanira	57	f	farmer	widow
6	Aphrodis Karamaga	28	m	farmer	married
7	Nyirakanyana	29	f	farmer	married
8	Baby Karamaga	5m	m		
9	Hesron Munyangabe	63	m	farmer	widower
10	Ousiel Hategekimana	31	m	herdsman	married
11	Son of Hategekimana	3	m		
12	Jean	36	m	farmer	married
13	Bernadette Mukazitoni	34	f	farmer	married
14	Nyirabucoci	7	f	student	
15	Pierre Rugamba	4	m		
16	Colette Mukundufite	37	f	farmer	widow
17	Thacienne	17	f	farmer	single
18	Mugema	55	m	herdsman	married
19	Mukankuranga	47	f	farmer	married
20	Ngendahayo	28	m	farmer	single
21	Athanase Bwana	66	m	herdsman	married
22	Esther Nyirabusimba	59	f	farmer	married
23	Gaspard Gatsitsi	54	m	farmer	married
24	Thérèse	47	f	farmer	married

25	Chantal	3	f		
26	Spéciose	25	f	farmer	married
27	Ngamije	30	m	farmer	single
28	Grégoire Kayijuka	60	m	herdsman	married
29	Agnès Mukamangara	46	f	farmer	married
30	Gorette Uwimana	11	f	student	
31	François Ukurikimfura	28	m	farmer	single
32	Kayigamba	28	m	farmer	married
33	Marguerite	25	f	farmer	married
34	Denis Kayigamba	4	m		
35	Claudine Kavigamba	2	f		
36	Munyurangabo	11	f	student	
37	Pascal Ndamage	35	m	herdsman	married
38	Candide Mukandirima	30	f	farmer	married
39	Mukamurenzi	9	f	student	
40	Nyirabunonko	6	f		
41	Mutsiri	1	m		
42	Etienne Nyirimbibi	65	m	herdsman	widower
43	Immaculée	27	f	farmer	married
44	Stanislas Nyakazungu	54	m	herdsman	married
45	Xavéra Nyirampirima	46	f	farmer	married
46	Pascal Buhigiro	30	m	shopkeeper	single
47	Modeste Gasagara	32	m	herdsman	married
48	Adrienne Uwamariya	28	f	farmer	married
49	Habimana	9	m	student	
50	Claude Murwanashyaka	24	m	herdsman	married
51	Odette	22	f	farmer	married
52	Karangwa	13	m	student	
53	Innocent Ngoga	27	m	herdsman	married
54	Régine Mukarutabana	25	f	farmer	married
55	Gakwerere	3	m		
56	Athanasie Ngoga	5m	f		
57	Rwakana Mutsiri	62	m	herdsman	married
58	Mukamusoni	57	f	farmer	married
59	Odette Muteteri	22	f	farmer	single
60	Mudori	26	f	farmer	single
61	Marcel Semutware	6	m		
62	Dative Mukandori	48	f	farmer	married
63	Emmanuel Kayinamura	26	m	herdsman	married
64	Mukeshimana	25	f	farmer	married
65	Anathalie Mukandekezi	22	f	farmer	single
66	Alphonse Habyarimana	20	m	student	single
67	Alphonsine Nyirajyambere	17	f	student	single
68	Marie Mukangango	14	f	student	
69	Mukamunana	9	f	student	
70	Nyirabigirimana	4	f		
71	Pierre Gakoko	2	m		
72	Gaudence Mukandirima	50	f	farmer	married
73	Edouard Kanyamiganda	27	m	herdsman	single
74	Narcisse kayiranga	23	m	farmer	single
75	Suzanne	31	f	farmer	
76	Mukashema	34	f	farmer	married
77	Murekatete	15	f	farmer	
78	Mukankomeje	12	f	student	
79	Ntigurirwa	8	m	student	
80	Damascène Cyiza	5	m		
81	Rutebuka	3	m		
82	Isaac Sebushishi	60	m	teacher	married
83	Eleda Mukakimanuka	52	f	farmer	married
84	Paul Bimenyimana	24	m	student	single
85	Muhire	30	f	farmer	married
86	Nyirangirimana	9	f	student	
87	Valence	6	m		
88	Kaduguri	3	m		
89	Mukeshimana	10	f	student	
90	Edouard Kazungu	65	m	herdsman	married
91	Stéphanie Nyirankesha	60	f	farmer	married
92	Casimir Munyandinda	25	m	farmer	single
93	Hategeka	28	m	herdsman	single
94	Eugénie Mukamuhizi	22	f	farmer	married
95	Eugénie Mukankuranga	30	f	farmer	married
96	Béatrice Mukankundiye	10	f	student	
97	Patricia Mukamwiza	8	f	student	
98	Patrice Ntaganda	6	m		
99	Marcel	3	m		
100	Jean Ndengiyinka	40	m	herdsman	married
101	Béata	15	f	student	
102	Alphonse Murenzi	13	m	student	
103	Mukasine	10	f	student	
104	Alfred	6	m		
105	Ruzindana	30	m	herdsman	married
106	Uwamariya	27	f	farmer	married
107	Félicitée Nyiramaberete	60	f	farmer	widow
108	Ntagozera	36	m	herdsman	married
109	Aimé Marie Mukankomeje	32	f	farmer	married
110	Callixte Runombe	11	m	student	
111	Matoroshi Ntakirutimana	15	f	student	
112	Claudine Ntagozera	9	f	student	
113	Louis Ntagozera	7	m	student	
114	Nadine Ntagozera	5	f		
115	Nicodème Ntagozera	2	m		
116	Kayumba Gasirikari	22	m	farmer	single
117	Jean Nyamuganza	58	m	herdsman	married
118	Catherine Mukakabano	52	f	farmer	married
119	Claver Karangwa	20	m	farmer	single
120	Candide Nyirajigo	20	f	farmer	single
121	Vérène Mukandayisenga	16	f	student	single
122	Ignace Munana	30	m	herdsman	married
123	Odette Mukamugema	28	f	farmer	married
124	Mukeshimana	3	f		
125	Marie Mukambishibishi	60	f	farmer	widow
126	Charles Rutiyimba	16	m	farmer	single
127	Ntagara	14	m	student	
128	Emile Kabasha	32	m	carpenter	single
129	Esther Mukangoga	68	f	farmer	widow
130	Cécile Mukamusoni	27	f	farmer	married
131	Augustin Ngirababyeyi	16	m	student	single
132	Spéciose Mukashema	12	f	student	
133	Marie Yamfashije	10	f	student	
134	Jacqueline Nzamukosha	8	f	student	
135	Vincent Nzasabimfura	7	m	student	
136	Jean Kabandana	35	m	herdsman	married
137	Hyacinthe Kangabe	32	f	farmer	married
138	Callixte Karangwa	9	m	student	
139	Charles Ndizeye	7	m	student	
140	Déogratias Muganga	38	m	herdsman	married
141	Adeline Mukarusanga	35	f	farmer	married
142	Mukeshimana	7	f	student	
143	Gasana	2	m		
144	Mukagashema	5	f		
145	Patrice Niyomushi	42	m	builder	married
146	Adeline Nyirampirima	35	f	farmer	married
147	Joséphine Mukarugwiza	16	f	student	single
148	Tite Nkurunziza	14	m	student	
149	Mukandamage	8	f	student	
150	Murindahabi	6	m		
151	Narcisse	67	m	farmer	married
152	Anastasie Karwoga	62	f	farmer	married
153	Colette Mukantaganda	24	f	farmer	divorced
154	Mukankundiye	5	f		
155	Mukankomeje	3	f		
156	Kayigamba	27	m	farmer	married
157	Mukagatwaza	4	f		
158	Karemangingo	2	m		
159	Eulade Kazungu	65	m	merchant	married
160	Ancille Nyirampirima	52	f	farmer	married
161	Alphonse Gatwaza	20	m	student	single
162	Dative Mukangemanyi	17	f	student	
163	Marcel Ntakirutimana	15	m	student	single
164	Harorimana	13	m	student	
165	André Shamukiga	60	m	herdsman	married
166	Julienne Mukarutabana	48	f	farmer	married
167	Christine Mukakabego	22	f	farmer	married
168	Jean Paul Byiringiro	1	m		
169	Vianney Sebatwa	29	m	farmer	single
170	Odette Mukashema	16	f	student	single
171	Mukamayire	14	f	student	
172	Budoziya	12	f	student	
173	Bakame	9	m	student	
174	Edith Murekatete	26	f	secretary	married
175	Ngoga Munyandinda	4	m		
176	Cassien Munyandinda	2	m		
177	Candide Mukabideri	26	f	farmer	married
178	Mujawamariya	3	f		
179	Gaudence Mukaruburika	60	f	farmer	widow
180	Thacienne Mukamurenzi	25	f	farmer	single
181	Rusingizandekwe	22	m	student	single
182	Jean Ncogoza	33	m	merchant	married
183	Winniphrida Kantashya	28	f	farmer	married
184	Boniface Ncogoza	4	m		
185	Didacienne Ncogoza	2	f		
186	Emmanuel Habiyambere	36	m	herdsman	married
187	Julienne	32	f	farmer	married
188	Ntezimana	5	m		
189	Mukankundiye	3	f		
190	Nyirabukara	2	f		
191	Célestine Ntagwarira	50	m	herdsman	married
192	Gertrude Nyiranzeyimana	47	f	farmer	married
193	Marcel Karimba	13	m	student	
194	Alphonsine	9	f	student	
195	Budoziya	7	f	student	
196	Ntezimana	5	m		
197	Bernard	2	m		
198	Assiel Gakeri	50	m	herdsman	married
199	Rose Mukarugwiza	48	f	farmer	married
200	Martin Hakizimana	28	m	farmer	single
201	Gaudence Mukamazimpaka	16	f	student	single
202	Gashema	10	m	student	
203	François Rusagara	46	m	herdsman	married
204	Adèle Mukabacondo	42	f	farmer	married
205	Canisius Kabayiza	24	m	farmer	single

206	Euphrasie Mukakaragwa	20	f	student	single
207	Dorothée Mukarwego	22	f	farmer	single
208	Jolie	16	f	student	single
209	Déogratias Kalisa	12	m	student	
210	Mukawera	8	f	student	
211	Murenzi	3	m		
212	Narcisse Karemera	35	m	herdsman	married
213	Gertrude Nyirahategeka	32	f	farmer	married
214	Annonciata Mukamasabo	11	f	student	
215	Immaculée	9	f	student	
216	Niyoyita	6	m		
217	Mujawamariya	3	f		
218	Cécile Karemera	3	f		
219	Anathalie Nyirabayi	56	f	farmer	widow
220	Innocent Nsengayire	14	m	student	
221	Evérienne Mukamuganga	47	f	farmer	married
222	Bagirinka	20	f	farmer	single
223	Jean Turikunkiko	25	m	merchant	single
224	Innocent Hakizimana	18	m	retailer	single
225	Caritas Mukamuzima	14	f	student	
226	Nkurikiyinka	5	m		
227	Marthe Nyiramategeko	38	f	farmer	married
228	Thacienne Mukamunana	19	f	farmer	single
229	Drocella Nyirahabimana	11	f	student	
230	Ntivuguruzwa	9	m	student	
231	Eliezer Nsanzurwimo	11	m	student	
232	Marguerite Mukandirima	50	f	farmer	married
233	Augustin Ndayisaba	25	m	farmer	single
234	Emmanuel Havugimana	15	m	farmer	
235	Denise Hategeka	2	f		
236	Athanase Ntaganzwa	57	m	herdsman	married
237	Immaculée Kamayogi	52	f	farmer	married
238	Béata Mukabera	30	f	farmer	
239	Thérèse	26	f	farmer	married
240	Anastasie Mukarwego	45	f	farmer	married
241	Annonciata Mukashema	15	f	farmer	
242	Frolide Mukamusoni	30	f	farmer	married
243	Eugénie Nyinawindinda	8	f	student	
244	Alphonsine Mukankubana	6	f		
245	Ignace Sibomana	4	m		
246	Daphrose Mukamwiza	2	f		
247	Musabende	14	f	student	
248	Hatunguramye	11	m	student	
249	Ntigurirwa	8	m	student	
250	Havugabaramye	4	m		
251	Majyambere	11	m	student	
252	Xaveri Rugaravu	35	m	herdsman	married
253	Daphrose Mukankaka	32	f	farmer	married
254	Munyinya	70	m	herdsman	widower
255	Cyprien Ntagozera	30	m	farmer	married
256	Vérène Mukamurangwa	28	f	farmer	married
257	Pascal	3	m		
258	Nyirahabimana	1	s		
259	Pascal Nkanika	27	m	herdsman	married
260	Béata Nyirapare	32	f	farmer	married
261	Ntigurwa	5	m		
262	Dismas Habiyambere	3	m		
263	Jean Kananura	40	m	herdsman	married
264	Bernadette Mukazitoni	35	f	farmer	married
265	Mugambi	11	m	student	
266	Mukamunana	9	f	student	
267	Bizuru	7	m	student	
268	Louis Kananura	3	m		
269	Hategeka	30	m	herdsman	married
270	Nyirabageni	28	f	farmer	married
271	Habyarimana	2	m		
272	Hesron Munyangabe	60	m	herdsman	married
273	Edmond Nyumbayire	35	m	merchant	married
274	Berna Nyinawindinda	32	f	merchant	married
275	Ildephonse Nsengimana	7	m	student	
276	Mujawamariya	5	f		
277	Dative Nyumbayire	3	f		
278	Cyprien Biregeya	56	m	herdsman	married
279	Madeleine Nyirabudederi	54	f	farmer	married
280	Béatrice Mukangango	18	f	student	single
281	Mukanzungize	16	f	student	single
282	Patricie Mukantabana	14	f	student	
283	Gaspard kayigamba	11	m	student	
284	Nzayibaza	70	m	herdsman	widower
285	Munyampama	35	m	farmer	single
286	Isidore Rugombashari	62	m	herdsman	married
287	Cécile Mukantaganzwa	58	f	farmer	married
288	Gérard Bazasangwa	26	m	herdsman	single
289	Thomas Kabwana	49	m	herdsman	married
290	Tite Gatarayiha	35	m	herdsman	married
291	Mukangango	30	f	farmer	married
292	Seromba	37	m	herdsman	married
293	Spéciose Mukarutabana	32	f	farmer	married
294	Colette Musabyimana	16	f	student	single
295	François Rugango	40	m	herdsman	married
296	Marguerite Mukandinda	37	f	farmer	married
297	Anésie Mukamurara	18	f	student	single
298	Kadiringo	16	f	student	single
299	Mukeshimana	8	f	student	
300	Nyakayiro	9	m	student	
301	Sibomana	7	m	student	
302	Régine Mukandori	42	f	farmer	married
303	Béatrice Mukangamije	20	f	farmer	single
304	Patricie	18	f	student	single
305	Gafirigita	14	m	student	
306	Nyiragafene	16	f	student	single
307	Déo Ngarambe	3	m		
308	Marguerite Mukandutiye	30	f	farmer	married
309	Xaverine Mukeshimana	13	f	student	
310	Emmanuelle M.mazimpaka	10	f	student	
311	Pascal Tuyisenge	6	m		
312	Thomas Bizimungu	4	m		
313	Philippe Nteziryayo	1	m		
314	Kamugwera	38	f	farmer	married
315	Madeleine Nyinawandori	20	f	farmer	single
316	Marianne Mukankanika	18	f	student	single
317	Mukamunana	16	f	student	single
318	Mukomeza	14	m	student	
319	Mutaganda	12	m	student	
320	Mukagasana	10	f	student	
321	Mukamurenzi	8	f	student	
322	Mukamuhire	6	f		
323	Boniface Kadaraza	35	m	herdsman	married
324	Spéciose Nyirakanyana	32	f	farmer	married
325	Habimana	15	m	student	
326	Gérard Gahamanyi	13	m	student	
327	Vénancie	11	f	student	
328	Nyirarusatsi	5	f		
329	Corneille Kadaraza	2	m		
330	Jean Habiyambere	55	m	herdsman	married
331	Thabithe	35	f	farmer	married
332	Emmanuel	8	m	student	
333	Mbarushimana	7	f	student	
334	Nyirabarerwa	60	f	farmer	widow
335	Martin Ndamage	35	m	herdsman	married
336	Eugénie Mukankusi	32	f	farmer	married
337	Mukarusanga	12	f	student	
338	Gaspard	9	m	student	
339	Dominique Ndamage	5	m		
340	Augustin Rutayisire	45	m	herdsman	married
341	Spéciose Mukabideri	41	f	farmer	married
342	Mukamurara	21	f	farmer	single
343	Jean Paul Ndagijimana	15	m	student	
344	Nyirakabea	12	f	student	
345	Védaste	10	m	student	
346	Gasana	8	m	student	
347	Claude	6	m		
348	Rwigamba	40	m	herdsman	married
349	Joséphine Mukaremera	37	f	farmer	married
350	Uwihaye	10	f	student	
351	Télésphore	6	m		
352	François Kabandana	27	m	herdsman	married
353	Catherine Kanakuze	24	f	farmer	married
354	Tharcisse	2	m		
355	Bernadette Mukazitoni	40	f	farmer	
356	Jacqueline Mujawayezu	15	f	student	
357	Uwimana	13	f	student	
358	Dancille Mukantagara	40	f	farmer	married
359	Eugénie Mukamudenge	22	f	farmer	single
360	Vestine Mukangwije	20	f	farmer	single
361	Cécile Mukamuhizi	18	f	student	single
362	Alphonsine Mukasine	12	f	student	
363	Damascène	2	m		
364	Innocent	2	m		
365	Elianne	26	f	farmer	married
366	Alphonse	6	m		
367	Sugabo	12	m	student	
368	Evérienne Mukasharangabo	24	f	farmer	divorced
369	Mutsiri	5	m		
370	Zirimwabagabo	35	m	herdsman	married
371	Caritas Mukamuhizi	28	f	farmer	married
372	Dunuri	8	m	student	
373	André Murakaza	48	m	carpenter	married
374	Xavéra Nyirajyambere	42	f	farmer	married
375	Mukagatana	15	f	student	
376	Patricie Mukamasabo	13	f	student	
377	Muhutu	9	m	student	
378	Nshimiye	6	m		
379	Anastasie Mukamuhigirwa	38	f	farmer	widow
380	Iyaremye	18	m	student	single
381	Havugimana	16	m	student	single
382	Suzanne	5	f		
383	Félicitée Nyirabwinturo	80	f	farmer	married
384	Fidèle Ngirinshuti	32	m	herdsman	married
385	Nyirankotsori	12	f	student	
386	Ousiel Nzamwita	35	m	herdsman	married
387	Damarce Mukandori	32	f	farmer	married

No.	Name	Age	Sex	Occupn.	Marital Status
388	Nyinawandori	9	f	student	
389	Nyirambeba	7	f	student	
390	Niyomugabo	5	m		
391	Casimir Nzamwita	2	m		
392	Catherine Kangwiza	25	f	farmer	single
393	Berna Kandanga	44	f	farmer	widow
394	Bikorimana	22	m	farmer	single
395	Eugénie Nyirambabazi	18	f	farmer	single
396	Espérance Nyirabutorano	14	f	student	
397	Thalienne Nyiramasirabo	35	f	farmer	married
398	Mukangarambe	18	f	farmer	single
399	Alphonsine Mukaminiza	16	f	student	single
400	Dedacienne Barayibaza	10	f	student	
401	Caritas Mukamunana	35	f	farmer	married
402	Innocent Nshimiye	14	m	student	
403	Rushingabiti	12	m	student	
404	Manyinya	9	m	student	
405	Nyiramana	7	f	student	
406	Louise Muzungu	3	f		
407	Cyprien Ntaganzwa	60	m	herdsman	married
408	Marthe Nyirabuseruka	50	f	farmer	married
409	Innocent Ndayisaba	20	m	herdsman	single
410	Havugimana	13	m	student	
411	Joséphine Mukandori	30	f	farmer	married
412	Niyomugabo	12	m	student	
413	Iyakagaba	9	m	student	
414	Mukankaka	7	f	student	
415	Mukankundiye	4	f		
416	Bizuru	1	m		
417	Charles Nzakamwita	60	m	herdsman	married
418	Lidie Mukangamije	50	f	farmer	married
419	Joseph Kayijuka	55	m	farmer	married
420	Costasie Kabega	50	f	farmer	married
421	Mukamwiza	18	f	student	single
422	Mukasine	15	f	student	
423	Albert Mutwa	12	m	student	
424	Nkecuru	6	f		
425	Kibwa	3	m		
426	Emile Kayijuka	2	m		
427	Innocent Munana	28	m	herdsman	married
428	Patricie Nyirankundiyeze	25	f	farmer	married
429	Ingabire	2	f		
430	Dancille Nyirandege	23	f	farmer	married
431	Odette Mashyaka	1	f		
432	Damien Munyurabatware	45	m	farmer	married
433	Marie Kabagwira	37	f	farmer	married
434	Colette	20	f	farmer	
435	Dunuri	9	m	student	
436	Mutsiri	7	m	student	
437	Dismas Rugigana	80	m	herdsman	married
438	Xaverine Nyiramugwera	55	f	farmer	married
439	Denis Buhundi	60	m	herdsman	married
440	Marguerite Kabayundo	55	f	farmer	married
441	Thérèse Cyurinyana	70	f	farmer	widow
442	Narcisse Ngarambe	18	m	farmer	single
443	Edison Muberanziza	32	m	herdsman	married
444	Dorothée Nyirabizimana	26	f	farmer	married
445	Nyiramwamira	6	f		
446	Gasaruhande	4	m		
447	Kibwa, son of Munyanziza	1	m		
448	Xaverine Mukankusi	35	f	farmer	married
449	François Nshimiye	12	m	student	
450	Alphonsine Mukandayisenga	5	f	student	
451	Aniseth Rangira	42	m	herdsman	married
452	Ancille Mukagasana	36	f	farmer	married
453	Alphonsine	14	m	student	
454	Ngiruwonsanga	11	m	student	
455	Dusenge	9	m	student	
456	Aloys	7	m	student	
457	Rangira Rukundo	3	m		
458	Védaste Ndangayija	40	m	herdsman	married
459	Philomène Mukanyemazi	32	f	farmer	married
460	Suzanne	11	f	student	
461	Ingabire	9	f	student	
462	Marcel Ngarukiye	6	m		
463	Nkulikiyinka	3	m		
464	Gérard Rwanyabuto	37	m	herdsman	married
465	Bernadette Mukayuhi	31	f	farmer	married
466	Mukandahinyuka	15	f	student	single
467	Nyirahabimana	9	f	student	
468	Marcel	7	m	student	
469	Hakizimana	5	m		
470	Théodore Rwanyabuto	3	m		
471	Albert Ndahimana	45	m	herdsman	married
472	Eugénie Mukagatare	38	f	farmer	married
473	Pascal	13	m	student	
474	Marie	4	f		
475	Mathias Maboneza	52	m	herdsman	married
476	Rose Kampogo	45	f	farmer	married
477	Rubyogo	10	m	student	
478	Emerthe	14	f	student	
479	Jeanne	8	f	student	
480	Thérèse Mboneza	4	f		
481	Tharcisse Segashi	75	m	herdsman	married
482	Xaverine Nyirarubabaza	70	f	farmer	married
483	Catherine Mukagatare	30	f	nurse	single
484	Canisius Mudahunga	35	m	farmer	married
485	Madeleine Uwimana	30	f	farmer	married
486	Nyiranshongore	8	f	student	
487	Muteteri	6	f		
488	Mudahunga	4	m		
489	Denis Mudahunga	2	m		
490	Jean Ndutiye	42	m	farmer	married
491	Césalie Mukantaganzwa	35	f	farmer	married
492	Semutakirwa	22	m	farmer	single
493	Gashema	20	m	farmer	single
494	Catherine	18	f	farmer	single
495	Félicitée Uwamariya	32	f	farmer	married
496	Sibomana	10	m	student	
497	Nyirabukara	8	f	student	
498	Emmanuel Ruvuzandekwe	6	m		
499	Mélanie	4	f		
500	Gasaruhande	2	m		
501	Paul Gakiza	80	m	herdsman	widower
502	Christine Mukandutiye	32	f	farmer	
503	Nyiranzage	5	f		
504	Dative Mukarukaka	30	f	farmer	
505	Musabyemariya	9	f	student	
506	Gasaruhande	6	m		
507	Jonas Habayo	32	m	herdsman	married
508	Berna Mukareta	40	f	farmer	married
509	Kabanja	20	m	farmer	single
510	Samuel Habineza	18	m	student	single
511	Murwanashyaka	16	m	student	single
512	Ndayisaba	6	m		
513	Béata	27	f	farmer	married
514	Kiromba Mukamana	7	f	student	
515	Tuyisenge	3	m		
516	Pascasie	1	f		
517	Mukamugema	55	f	farmer	divorced
518	Nyirakanani	7	f	student	
519	Samuel Kanuni	60	m	herdsman	married
520	Marguerite Mukandekezi	57	f	farmer	married
521	Julienne Mukandamage	30	f	farmer	married
522	Catherine Izabiriza	27	f	farmer	single
523	Immaculée Mukashyaka	14	f	student	
524	Mushimiyimana	9	f	student	
525	Mathieu Segatare	48	m	herdsman	married
526	Phaïna	38	f	farmer	married
527	Nyiranzage	12	f	student	
528	Donatilla	7	f	student	
529	Donatha	5	f		
530	Angès	3	f		
531	Tamuriza Mukaremera	30	f	farmer	
532	Rubyogo Ngiruwonsanga	7	m	student	
533	Assiel Murinanashaka	65	m	farmer	single
534	Stanislas Segasagara	45	m	herdsman	married
535	Thacienne Mukangango	38	f	farmer	married
536	Odette mukangambe	18	f	farmer	single
537	Nyirambeba Mukarubayiza	16	f	student	single
538	François Rukara	14	m	student	
539	Jean	12	m	student	
540	Nyirankware	5	f		
541	Jolie Segasagara	2	f		
542	Claver Sekaziga	34	m	herdsman	married
543	Anastasie Kaburangha	32	f	farmer	married
544	Hélène	11	f	student	
545	Mukamuganga	9	f	student	
546	Anathalie	7	f	student	
547	Emmanuel Nemeye	5	m		
548	Pascal Rukundo	1	m		
549	Antoine Kambari	32	m	farmer	married
550	Marie	26	f	farmer	married
551	Nyirabazungu	5	f		
552	Nyirabizimana	2	f		
553	Cécile	50	f	farmer	widow
554	Ignace	18	m	farmer	single
555	Burimwinyundo	20	m	farmer	single
556	Frédéric Kamanzi	62	m	herdsman	married
557	Damarce Mukaruberwa	54	f	farmer	married
558	Béatha Mukangwije	18	f	student	single
559	Appolinaire Ntagara	22	m	farmer	single

1.1.3 Cellule Kigarama

No.	Name	Age	Sex	Occupn.	Marital Status
1	Thomas Rugwizangoga	55	m	herdsman	married
2	Anastasie Kabayundo	45	f	farmer	married
3	Marie Murorunkwere	13	f	student	

4	Niyonteze Bizuru	11	m	student	
5	Nyirambaragasa	9	f	student	
6	François Gahamanyi	45	m	herdsman	married
7	Espérance Kangwiza	30	f	farmer	married
8	Nyirankotsori	9	f	student	
9	Maningiri	7	f	student	
10	Cyprien Senguge	58	m	herdsman	married
11	Albert	36	m	farmer	married
12	Modeste	25	m	farmer	single
13	Théophile Kabayiza	40	m	herdsman	married
14	Patricie Mukagatare	35	f	farmer	married
15	Thaddée	10	m	student	
16	Théophile Ukurikiyimfura	8	m	student	
17	Alphonse	3	m		
18	Marie Uwihezuye	60	f	farmer	widow
19	Perpétuée Mukagatana	27	f	farmer	
20	Daniel Munyanganji	77	m	herdsman	married
21	Ngamije	45	m	farmer	single
22	Modeste Sebuhoro	37	m	herdsman	married
23	Bernadette Mukashema	35	f	farmer	married
24	Alphonse Shabo	10	m	student	
25	Nyirabwo Neye	9	f	student	
26	Bayingana	6	m		
27	Habimana	4	m		
28	Casimir Munyandinda	55	m	teacher	married
29	Marthe Mukabutera	50	f	farmer	married
30	Jeanne d'Arc Iyadede	28	f	student	
31	Adolphe Rulinda	24	m	student	single
32	Murorukwbre Nyiramasaro	21	f	student	single
33	Mubashankwaya Mupeyi	19	m	farmer	single
34	Munyandinda Muzehe	17	m	student	single
35	Grégoire Nunyandinda	14	m	student	
36	Uwimana	8	f		
37	Jean Mukomangashya	72	m	herdsman	married
38	Marguerite Mukabadege	67	f	farmer	married
39	Louis Ntagara	32	m	herdsman	married
40	Patricie Nyirahabiyambere	28	f	farmer	married
41	Gihahira	5	m		
42	Nyirapironi	3	f		
43	Veronique Nyirakagusa	65	f	farmer	widow
44	Aloys Niyibigira	35	m	herdsman	married
45	Winniphrida Mukakimanuka	9	f	student	
46	Patricie	6	f		
47	Musonera Sehuku	45	m	farmer	married
48	Mukashema	32	f	farmer	married
49	Nyirabare	11	f	farmer	
50	Maningira	2	f		
51	Joséphine	23	F	farmer	married
52	Gespard Sibomana	2	m		
53	Thierry Habiyambere	7 days	m		
54	Marianne Nyirakagoro	60	f	farmer	widow
55	Anastase Munyabagisha	31	m	herdsman	married
56	Alphonse Nshimiyimana	5	m		
57	François Munyakazi	38	m	herdsman	married
58	Pascasie Nyirahabimana	34	f	farmer	married
59	Joséphine Mukashema	11	f	student	
60	Winniphrida Yankurije	9	f	student	
61	Rutenderi	7	m	student	
62	Delina	5	f		
63	Gaspard	3	m		
64	Son of Munyakazi	1 day	m		
65	Simon Musominari	28	m	herdsman	married
66	Vérène Nyirankwavu	27	f	farmer	married
67	Anastasie Nyirabuhoro	1	f		
68	Marcel Nsanzurwimo	35	m	herdsman	married
69	Patricie	34	f	farmer	married
70	Bikorimana	8	m	student	
71	Mukantwari	6	f		
72	Paul Gakwaya	70	m	herdsman	married
73	Léocadie Madame	60	f	farmer	married
74	Chantal Nyirandame	21	f	student	single
75	Félicitée Mukankaka	20	f	farmer	single
76	Bwanakweri	45	m	herdsman	married
77	Catherine	41	f	farmer	married
78	Thérèse Mukankusi	22	m	farmer	single
79	Innocent	15	m	student	
80	Odette	8	f	student	
81	Cyriaque	6	m		
82	Aimé Marie Muukandahiriwe	4	f		
83	Buwanakweri's baby	3m	f		
84	Mbaraga	40	m	herdsman	married
85	Xaverine Nyiramadirida	38	f	farmer	married
86	Rugwizangoga	10	m	student	
87	Gasurira	8	m	student	
88	Kazungu	6	m		
89	Nyirabazungu	4	f		
90	Martin Kadaraga	38	m	herdsman	married
91	Verène	35	f	farmer	married
92	Mukamuhigirwa	57	f	farmer	widow
93	Eugénie Mukantabana	23	f	farmer	single
94	Mukantaganda	11	f	student	
95	Spéciose Mukantaganda	25	f	farmer	married
96	Baby of Mukantaganda	3days	m		
97	Berchamans Rwamunyana	67	m	herdsman	married
98	Nyirakanyenzi	60	f	farmer	married
99	Habyarimana	20	m	student	single
100	Bagemahe	37	m	herdsman	married
101	Xaverine	32	f	farmer	married
102	Adalie	11	f	student	
103	Njogori	5	m		
104	Nyiramwamira	3	m		
105	Cécile	43	f	farmer	married
106	Immaculée Nyirahabimana	8	f	student	
107	Siméon Ruzindana	27	m	herdsman	married
108	Cécile	23	f	farmer	married
109	Félicitée Mukantaganda	24	f	farmer	married
110	Spéciose Mukandori	30	f	teacher	married
111	Ntagara's son	1	m		
112	Partrice Mutaganda	38	m	herdsman	married
113	Gaspard Munyansanga	35	m	herdsman	married
114	Gaudence Mukamudenge	35	f	farmer	married
115	Colette	28	f	farmer	married
116	Edith Nyiransabimana	26	f	farmer	single
117	Pascasie Mukarusine	27	f	farmer	married
118	Gafirigita	4	m		
119	Félicitée Mukakabano	60	f	farmer	widow
120	Vincent Nzabitega	26	m	farmer	single
121	Simon Kabigi	65	m	herdsman	widower
122	Wenceslas	24	m	herdsman	married
123	Patricie Makantagwabira	20	f	farmer	married
124	Pascal Mutuyeyezu	54	m	herdsman	married
125	Dative Makabaziga	48	f	farmer	married
126	Elizabeth Mukerinka	16	f	student	single
127	Immaculée Mukankaka	26	f	student	
128	Mukankaka's son	1 m	m		
129	Pasteur Ntaganda	52	m	herdsman	married
130	Mukamusana	34	f	farmer	married
131	Déogratias Kayihura	24	m	student	single
132	Edouard Karimba	20	m	student	single
133	Claver Kayijaho	16	m	student	single
134	Catherine Murekatete	7	f		
135	Gorette Bucyedusenge	2	f		
136	Régine Nyirakabano	80	f	farmer	widow
137	Alphonsine Mukabideri	24	f	farmer	married
138	Evariste Habimana	1	m		
139	Bizimana Rudomore	12	m	farmer	
140	Makamurangwa	8	f		
141	Ndwaniye Rutaburanubwiza	35	m	herdsman	married
142	Mukagatare	30	f	farmer	married
143	Mukamazimpaka	6	f		
144	Judith Senyenzi	31	f	farmer	married
145	Hélène Mukeshimana	5	f		
146	Nsabimana	3	m		
147	Célestin Musonera	45	m	herdsman	married
148	Agnès Nyirakanani	35	f	farmer	married
149	Françoise Nyirahabimana	17	f	farmer	single
150	Ukurikiyimfura	7	m	student	
151	Hélène	5	f		
152	Appolinaire Kabindo	60	m	herdsman	married
153	Ancille Nyirabahozi	55	f	farmer	married
154	Léoncie Nyirabahire	23	f	farmer	single
155	Marcel Nzamwita	18	m	farmer	single
156	Clémentine	3	f		
157	Claver Kayigamba	28	m	herdsman	married
158	Marthe Mukantagara	26	f	farmer	married
159	Nyirahabimana	2	f		
160	Madeleine Mukarugwiza	45	f	farmer	widow
161	Niyomugabo	15	m	farmer	single
162	Busharire Ndagijimana	22	m	farmer	single
163	Migambi	10	m	student	
164	Rutamu	6	m		
165	Nyiramasimba	3	f		
166	Anastase Mutaganda	40	m	herdsman	married
167	Marthe Mukakalisa	33	f	farmer	married
168	Mukurarinda	72	m	herdsman	married
169	Berna Karuyonga	63	f	farmer	married
170	Samuel Sibomana	16	m	student	single
171	Thacienne	20	f	farmer	single
172	Catherine	33	f	farmer	married
173	Ntamabyariro	11	m	student	
174	Gatembangara	8	m	student	
175	Masimbi	6	f		
176	Esther Nyirahabayo	65	f	farmer	widow
177	Agnès Nyirakanyange	40	f	farmer	married
178	Jeannette Nyirasogi	5	f		
179	Silas Mukaragajekule	76	m	herdsman	married
180	Adrienne	42	f	farmer	married
181	Harerimana	14	m	student	
182	Emmanuel Hakizimana	12	m	student	
183	Thacienne	31	f	farmer	married
184	Mukarukaka	3	f		
185	Judith	40	f	farmer	married

186	Nyirankotsori	6	f		
187	Mukankaka	8	f	student	
188	Mikwege	6	m		
189	Félicien	3	m		
190	Thomas Bizimana	25	m	farmer	married
191	Martin Karekezi	64	m	farmer	married
192	Madeleine	58	f	farmer	married
193	Butera	34	m	farmer	single
194	Anastasie Mukandinda	26	f	farmer	
195	Kanziga	59	f	farmer	married
196	Hesron	24	m	farmer	single
197	Tharcisse Gacanyi	16	m	farmer	single
198	Assinapole	20	m	farmer	single
199	Bidega	14	m	farmer	
200	Nyumbayire	4	m		
201	Nyiribakwe	75	m	herdsman	married
202	Madidi	28	f	farmer	single
203	Jean Damascène Kabanda	42	m	herdsman	married
204	Cécilie Mukakabera	30	f	farmer	single
205	Costasie Makarukaka	27	f	farmer	married
206	Ildephonse Hitimana	9	m	student	
207	Hakizimana	2	m		
208	André Vuguziga	4	m		
209	Varène	1	f		
210	Jeannette Nyiramapironi	14	f	student	
211	Rose Nyirabukara	80	f	farmer	widow
212	Nsanzurwimo	28	m	farmer	married
213	Mahura	11	m	student	
214	Bizuru	9	m	student	
215	Rubyogo	6	m		
216	Macibiri	4	f		
217	Michel	8	m	student	
218	Félicitée Kanakuze	41	f	farmer	married
219	Angélique Mukarunyange	19	f	student	single
220	Sekaduri	17	m	student	single
221	Nsengiyumva	15	m	student	
222	Manzi	13	m	student	
223	Nyirakinazi	9	f	student	
224	Seth Majabo	76	m	herdsman	married
225	Marthe Nyiramanyenzi	69	f	farmer	married
226	Abraham Gisoma	72	m	herdsman	married
227	Nyirajabiro	65	f	farmer	married
228	Callixte Munyanshongore	22	m	herdsman	single
229	Vérédianne	43	f	farmer	married
230	Emmanuel	13	m	farmer	
231	Gacaka	16	m	farmer	single
232	Kantarama	14	f	student	
233	Zacharie Karangwa	36	m	herdsman	married
234	Mukarutabana	34	f	farmer	married
235	Rutenderi	7	m	student	
236	Mukawera	10	f	student	
237	Silas Karangwa	1	m		
238	Munyambibi	58	m	herdsman	married
239	Kamatamu	50	f	farmer	married
240	Emmanuel Ndayisaba	26	m	farmer	married
241	François Habimana	24	m	farmer	single
242	Assiel	22	m	farmer	single
243	Jean	9	m	student	
244	Félicitée Kambayire	75	f	farmer	widow
245	Colette Nyiramusugi	26	f	teacher	single
246	Modeste Higiro	40	m	herdsman	married
247	Prudence Mukandinda	35	f	farmer	married
248	Thérèse Mukankubana	11	f	student	
249	Claude Sakufi	9	m	student	
250	Ayinkamiye	7	f	student	
251	Nkurikiyinka	3	m		
252	Albert Higiro	5 m	m		
253	Adèle	35	f	farmer	married
254	Gaspard Nsengimana	9	m	student	
255	Bimenyimana	4 m	m		
256	Emmerthe Nyinawumuntu	30	f	farmer	married
257	Eugénie Uwantege	11	f	student	
258	Bernard Mafene	9	m	student	
259	Inkotanyi	6	f		
260	Nyiramitega	4	f		
261	Kagufi	2	f		
262	Michel Nzabahimana	28	m	herdsman	married
263	Béatrice Nyirahabimana	26	f	farmer	married
264	Macibiri Ntakirutimana	1	m	farmer	
265	Mukaremera	30	f	farmer	widow
266	Muhawenimana	11	m	student	
267	Nyinawumuntu	7	f	student	
268	Kagarara	2	m		
269	Matemeri	4	f		
270	Ezechias Mugambira	50	m	herdsman	married
271	Pauline Kanyonga	46	f	farmer	married
272	Innocent Ngirabatware	20	m	farmer	single
273	Matoroshi	8	m	student	
274	Ildephonse Karangwa	1	m		
275	Vianney	5	m		
276	Vérène Mukakimonyo	20	f	farmer	married
277	Yamfashije	1.5	f		
278	Winniphrida Mukamwiza	18	f	student	single
279	Célestin Kamugundu	45	m	herdsman	married
280	Vérèdianne Mukamugema	40	f	farmer	married
281	Louis Karemera	20	m	farmer	single
282	Mukamudenge	18	f	student	single
283	Gaspard Mbarushimana	16	m	student	single
284	Jacqueline	12	f	student	
285	Thomas Kadaraza	35	m	herdsman	married
286	Judith Nyirabakiga	30	f	farmer	married
287	Kanonko	7	m	student	
288	Havugimana	5	m		
289	Thacien Kadaraza	5 m	m		
290	Nyirarubindo	80	f	farmer	widow
291	Narcisse Kazungu	38	m	herdsman	married
292	Winniphrida Mukantabana	30	f	farmer	married
293	Caritas	8	f	student	
294	Hakizimana	7	m	student	
295	Elianne Nyirabagenzi	40	f	farmer	widow
296	Nyirantoke Mukamazimpaka	8	f	student	
297	Hasekukize	7	f	student	
298	Xaveri Sekaganda	35	m	herdsman	married
299	Marianne Nyiramakende	25	f	farmer	married
300	Rusine	3	m		
301	Zacharie Kageruka	43	m	herdsman	married
302	Rose	37	f	farmer	married
303	Alphonse	10	m	student	
304	Nyiransabimana	9	f	student	
305	Kanungeri	3	f		
306	Adeline Nyirabundoyi	37	f	farmer	married
307	Sophie	45	f	farmer	widow
308	Gafupi	3	m		
309	Emmanuel Ngiruwonsanga	16	m	farmer	single
310	Busugugu	9	m	student	
311	Thaddée Munyampenda	40	m	herdsman	married
312	Xavéra	39	f	farmer	married
313	Mbendegezi	9	f	student	
314	Nyirambeba	8	f	student	
315	Jacqueline	6	f		
316	Etienne Ngirabatware	26	m	herdsman	widower
317	Munyakaragwe	37	m	herdsman	married
318	Mukamukomeza	30	f	farmer	married
319	Emmanuel Ngiruwonsanga	10	m	student	
320	Rugasira	43	m	herdsman	married
321	Julienne Uzamukunda	40	f	farmer	married
322	Félicitée Nyirabatsinda	13	f	student	
323	Catherine	10	f	student	
324	Havugimana	8	m	student	
325	Kanonko	7	f	student	
326	Dugiri	4	f		
327	Edmond Twamugabo	50	m	herdsman	married
328	Evérienne Nyiramafaranga	47	f	farmer	married
329	Innocent Muhire	5	m		
330	Anastase Rwagacuzi	25	m	herdsman	married
331	Kandame	27	f	farmer	married
332	Donatille Nyirajeri	5	f		
333	Jacqueline	3	f		
334	Agnès Mukantaho	26	f	farmer	married
335	Esther Mukarusanga	40	f	farmer	widow
336	Nyirabizimana	10	f	student	
337	Agathe Mukarukaka	37	f	farmer	widow
338	Bikorimana	10	m	student	
339	Spéciose	9	f	student	
340	Marianne Mukarusanga	60	f	farmer	widow
341	Ruganzabahunde	32	m	herdsman	married
342	Léoncie Nyirabagwiza	75	f	farmer	widow
343	Elianne Mukamunana	50	f	farmer	married
344	Caritas Mukangarambe	27	f	farmer	single
345	Assiel Ngirinshuti	21	m	farmer	single
346	Winniphrida mukamasabo	19	f	farmer	single
347	Narcisse Ntibarutimana	17	m	student	single
348	Gaudence Mukamazimpaka	11	f	student	
349	Augustin Kagemana	9	m	student	
350	Nyirahabimana	6	f		
351	Elianne Mukamwiza	20	f	farmer	married
352	Emmanuel Ntirenganya	2.5	m		
353	Sibomana	1	m		
354	Félicitée Kankuyo	54	f	farmer	married
355	Uzabakiriho	12	m	student	
356	Catherine Mukagatare	9	f	student	
357	Samuel Karangwa	33	m	herdsman	married
358	Winniphrida Mukanyemera	33	f	farmer	married
359	Harerimana	9	m	student	
360	Jacqueline Uwamariya	7	f	student	

1.1.4 Cellule Gitwa

No.	Name	Age	Sex	Occupn.	Marital Status

1	Evérienne Kabera	47	f	farmer	married
2	Bèatrice Mukarusanga	28	f	accountant	single
3	Odette Mukarwego	20	f	farmer	single
4	Mukeshimana	12	f	student	
5	Tuyishime	3	m	student	
6	Sala	1	f	student	
7	Rukara	40	m	herdsman	married
8	Agnès Mukamudenge	38	f	farmer	married
9	Adriane Mukamunana	14	f	student	
10	Yamfashije	12	f	student	
11	Mukantabana	10	f	student	
12	Mutambazi	3	m	student	
13	Nicodème Rwamparage	70	m	herdsman	married
14	Nyiramafurebo	67	f	farmer	married
15	Nyirabahunde	80	f	farmer	widow
16	Judith	22	f	farmer	married
17	Mazuru	1	m	farmer	
18	Lèonidas Munyankindi	3	m	farmer	
19	Zacharie Kayenge	52	m	herdsman	married
20	Elina Kamatamu	45	f	farmer	married
21	François Nkusi Mikwenge	30	m	student	single
22	Joséphine Mukantwari	8	f	student	
23	Thaddée Mubiligi	50	m	shopkeeper	married
24	Mukarugagi	47	f	farmer	married
25	Alphonsine Nyirabarenzi	30	f	student	single
26	Agathe Mukamurenzi	27	f	student	single
27	Caritas Musabyimana	20	f	student	single
28	Xavéra	10	f	student	
29	Slyvain Sebabumbyi	10	m	student	
30	Espèrance Mukankanika	15	f	student	
31	Ezechiel Kayumba	35	m	herdsman	married
32	Immaculèe	35	f	farmer	married
33	Sarigoma	7	f	student	
34	Munanira	5	m	student	
35	Angèlique Mukaribanje	30	f	farmer	married
36	Pascal Bikorimana	12	m	student	
37	Buregeya	2	m		
38	Augustin Sibomana	27	m	herdsman	married
39	Joséphine	1	f		
40	Samson Rwigemera	32	m	herdsman	married
41	Ingabire	5	f		
42	Nyiramazuru	3	f		
43	Félicitée Nyirakanyana	35	f	farmer	widow
44	Nyirantoki	8	f	student	
45	Muzungu	6	m	student	
46	Rutwe	4	m		
47	Nyirajeri	2	f		
48	Pauline Munyandamutsa	2	f		
49	Mukabaziga	55	f	farmer	widow
50	Segasagara	62	m	herdsman	married
51	Marthe Mukankwanya	40	f	farmer	married
52	Jason Gatsimbanyi	33	m	herdsman	married
53	Thérèse Mukabitega	27	f	farmer	married
54	Rubyogo	7	m	student	
55	Gasurira	5	m	student	
56	Bujenderi	3	f		
57	Euphrasie Mukamukomeza	40	f	farmer	married
58	Elièziel Niyitegeka	15	m	student	
59	Nyirantamanji Mukangumije	10	f	student	
60	Rose Mukantwari	5	f	student	
61	Gérard	8	m	student	
62	Védaste Kabanda	7d	m		
63	Eliezer Buregeya	27	m	herdsman	married
64	Prudence Mukagatare	22	f	farmer	married
65	Uwimana	1	f		
66	Thomas Rubuguza	32	m	herdsman	married
67	Everiènne Mukankubana	26	f	farmer	married
68	Rubwana	3	m		
69	Inkotanyi	2	m		
70	Esther Mukandirima	50	f	farmer	widow
71	Aphrodis Ruzibiza	22	m	farmer	single
72	Abraham Semanza	70	m	herdsman	widower
73	Venance Mukamuhire	27	f	farmer	married
74	Nyirabazungu	2	f		
75	Adeline Nyirakwibuka	70	f	farmer	widow
76	Hana Mukarasharangabo	80	f	farmer	married
77	Esdras Mushimiyimana	8	m	student	
78	Bayiringire	4	m		
79	Ngezahayo	6	m	student	
80	Nyirahabimana	1	f		
81	Efesto Kaberuka	50	m	herdsman	married
82	Thaddée Kangabe	43	f	farmer	married
83	Céléstin Bizimana	14	m	student	
84	Pascal Habiyambere	7	m	student	
85	Venancie Nyiranguge	50	f	farmer	widow
86	Rudandaza Sabayiro	30	m	farmer	single
87	Esther	25	f	farmer	married
88	Nyiramwamira	5	f		
89	Nyirabukara	1	f		
90	Candide	23	f	farmer	married
91	Damascène Habiyambere	2	m		
92	Samuel Habimana	27	m	herdsman	married
93	Jacqueline Mukashyaka	21	f	farmer	married
94	Aloys Habimana	4	m		
95	Adalie Mukayoboka	35	f	farmer	married
96	Immaculée	8	f	student	
97	Muzungu	6	m		
98	Mbindigiri	4	f		
99	Mukabuduwe	35	f	farmer	married
100	Ndikubwimana	6	m		
101	Mukankundiye	4	f		
102	Balthazar Senkware	71	m	herdsman	married
103	Thaciènne Mukabacondo	60	f	farmer	married
104	Simon Seyeze	65	m	herdsman	married
105	Julienne Nyiramparamage	60	f	farmer	married
106	Béata Mukamudenge	18	f	farmer	single
107	Casimir Ndongozi	16	m	farmer	single
108	Damascène Mugarura	12	m	student	
109	Béatrice Nyirajyambere	21	f	farmer	married
110	Mukamwiza	2	f		
111	Damascène Senkuba	45	m	herdsman	married
112	Eugénie Mukankubana	29	f	farmer	married
113	Gashikori	2	f	student	
114	Célestin	7	m	student	
115	Sebuhoro	87	m	herdsman	married
116	Mbibiri	65	f	farmer	married
117	Samuel Ntashamaje	21	m	farmer	single
118	Mukeshimana	17	f	student	single
119	Félicitée Mukarutezi	65	f	farmer	widow
120	Sylvère Mahindigiri	28	m	farmer	single
121	Rwagasana	35	m	herdsman	married
122	Marthe Mukarushema	30	f	farmer	married
123	Ngiruwonsanga	9	m	student	
124	Jeanne d'Arc Rwagasana	3	f		
125	Isacar Gahiro	50	m	herdsman	married
126	Suzanne	40	f	farmer	married
127	Damarce Mukansanga	17	f	farmer	single
128	Mukeshimana	15	f	student	
129	Mukankusi	12	f	student	
130	Sebushishi	8	f	student	
131	Evariste Kayinamura	45	m	herdsman	married
132	Donatilla Mukagatare	35	f	farmer	married
133	Innocent	13	m	student	
134	Nsabimana	11	m	student	
135	Assiel Kabanda	55	m	shopkeeper	married
136	Marcianne Kantarama	50	f	farmer	married
137	Rugwizangoga	30	m	student	single
138	Béata Mukanyemera	24	f	student	single
139	Binwangari	14	m	farmer	
140	Gaudence Mukalindiro	38	f	farmer	married
141	Rubyogo Nsabihimana	38	f	farmer	married
142	Mukabine	14	f	student	
143	Fidèle Muhutu	10	m	student	
144	Eugénie	8	f	student	
145	Kabagwiza Nyirakiromba	35	f	farmer	married
146	Célestin	56	m	carpenter	married
147	Anastasie Nyirabizimana	50	f	farmer	married
148	Vincent Rutayisire	27	m	farmer	
149	Mutwa	17	m		
150	Niyonteze	4	m		
151	Thamale Mukandinda	38	f	farmer	single
152	Habimana	23	m	farmer	single
153	Mukashema	20	f	farmer	single
154	Kamatete	16	f	student	single
155	Maribori	10	f	student	
156	Mabwa	6	f		
157	Mukamudenge	26	f	farmer	married
158	Adèle Nyirahabimana	40	f	farmer	widow
159	Xaveri	16	m	student	single
160	Drocella Byandagara	6	f		
161	Mukansanga	12	f	farmer	
162	Nsengiyumva	6	m		
163	Pierre Nzakamwita	40	m	herdsman	married
164	Béata Uwiturije	25	f	farmer	married
165	Nyirabukara	13	f	student	
166	Narcisse	20	m	far,er	single
167	Nyirandagije	80	f	farmer	widow
168	Bernadette Mukamfizi	13	f	student	
169	Ignace	10	m	student	
170	Nyirabazungu	8	f	student	
171	Nyirahabimana	5	f		
172	Akimpaye	1	m		
173	Mukamugenzi	30	f		single
174	Ousiel Birara	54	m	herdsman	married
175	Rose Nyiransaba	48	f	farmer	married
176	Pascal Munyaneza	24	m	herdsman	single
177	Marguerite Mukamurangwa	28	f	farmer	single
178	Evariste Habimana	20	m	farmer	single
179	Mathias Higiro	15	m	student	
180	Vénancie Mukankundiye	13	f	student	
181	Nyirakuba Mukamana	6	f		

182	Ndayisaba	4	m		
183	Louise Birara	1	f		
184	Domitilla Kampirwa	30	f	farmer	married
185	Tharcisse Gakuba	25	m	farmer	single
186	Anastase Kandekwe	41	m	herdsman	married
187	Anastasie Mukamuyoboke	36	f	farmer	married
188	Athanase Mudacumura	14	m	student	
189	Costasie Mukakinani	12	f	student	
190	Immaculée Murorukwere	9	f	student	
191	Augustin Musabyimana	6	m		
192	Rose Mukandori	3	f		
193	Biregeya	36	m	farmer	married
194	Agnès Mukaruziga	30	f	farmer	married
195	Seromba	4	m		
196	Esther Nyirarukundo	2	f		
197	Etienne Musonera	36	m	herdsman	married
198	Prudence Nyiramuruta	24	f	farmer	married
199	Thérèse Nyirantarama	5	f		
200	Marianne Uwimana	2	f		
201	Edouard Munyampama	28	m	herdsman	married
202	Mukandinda	22	f	farmer	married
203	Aminadabu Rwanyabugigira	80	m	herdsman	married
204	Thérèse Nyirankuriza	70	f	farmer	married
205	Ntezamaso	16	m	student	single
206	Maromba	13	f	student	
207	Mutiganda	37	m	herdsman	married
208	Chrésie Mukaremera	80	f	farmer	married
209	Ndimubanzi	5	m		
210	Nyiransabimana	1	f		
211	Marthe Nyiragukura	38	f	farmer	married
212	Pascal Utazirubanda	7	m	student	
213	Claver Nsengiyumva	5	m		
214	Marguerite	15	f	student	single
215	Nyirambera	3	f		
216	Ngarambe	2	m		
217	Denis Rumenerangabo	45	m	herdsman	married
218	Rose Mukamugenzi	39	f	farmer	married
219	Mukamunana	9	f	student	
220	Mukarugwiza	3	f		
221	Mukamugemanyi	6	f		
222	Nyirarukundo	2	f		
223	Hitimana	60	m	herdsman	married
224	Azelle Nyirankusi	57	f	farmer	married
225	Nyirangezahayo	8	f	student	
226	Anastasie Kabera	26	f	farmer	married
227	Pascasie Mukashyaka	8	f	student	
228	Louis Murwanashyaka	6	m	student	
229	Théodore Ngiruwonsanga	3	m		
230	Sophie Mukabitega	40	f	farmer	widow
231	Joséphine Ntihabose	13	f	farmer	
232	Buforode	5	m		
233	Budariro	3	m		
234	Bideri	24	m	farmer	single
235	Nyirampeta	55	m	farmer	single
236	Alphonsine Mukansoro	14	f	student	
237	Banamwana	12	m	student	
238	François Karemera	40	m	herdsman	married
239	Espérance Mukazimurinda	35	f	farmer	married
240	Niyomugabo	2	m		
241	Marcel Munyurangabo	8	m	student	
242	Niyomugabo	6	m	student	
243	Mukangango	2	f		
244	Thomas Birara	50	m	herdsman	married
245	Xaverine Nyiramajangwe	45	f	farmer	married
246	Eugénie Mukashema	15	f	student	
247	Daphrose Mukabutera	13	f	student	
248	Anathalie Uwantege	10	f	student	
249	Mbindigiri	7	m	student	
250	Mukakarori	5	f		
251	Nyirantarama	80	f	farmer	widow
252	Augustin Gatwaza	30	m	student	single
253	Samuel Kanyemera	30	m	herdsman	married
254	Mukarugaba	27	f	farmer	married
255	Mukeshimana	10	f	student	
256	Ndutiye	6	m		
257	Rugwizangoga	26	m	herdsman	single
258	Munyurangabo	24	m	herdsman	married
259	Uwihoreye	22	f	farmer	married
260	Uwayisenga	3	f		
261	Mukabyagaju	27	f	farmer	married
262	Nkurunziza	2	m		
263	Aminadabu Gasagara	60	m	herdsman	married
264	Nyakarundi	34	m	herdsman	married
265	Kwitegetse	14	f	student	
266	Ndagije	6	m		
267	Ntihemuka	4	m		
268	Bayisenge	2	f		
269	Rutugame	28	m	farmer	married
270	Rusohoka	10	m	student	
271	Nyirabavuka	50	f	farmer	widow
272	Claver Mugengano	29	m	herdsman	single
273	Nyakana	27	m	farmer	single
274	Patricie Mnkantagwabira	20	f	farmer	single
275	Nsengiyumva	18	m	herdsman	single
276	Uwanyirigira	26	f	farmer	married
277	Nyiramapori	3	f		
278	Daphrose Nyamuhenda	1	f		
279	Amos Gahamanyi	38	m	herdsman	married
280	Xaverine Mukandema	33	f	farmer	married
281	Matoroshi	12	m	student	
282	Donatille	10	f	student	
283	Nvirabukara	8	f	student	
284	Abel Ngendahayo	60	m	herdsman	widower
285	Mugambi	10	m	student	
286	Thérèse Gahamanyi	6	f	student	
287	Chantal Gahamanyi	4	f		
288	Pauline Gahamanyi	2	f		
289	Mukamudenge	7	f	student	
290	Modeste Munyangabe	72	m	herdsman	married
291	Esther Kwitegetse	70	f	farmer	married
292	Martin Bugingo	15	m	student	
293	Mukantabana	13	f	student	
294	Rachel	10	f	student	
295	Fidèle	8	m	student	
296	Mukandori	16	f	student	single
297	Thomas Ndamage	40	m	herdsman	married
298	Elianne Mukankaka	38	f	farmer	married
299	Mukankundiye Gashikori	8	f	student	
300	Ndayisaba	6	m		
301	Uwayisenga	3	m		
302	Marianne Uwababyeyi	20	f	farmer	married
303	Madeleine Kamananga	60	f	farmer	widow
304	Bernadette Mukambungo	18	f	student	single
305	Hérédion Nteziryayo	30	m	herdsman	married
306	Esther Mukakarera	27	f	farmer	married
307	Jacqueline Mukamihigo	7	f	student	
308	Nzaramba	5	m		
309	Daphrose Nteziryayo	3	f		
310	Adeline Mukamuhizi	27	f	farmer	divorced
311	Debora Kamayanja	50	f	farmer	divorced
312	Munyabarame	60	m	herdsman	married
313	Amelie Uzamushaka	55	f	farmer	married
314	Narcisse Gakwavu	18	m	farmer	single
315	Dative Yankuriki	16	f	student	
316	Bavakure	14	m	student	
317	Casimir Nyumbayire	12	m	student	
318	Dorothée Yamfashije	10	f	student	
319	Emmanuel	4	m		
320	Berna Mukantagwabira	40	f	farmer	married
321	Frodouald Byandagara	13	m	student	
322	Odette Nyiramadenderi	10	f	student	
323	Donatha Mukankuka	4	f		
324	Donatha Hategeka	5	f		
325	Louise Hategeka	2	f		
326	Nyiramwamira	6	f		
327	Thérèse Mukankubito	50	f	farmer	divorced
328	Colette	15	f	student	
329	Nyirabiguri	13	f	student	
330	Dorothée	8	f	student	
331	Nyiramujyambere	80	f	farmer	widow
332	Odette Rwakayiro	5	f		
333	Nyiramakondera	2	f		
334	Hérédion Munyakanyamibwa	60	m	herdsman	married
335	Suzanne Nyiranyamibwa	55	f	farmer	married
336	Pascasie Mukamurigo	20	f	farmer	single
337	Assiel Rwakayiro	38	m	herdsman	married
338	Marcianne Nukankubana	32	f	farmer	married
339	Thomas	7	m	student	
340	Marcianne Mukafurere	18	f	student	single
341	Daphrose Uwimana	16	f	student	single
342	Esdras	13	m	student	
343	Marianne	9	f	student	
344	Ezéchiel	7	m	student	
345	Marcelline Munyakayanza	5	f		
346	Ezechiel Habayo	50	m	herdsman	married
347	Euphrasie Mukamudenge	48	f	farmer	married
348	Anastase Murwanashyaka	22	m	farmer	single
349	Joséphine Mukamwiza	20	f	farmer	single
350	Mukamasaro	16	f	student	single
351	Zilipa Nyirangeri	30	f	farmer	married
352	Sugabo	13	m	student	
353	Karake	9	m	student	
354	Mukeshimana	4	f		
355	André Munyantarama	70	m	herdsman	married
356	Immaculée Nyirabasuku	60	f	farmer	married
357	Alphonsine Cyurinyana	17	f	student	single
358	Patricie Mukarugwiza	20	f	farmer	single
359	Nyiramayira	15	f	student	
360	Ezechias Ziruguru	35	m	herdsman	married
361	Xaverine Mukangarambe	32	f	farmer	married
362	Nyirahabimana	8	f	student	
363	Nyiramazuru	6	f	student	

364	Dominique Ziruguru	3	m		
365	Julienne Mukamudenge	32	f	farmer	married
366	Pascal Museruka	12	m	student	
367	Mukamugema	7	f	student	
368	Eugénie	5	m		
369	Hesron Munyambibi	71	m	herdsman	married
370	Rosalie Nyankobwa	68	f	farmer	married
371	Alphonsine Bugenimana	9	f	student	
372	Ephrem Butera	38	m	herdsman	married
373	Xavéra Mukarugaba	30	f	student	married
374	Mbonabucya	14	m	student	
375	Aphrodis Bizumuremyi	8	m	student	
376	Dènise Butera	4	f		
377	Athanasie Butera	1	f		
378	Ngarambe	40	m	herdsman	married
379	Nyiramwamira	13	f	student	
380	Sugabo	8	m	student	
381	Rudagari	11	f	student	
382	Marc Nkunziryo	73	m	herdsman	married
383	Marthe Kangondo	68	f	farmer	married
384	Jean-Damascène Munyaneza	18	m	student	single
385	Béata Mukarukaka	16	f	student	single
386	Simon Habiyambere	24	m	herdsman	married
387	Mukeshimana	22	f	farmer	married
388	Rwigimba	75	m	herdsman	married
389	Xaverine Nyirafuku	70	f	farmer	married
390	Ousiel Ngirumwami	35	m	farmer	single
391	Marcel Ndayisaba	20	m	farmer	single
392	Ndwanije	40	m	herdsman	married
393	Euphrasie Mukabitega	30	f	farmer	married
394	Isacar Ngamije	37	m	herdsman	married
395	Anastase Mukagakombe	35	f	farmer	married
396	Bikorimana	8	m	student	
397	Ruhana	6	m		
398	Nzabihimana	3	m		
399	Zilipa Mukamukomeza	56	f	farmer	married
400	Ntirenganya	15	m	student	
401	Thomas Munyaneza	1	m		
402	Joséphine Nyirantagorama	20	f	farmer	married
403	Antoine Hitimana	75	m	herdsman	married
404	Ezechias Bucyana	45	m	herdsman	married
405	Thabithe Mukamudenge	72	f	farmer	married
406	Aron Segatarama	20	m	farmer	single
407	Mukangango	17	f	farmer	single
408	Sindikubwabo	14	m	student	
409	Nzamurambaho	12	m	student	
410	Bwisore	4	m		
411	Elizaphane Munyaragisha	40	m	herdsman	married
412	Gaudence	38	f	farmer	married
413	Mukantabana	10	f	student	
414	Frodouald	6	m		
415	Edouard Munyabagisha	3	m		
416	Callixte Munyabagisha	1	m		
417	Busugugu	30	m	herdsman	married
418	Erina Mukakabaka	27	f	farmer	married
419	Habimana	4	m		
420	Rose Kayumba	2	f		
421	Jacques Fundi	70	m	herdsman	married
422	Marguerite Makumi	65	f	farmer	married
423	Kamanzi	16	f	student	single
424	Mukamwiza	14	f	student	
425	Nyirakamagaza	12	f	student	
426	Ishimwe	10	m	student	
427	Phanie Munyankindi	50	m	herdsman	married
428	Marthe Kabagwiza	45	f	farmer	married
429	Gaspard Nzabahimana	22	m	farmer	single
430	Boniface Ruhezamihigo	18	m	farmer	single
431	Rachel Mukamugema	30	f	farmer	divorced
432	Innocent	5	m		
433	Heredi	3	m		
434	Gahima	1	m		
435	Nyirankima	7	f	student	
436	Ousiel Kampayana	40	m	herdsman	married
437	Concessa Nyirampakanije	37	f	farmer	married
438	Majyambere	10	m	student	
439	Sinderibuye	8	m	student	
440	Mayira	6	m		
441	Didace Muberankiko	3	m		
442	Munyakazi	45	m	herdsman	widower
443	Athanase Mutezintare	17	m	farmer	single
444	Muberangango	15	m	student	
445	Louis Muberankiko	10	m		
446	Kadaraza	35	m	herdsman	married
447	Mukangango	32	f	farmer	married
448	Alphonse Kadaraza	1	f		

1.1.5 Cellule Uwingabo

No.	Name	Age	Sex	Occupn.	Marital Status
1	Simon Kajonge	70	m	herdsman	married
2	Domitilla Zaninka	65	f	farmer	married
3	Odette Kampogo	20	f	farmer	single
4	Nyiramanzi	9	f	student	
5	Nyirahabimana	4	f		
6	Munyampara	32	m	herdsman	married
7	Eugénie Mukansonera	25	f	farmer	married
8	Nyirahabimana	3	f		
9	Munyampara	6m	f		
10	Muganga	33	m	farmer	married
11	Mukamarara	24	f	farmer	married
12	Louis Muganga	4m	f		
13	Joséphine Mukasharangabo	48	f	farmer	widow
14	Xaverine Murorukwere	25	f	farmer	single
15	Cyrille Nsabimana	22	m	herdsman	single
16	Anathalie Mukamwiza	18	f	farmer	single
17	Ndagije	29	m	herdsman	married
18	Mukansonera	23	f	farmer	married
19	Mihigo	72	m	herdsman	married
20	Aloys	1	m		
21	Kabahizi	20	f	farmer	single
22	David Kayijaho	29	m	herdsman	single
23	Nyirasugi	78	f	farmer	widow
24	Isacar Munyandinda	46	m	herdsman	married
25	Caritas Mukakamari	37	f	farmer	married
26	Ngezehayo	1	m		
27	Nyiranzeyimana	8	f	student	
28	Dative Munyandinda	3	f		
29	Denis munyandinda	1	m		
30	Murengera	70	m	herdsman	married
31	Mukarusanga	67	f	farmer	married
32	Innocent Ndayisaba	21	m	student	single
33	Murwanashyaka	16	m	student	single
34	Marcianne	11	f	student	
35	Silas Ngiruwonsanga	47	m	herdsman	married
36	Nyirajyambere	44	f	farmer	married
37	Musabyimana	15	f	student	
38	Mukandori	13	f	student	
39	Shyirambere	11	m	student	
40	Mukangarambe	8	f	student	
41	Spéciose Mukangarambe	7	f	student	
42	Mukeshimana	5	f	student	
43	Simon Rwigamba	34	m	herdsman	married
44	Spéciose Rwigamba	30	f	farmer	married
45	Alphonsine Rwigamba	4	f		
46	Théodore Rwigamba	8m	m		
47	Appolinaire Ntambiye	75	m	herdsman	widower
48	Faustin Murigande	60	m	herdsman	married
49	Mukankuba	58	f	farmer	married
50	Hategekimana	21	m	farmer	single
51	Basile	12	m	student	
52	Samvura	73	m	herdsman	married
53	Julienne Nyiramnguera	65	f	farmer	married
54	Euphrasie Nyirabagemahe	20	f	farmer	single
55	Evariste Songa	32	m	herdsman	married
56	Dorothée Iribagiza	28	f	farmer	married
57	Kayirabo	45	m	herdsman	widower
58	Muhigirwa	47	m	herdsman	married
59	Thérèse	44	f	farmer	married
60	Vérène Mukamunana	20	f	farmer	single
61	Dancilla Mukandori	17	f	farmer	single
62	Immaculée	14	f	student	
63	Claver	12	m	student	
64	Ntakuritimana	5	m		
65	Kambayire	85	f	farmer	married
66	Rwabukwisi	60	m	herdsman	married
67	Nirere	57	f	farmer	married
68	Ndagije	12	m	student	
69	Joséphine Mukabutera	66	f	farmer	married
70	Thomas Gashakamba	46	m	herdsman	married
71	Marcianne Mukandirima	42	f	farmer	married
72	Samuel Sindayigaya	8	m	student	
73	Nyirantenderi	5	f		
74	Zéphanie Nyakagabo	48	m	herdsman	married
75	Adèle Kamugwera	45	f	farmer	married
76	Esdras Musabyimana	20	m	farmer	single
77	Ntakuritimana	17	m	farmer	single
78	Nyirahakizimana	11	f	student	
79	Nsengimana	6	m	student	
80	Nyakagabo	3	m	student	
81	Harerimana	26	m	herdsman	married
82	Eugénie Mukaremera	23	f	farmer	married
83	Etienne Ndwaniye	48	m	herdsman	married
84	Mukagasana	45	f	farmer	married
85	Nkusi	22	m	farmer	single

86	Nyirahategeka	18	f	farmer	single
87	Callixte Ndahayo	13	m	student	
88	Mushimiyimana	10	f	student	
89	Niyonsaba	6	f		
90	Mukasine	3	f		
91	Niyomugabo	9m	m		
92	Nyiranyange	60	f	farmer	married
93	Emmanuel Ndahimana	46	m	herdsman	married
94	Costasie Mukamasabo	40	f	farmer	married
95	Nikuze	9	f	student	
96	Bizimana	7	m	student	
97	Césalie Ndahimana	5	f		
98	Cansilde Ndahimana	3	f		
99	Thomas Ndahimana	1	m		
100	Phénéas Karama	35	m	herdsman	married
101	Natalie Nyirangeri	30	f	farmer	married
102	Nyirangunzu	4	f		
103	Karama	6m	f		
104	Ezechias Birara	30	m	herdsman	married
105	Odette Mukankundiye	27	f	farmer	married
106	Nyirambengere	3	f		
107	Birara	2	f		
108	Birara	7m	f		
109	Annonciata Nyirantoki	32	f	farmer	married
110	Mukamunana	8	f	student	
111	Habimana	5	m		
112	Sylvère	3	f		
113	Thacienne	30	f	farmer	married
114	Munyaburanga	5m	f		
115	Assiel Mudacumura	40	m	herdsman	married
116	Thacienne Mukamashyaka	36	f	farmer	married
117	Mukeshamariya	10	f	student	
118	Alphonse	8	f	student	
119	Catherine	6	f		
120	Mudacumura	3	m		
121	Nyirabuseruka	42	f	farmer	widow
122	Nyiransabimana	10	f	student	
123	Alphonse	7	m	student	
124	Rubyogo	4	m		
125	Ruhinja	1	m		
126	Ruhanamirindi	78	m	herdsman	widower
127	Anastasie Gasasira	26	m	farmer	single
128	Kayumba	16	m	farmer	single
129	Uwimana	12	f	student	
130	Rutayisire	20	m	student	single
131	Gasore	17	m	student	single
132	Gatarayiha	32	m	herdsman	married
133	Uwimana	20	f	farmer	married
134	Gatarayiha	1	m		
135	Nyirahategeka	40	f	farmer	married
136	Mukansnga	16	f	student	single
137	Marthe Nyiransengima	9	f	student	
138	Mukamugenga	7	f	student	
139	Nyirahabimana	28	f	farmer	married
140	Céléstin Munyampeta	70	m	herdsman	married
141	Winniphrida Karagwiza	60	f	farmer	married
142	Kabagema	40	m	farmer	married
143	Mukakamana	36	f	farmer	married
144	Mukantwari	9	f	student	
145	Mukamana	7	f	student	
146	Nayirarora	4	m		
147	Kabagema	1	m		
148	Karemera	44	m	herdsman	married
149	Léocadie Mukamudenge	40	f	farmer	married
150	Ndayisaba	8	m	student	
151	Gafirigita	5	m		
152	Alphonsine	3	f		
153	Tuyisenge	1	f		
154	Kadabagizi	58	f	farmer	widow
155	Mukarurangwa	20	f	farmer	single
156	Nyiramataza	62	f	farmer	widow
157	Hagenga	55	m	farmer	married
158	Adèle Kamugwera	50	f	farmer	married
159	Mukamana	3	f		
160	Kabarira	28	m	farmer	married
161	Marie	26	f	farmer	married
162	Marthe	55	f	farmer	widow
163	Nyirakamondo	40	f	farmer	widow
164	Isacar	15	m	student	
165	Rusodoka	8	m	student	
166	Munyurangabo	45	m	herdsman	married
167	Mukamunana	40	f	farmer	married
168	Nyiramwamira	10	f	student	
169	Rukara	3	m		
170	Nyiraromba	42	f	farmer	widow
171	Munyurangabo	4	m		
172	Déo Munyurangabo	1	m		
173	Segatsama	78	m	herdsman	married
174	Nyirakariza	74	f	farmer	married
175	Bisangwa	32	m	herdsman	single
176	Munyanshongore	68	m	herdsman	married
177	Belancille Mukandera	65	f	farmer	married
178	Mukabutera	26	f	farmer	single
179	Mukakamana	20	f	farmer	single
180	Nyiranzeyimana	17	f	farmer	single
181	Xavier Nzamwita	45	m	herdsman	married
182	Madeleine Mukamuganga	40	f	farmer	married
183	Bududuri	10	m	student	
184	Canisius	7	m	student	
185	Jean Kayumba	39	m	herdsman	married
186	Adalie Mukamukomeza	35	f	farmer	married
187	Nyiranzeyimana	8	f	student	
188	Mukamwiza	5	f		
189	Aphrodis	2	m		
190	Patrice Nyirashyaka	25	m	herdsman	married
191	Bikorimana	5m	m		
192	Gasarabwe	44	m	herdsman	married
193	Vérène Nyirabakiga	40	f	farmer	married
194	Marcel	10	m	student	
195	Nyirabarundi	7	f	student	
196	Yambabariye	4	f		
197	Gasarabwe	2	f		
198	Kabeba	40	m	herdsman	married
199	Madame Kabeba	25	f	farmer	married
200	Madeleine Kabeba	2	f		
201	Mukanzigiye	35	f	farmer	married
202	Rwimana	13	f	student	
203	Gasimba	10	m	student	
204	Mukamuhizi	8	f	student	
205	Nsengiyumva	5	m		
206	Nirere	2	f		
207	Museruka	36	m	herdsman	married
208	Mukambaraga	30	f	farmer	married
209	Aphonse	7	m	student	
210	Seruryogo	5	m		
211	Gasongo	3	m		
212	Museruka	1	f		
213	Gaudance Nyirambabazi	28	f	farmer	married
214	Nyirahabiyaremye	7	f	student	
215	Ndikubwimana	4	m		
216	Nshimiyimana	2	m		
217	Uzziel Nyagahigi	38	m	herdsman	married
218	Nadine	1	f		
219	Biziyaremye	9	m	student	
220	Mukamana	7	f	student	
221	Mukandayisenga	5	f		
222	Nyagahigi	3	m		
223	Drocella Nyagahigi	1	f		
224	Aron Gasana	33	m	herdsman	married
225	Anastasie Mukakamari	28	f	farmer	married
226	Sibomana	9	m	student	
227	Odette	7	f	student	
228	Nkotanyi	3	f		
229	Simon Kagorora	65	m	herdsman	married
230	Damarce Mukara	55	f	farmer	married
231	Ayinkamiye	20	f	farmer	single
232	Marguerite Mukabaziga	40	f	farmer	widow
233	Niyigena	8	f	student	
234	Bikorimana	3	m		
235	Kagorora	1	m		
236	Odette Mukamana	12	f	student	
237	Semanyenzi	9	m	student	
238	Patricie	4	f		
239	Nyirahabayo	2	f		

1.1.6 Cellule Muhingo

No.	Name	Age	Sex	Occupn.	Marital Status
1	Callixte	25	m	herdsman	married
2	Byiringiro	4	m		
3	Dusabende	3	f		
4	Marc Ncogoza	58	m	farmer	married
5	Béatrice Nyirabije	40	f	farmer	married
6	Mpakaniye	20	m	farmer	single
7	Samson	10	m	student	
8	Sylvère Kibenji	6	m		
9	Matoroshi	4	m		
10	Berchmans Kimenyi	54	m	herdsman	married
11	Annonciata Mukabera	48	f	farmer	married
12	Pascal Nsengumuremyi	15	m	student	
13	Yankurije	12	f	student	
14	Ndikubwayo	9	m	student	
15	Ayinkamiye	7	m	student	
16	Sylvère Matoroshi	5	m	student	
17	Ruhigira	50	m	herdsman	married
18	Nyirangoga	46	f	farmer	married
19	Jean Yankurije	36	m	farmer	single
20	Nsengiyumva	32	m	farmer	single

No.	Name	Age	Sex	Occupn.	Marital Status
21	Bénoît Gatwaza	35	m	councillor	married
22	Thérèse Mukaruziga	32	f	farmer	married
23	Ntakuritimana	12	m	student	
24	Uwamahoro	5	f		
25	Nyirandenzaho	7	f	student	
26	Habimana	10	m	student	
27	Damarce Mukamugema	55	f	farmer	married
28	Bernard Kanamugire	30	m	teacher	single
29	Béatrice Mukamudenge	20	f	student	single
30	Baziga	50	m	herdsman	married
31	Nteziryayo	11	m	student	
32	Habimana	9	m	student	
33	Nyiranteziryayo	4	f		
34	Ruhashumukore	65	m	herdsman	married
35	Nyiratabaruka	52	f	farmer	married
36	Michel Makuza	30	m	mechanic	married
37	Mukakabego	45	f	farmer	married
38	Chantal	13	f	student	
39	Emmanuel	10	m	student	
40	Antoine Makuza	8	m	student	
41	Léonce Makuza	6	f		
42	Didiane Makuza	4	f		
43	Paul Ntabwoba	80	m	herdsman	married
44	Mariane Nyakayiru	70	f	farmer	married
45	Sebakabura	58	m	farmer	married
46	Spéciose Mukandanga	20	f	farmer	
47	Mathias Iyakaremye	23	m	herdsman	married
48	Mukagasana	22	f	farmer	married
49	Patrice Rucyesha	70	m	herdsman	married
50	Anastase Nyirabarame	60	f	farmer	married
51	Sibomana	20	m	farmer	single
52	Ntamugeri	10	m	student	
53	Mukarwego	38	f	farmer	married
54	Esther Mukashema	13	f	student	
55	Nyiransengimana	8	f	student	
56	Hakizimana	11	m	student	
57	Ndababonye	5	m		
58	Marie	2	f		
59	Nkusi	30	m	farmer	married
60	Uzziel Munyantarama	35	m	herdsman	married
61	Frodouald Habimana	12	m	herdsman	
62	Bikorimana Nyandwi	3	m		
63	Ntakuritimana	1	m		
64	Karwoga	40	f	farmer	single
65	Mukarukaka	39	f	farmer	married
66	Nyiransengimana	10	f	student	
67	Nshimiyimana	5	m		
68	Colette Mukagatare	9	f	student	
69	Ndikuwimana	6	m		
70	Godelièvе Ingabire	3	f		
71	Emmanuel Uwamahoro	2	f		
72	Ngirumwami	40	m	farmer	married
73	Marianne Nyirankuriza	40	f	farmer	married
74	Judith	22	f	farmer	single
75	Bernadette	24	f	farmer	single
76	Havugimana	13	m		
77	Muhigirwa Muzehe	3	m		
78	Etienne Munyanzira	50	m	herdsman	married
79	Bernadette Mukarugwiza	10	f	student	
80	Niyonzima	5	m		
81	Sibomana	3	m		
82	Nyirakanani	18m	f		
83	Consolée Mukamana	5	f		
84	Céléstin Havugimana	11	m	student	
85	Munyaneza	5	m		
86	Marc Busizori	40	m	herdsman	married
87	Cécile Mukandekezi	35	f	farmer	married
88	Euphrasie Nyirangwijuruvu	12	f	student	
89	Pascasie Ntirera	10	f	student	
90	Consolée Nyirahabineza	4	f		
91	François	2.5	m		
92	Pierre	18m	m		
93	Elie Karimunda	35	m	farmer	married
94	Nyiramajangwe	26	f	farmer	married
95	Serufigi	40	m	herdsman	married
96	Rose Murengayire	38	f	farmer	married
97	Vérène Nyiramporayonzi	18	f	farmer	single
98	Chadrac	8	m	student	
99	Zaburi Bazimaziki	5	m		
100	Sahinkuye	80	m	herdsman	married
101	Thérèse Nyirasugi	60	f	farmer	married
102	Ngwije	22	m	farmer	single
103	Aloys Munyarubuga	48	m	herdsman	married
104	Pascasie Mukankaka	40	f	farmer	married
105	Eugénie	23	f	farmer	single
106	Vincent	21	m	farmer	single
107	Nirere	19	f	farmer	single
108	Niyonzima	17	m	student	single
109	Thomas Kayijuka	57	m	herdsman	married
110	Mukandirima	54	f	farmer	married
111	Canisius	28	m	farmer	single
112	Athanase	21	m	farmer	single
113	Athanase	20	f	student	single
114	Hitimana	19	m	student	single
115	Anésie	17	f	student	single
116	Samuel Nyirintwari	65	m	herdsman	married
117	Ntirenganya	23	m	herdsman	single
118	Mukarugaba	17	f	farmer	single
119	Kabasire	30	m	herdsman	married
120	Gahindabuye	25	m	student	single
121	Nyiranturege	15	f	farmer	
122	Nsabimana	33	m	herdsman	married
123	Nyrabakiga	31	f	farmer	married
124	Rukara	13	m	student	
125	Mafene	12	m	student	
126	Nyirabukara	10	f	student	
127	Kabano	40	m	farmer	married
128	Kwitegetse	40	f	farmer	widow
129	Bakame	60	m	farmer	married
130	Nuwayo	14	f	student	
131	Nyiramahabari	17	f	student	single
132	Murengera	34	m	herdsman	married
133	Madeleine	31	f	farmer	married
134	Mbaraga	2	m		
135	Nkeramihigo	45	m	farmer	married
136	Kamatamu	49	f	farmer	widow
137	Ignace Ibambasi	33	m	herdsman	married
138	Thérèse	20	f	farmer	married
139	Uwimana	6	f		
140	Bikorimana	3	m		
141	Charles	38	m	herdsman	married
142	Mukamazimpaka	35	f	farmer	married
143	Béata	14	f	student	
144	Théogène	12	m	student	
145	Alphonse	9	m	student	
146	Espérance	7.5	f	student	
147	Colette	4.5	f	student	
148	Sophie Nyirankurira	40	f	farmer	married
149	Mukamanzi	37	f	farmer	married
150	Emmanuel Nsengiyumna	13	m	student	
151	Innocent Mushimiyimana	8	m	student	
152	Nyirambonigaba	6	f		
153	Ntakirutimana	5	m		
154	Nyirahabineza	2.5	f		
155	Esron Hangare	70	m	herdsman	married
156	Madeleine Nyirabucura	65	f	farmer	married
157	Phénéas Sebarinda	30	m	herdsman	married
158	Odette Nyirajyambere	25	f	farmer	married
159	Xavéra Nyirasinamenye	11	f	student	
160	Mukangemanyi	7	f	student	
161	Elianne Mukangwije	9	f	student	
162	Mushimiyimana	5	f		
163	Dominique Ntibagwe	23	m	herdsman	married
164	Pascasie Uwiragiye	23	f	farmer	married
165	Nyiransabimana	4	f		
166	Ndagijimana	2	m		
167	Drocella	7m	f		
168	Aminadabu Rwayitare	52	m	farmer	single
169	Régine Mukarutabana	40	f	farmer	married
170	Njyrajyambere	21	f	farner	single
171	Mukamudenge	19	f	farmer	single
172	Joseph	12	m	student	
173	Silas Mpakaniye	16	m	student	single
174	Karimba	55	m	farmer	married
175	Elianne Mukankabura	54	f	farmer	married
176	Simon Haragirimana	20	m	farmer	single
177	Abel Rubambari	18	m	student	single
178	Enos	12	m	student	

1.1.7 Cellule Gasata

No.	Name	Age	Sex	Occupn.	Marital Status
1	Gitaminzi	14	m	student	
2	Jonas	15	m	student	
3	Nyirahabimana	21	f	farmer	single
4	Bakame	9	m	student	
5	Kamanzi	45	m	herdsman	married
6	Niyizimigambi	7	m	student	
7	Rwagacuzi	55	m	herdsman	married
8	Mukangamije	56	f	farmer	married
9	Shamukiga	36	m	herdsman	single
10	Nzamwita	24	m	herdsman	single
11	Mukamparamage	20	f	farmer	single
12	Mukamugenga	14	f	student	
13	Munyakabungo	50	m	herdsman	married
14	Kamayanja	40	f	farmer	married
15	Nyirahabineza	12	f	student	
16	Mukarubayiza	24	f	farmer	single
17	Uwimana	13	f	student	

18	Marie Mukasine	27	f	farmer	married
19	Mukakamana	9	f	student	
20	Mukantwari	7	f	student	
21	François Nshimiyimana	5	m		
22	Pierre Nyirinkindi	2.5	m		
23	Augustin Ntagugura	60	m	herdsman	married
24	Gaudence Nyirantama	49	f	farmer	married
25	Makuza	23	m	farmer	single
26	Ngarambe	20	m	farmer	single
27	Mukangarambe	15	f	student	
28	Marie Mukankusi	41	f	farmer	married
29	Frodouald Nkurunziza	16	m	student	single
30	Sibomana	10	m	student	
31	Emmanuel Munyaneza	11	m	student	
32	Mukamashyaka	6	f		
33	Uwimana	3	f		
34	Mukankomeje	7	f	student	
35	Mukantamage	60	f	farmer	married
36	Munyaruguru	23	m	herdsman	single
37	Sematore	50	m	herdsman	married
38	Mukankubito	48	f	farmer	married
39	Hategekimana	16	m	student	single
40	Nyitwayiki	8	m	studen6t	
41	Mukankusi	5	f	student	
42	Hakizimana	3	m		
43	Murwanashyaka	19	m	farmer	single
44	Ngarambe	38	f	farmer	married
45	Nyirangezahayo	12	f	student	
46	Mukamugunga	38	f	farmer	married
47	Ndagijimana	6	m	student	
48	Uwera	2	f		
49	Munyabagisha	37	m	farmer	married
50	Nyirabagwiza	32	f	farmer	married
51	Nyiransabimana	8	f	student	
52	Nyirahategeka	1	f		
53	Rusagara	40	m	farmer	married
54	Mukansonera	35	f	farmer	married
55	Nyirindamutsa	10	m	student	
56	Ngendayihimana	7	m	student	
57	Nsengiyumva	5	m		
58	Rukundo	2	m		
59	Ntamakemwa	45	m	herdsman	married
60	Mukantabana	42	f	farmer	married
61	Ndayisaba	15	m	student	
62	Tuyisenge	7	m	student	
63	Ntakirutimana	5	m		
64	Bugingo	1	m		
65	Nkubana	55	m	herdsman	married
66	Mukasubika	45	f	farmer	married
67	Emmanuel	16	m	farmer	single
68	Nyiransabimana	4	f		

1.2 Sector Musenyi

1.2.1 Cellule Karama

No.	Name	Age	Sex	Occupn.	Marital Status
1	Marie Nyiramafurebo	45	f	farmer	married
2	Eugénie Mukamarara	20	f	farmer	single
3	Ndayisaba Serubyogo	17	m	farmer	single
4	Nkurunziza	12	m	student	
5	Mapironi	15	m	student	
6	Gafuku	16	m	student	single
7	Ngezahayo	12	m	student	
8	Rachel	9	f	student	
9	Joseph Munyanshongore	48	m	herdsman	married
10	Immaculée	40	f	farmer	married
11	Emmanuel Ngendahimana	22	m	student	single
12	Nyirabukara	10	f	student	
13	Nyirabazungu	8	f	student	
14	Munyansanga	32	m	herdsman	married
15	Odette	27	f	farmer	married
16	Léoncie	75	f	farmer	widow
17	Ruzindori	9	m	student	
18	Rukara	7	m	student	
19	Judith	35	f	farmer	divorced
20	Nyiranturege	15	f	student	
21	Pascal	4	m	student	
22	Déo Munyanshongore	2	m	student	
23	Claver Karemera	40	m	herdsman	married
24	Kandirima	35	f	farmer	married
25	Kabagwira	20	f	farmer	single
26	Fabien	17	m	farmer	
27	Callixte	13	m	student	
28	Casimir Mugimbaho	50	m	herdsman	married
29	Frolide	45	f	farmer	married
30	Uwizeye Nyirabukara	20	f	farmer	single
31	Kabagwiza	15	f	student	
32	Nyiranturege	8	f	student	
33	Christine	11	f	student	
34	Narcisse Gasana	37	m	herdsman	married
35	Marcianne	35	f	farmer	married
36	Marceline	19	f	farmer	single
37	Rugwizangoga	14	m	student	
38	Mukabutera	10	f	student	
39	Gaspard	8	m	student	
40	Benoît Higiro	32	m	farmer	married
41	Rudomoro	6	m		
42	Rutayisire	8	f	student	
43	Mukankundiye	6	f		
44	Kamanzi	70	m	herdsman	married
45	Véronique	65	f	farmer	married
46	Nyirahabimana	13	f	student	
47	Thomas Munyakayanza	35	m	farmer	married
48	Colette	28	f	farmer	married
49	Odette Kagorora	38	f	farmer	married
50	Davide Kagorora	7	m	student	
51	Odette	26	f	farmer	married
52	Jean Mudenge	2	m		
53	Jérôme Mbarubukeye	40	m	herdsman	married
54	Marie-Thérèse Mukankusi	40	f	farmer	married
55	Mukabihizi	28	f	farmer	married
56	Ingabire	10	f	student	
57	Liberata	7	f	student	
58	Marceline	5	f		
59	Nyirahabimana	3	f		
60	Mami Mbarubukeye	1	f		
61	Philippe Gasagara	44	m	builder	married
62	Marthe Nyirabucanda	40	f	farmer	married
63	Uwanmariya Mukaruberwa	18	f	student	single
64	Murekatete	15	f	student	
65	Nsengiyumva	12	m	student	
66	Pascal Ndayisaba	28	m	farmer	single
67	Winniphrida	22	f	farmer	married
68	Narcisse Rwabukwisi	65	m	herdsman	married
69	Thérèse Madame	58	f	farmer	married
70	Aphrodis Kagororora	37	m	herdsman	married
71	Anésie	32	f	farmer	married
72	Matoroshi	11	m	student	
73	Ndamage	34	m	herdsman	married
74	Celine	6	f		
75	Mukandori	28	f	farmer	married
76	Béata	11	f	student	
77	Isacar	9	m	student	
78	Cyprien Nzabahimana	80	m	herdsman	married
79	Esther Nyirantama	65	f	farmer	married
80	Gaspard Musazi	35	m	farmer	married
81	Marguerite	27	f	farmer	married
82	Martin	2	f		
83	Dominique	25	m	herdsman	married
84	Daphrose	22	f	farmer	married
85	Christophe	1	m		
86	Xaveri Muberankiko	50	m	herdsman	married
87	Prudence Mukandori	45	f	farmer	married
88	Innocent Ngarambe	25	m	herdsman	single
89	Emmanuel	10	m	student	
90	Matoroshi	7	m	student	
91	Edouard Munyampama	60	m	herdsman	married
92	Prudence Mukangwije	57	f	farmer	married
93	Anatole	24	m	farmer	single
94	Antoinette	26	f	farmer	married
95	Jean Claude	19	m	student	single
96	Pangarasi	11	m	student	
97	Berthe	9	f	student	
98	Mudenge	13	m	student	
99	Gakwenderi	7	m	student	
100	Marcienne Mukamazimpaka	24	f	farmer	married
101	Martin	2	m		
102	Straton Munyandamutsa	46	m	herdsman	married
103	Immaculée Nyirarwamo	30	f	farmer	married
104	Ntihemuka	9	m	herdsman	
105	Elianne	31	f	farmer	married
106	Ntihemuka	8	m	student	
107	Rosalie Mukandayisenga	12	f	student	
108	Niyomugabo	7	m	student	
109	Eugénie Kandame	18	f	farmer	married
110	Françoise	3	f		
111	Colette Mukamusoni	33	f	farmer	widow
112	Anastase Mazimpaka	17	m	student	single
113	Macibiri	10	f	student	
114	Nyiranturege	8	f	student	
115	Dative	32	f	farmer	
116	Marc Bimenyimana	7	m	student	
117	Pascasie	4	f		
118	Nyirahabimana	2	f		
119	Bigambazi	30	m	farmer	married
120	Chrésie	27	f	farmer	married

121	Damarce Kabuyundo	65	f	farmer	widow
122	Rugwizangoga	30	m	farmer	single
123	François Munyansanga	32	m	farmer/carpenter	married
124	Judith Uwimana	27	f	farmer	married
125	Emmanuelie Murorukwere	6	f		
126	Jean Baptiste	4	m		
127	Olivier Munyansanga	2	m		
128	André Ntagara	65	m	herdsman	married
129	Eugénie Kansinga	26	f	student	single
130	Denis Munyapeza	32	f	farmer/builder	married
131	Léocardie Mukecuru	62	f	farmer	married
132	Rachel Nyirahabimana	23	f	farmer/tailor	married
133	Pélagie Mukamukomeza	20	f	student	single
134	Thérèse	21	f	farmer	married
135	Musirikari	35	m	herdsman	married
136	Berthe	32	f	farmer	married
137	Nyirabunonko	14	f	student	
138	Tharcisse	12	m	student	
139	Elie Bizuru	8	m	student	
140	Masumbuko	6	m	student	
141	Alphonsine Musirikari	2	f		
142	Marie Nyirabushungwe	80	f	farmer	widow
143	Sala	28	f	farmer	married
144	Nyiramwamira	12	f	student	
145	Rubyogo	10	m	student	
146	Niyomugabo	6	m		
147	Adèle Nyirabakorahe	50	f	farmer	widow
148	Béatrice	20	m	farmer	single
149	Hélène Mukagatare	30	f	farmer	married
150	Ndangamira Rudomoro	15	m	student	
151	Prisca Nyirabishati	70	f	farmer	widow
152	Gakwaya	35	m	herdsman	married
153	Immaculée	30	f	farmer	married
154	Mujawayezu	16	f	student	
155	Sebirondo	14	m	student	
156	Daughter of Niyonzima	10	f	student	
157	Ndayisaba	22	m	farmer	single
158	Habimana	13	m	student	
159	Rudomoro	16	m	student	single
160	Nyirahabimana	18	f	farmer	single
161	Igance Ndahimana	20	m	herdsman	married

1.2.1 Cellule Karama (continued)

No.	Name	Age	Sex	Occupn.	Marital Status
1	Canisius Kanamugire	45	m	herdsman	married
2	Mukarubayiza	40	f	farmer	married
3	Fidèle Bidori	20	m	herdsman	single
4	Mukamurenzi	18	f	farmer	single
5	Bernard Mudondori	14	m	student	
6	Bigirimana	12	m	student	
7	Mukamana	10	f	student	
8	Hakizimana	7	m	student	
9	François Rucyeribuga	30	m	herdsman	married
10	Kampogo	25	f	farmer	married
11	Habiyambere	7	m	student	
12	Mukandayisenga	5	f		
13	Seneza	2	m		
14	Mukabaziga	60	f	farmer	married
15	Nyirampeta	45	f	farmer	married
16	Gatwa	17	m	farmer	single
17	Nzabahimana	14	m	student	
18	Bimenyimana	12	m	student	
19	Nyirabasinga	6	f		
20	Ndahayo	2	m		
21	Nyirahabiyambere	60	f	farmer	married
22	Hatungimana	25	m	farmer	single
23	Ngabonziza	60	m	herdsman	married
24	Gakwaya	25	m	herdsman	married
25	Kayijuka	45	m	herdsman	married
26	Nyiramwiza	42	f	farmer	married
27	Monique	10	f	student	
28	Sibomana	7	m	student	
29	Mukaragandekwe	55	m	herdsman	married
30	Mukagatare	45	f	farmer	married
31	Mukamurangwa	25	f	farmer	single
32	Hanyurijyayo	15	m	student	
33	Kanakuze	10	f	student	
34	Straton Nzarubara	50	m	herdsman	married
35	Nyiraneza	15	f	student	
36	Kabanda	47	m	herdsman	married
37	Uzayisenga	10	f	student	
38	Ntagwabira	16	m	farmer	single
39	Ndangayija	14	m	student	
40	Niyonzima	11	m	student	
41	Nkurunziza	5	m		
42	Césalie	8	f	student	
43	Nyirankwavu	6	f	student	
44	Cyrille Bangana	23	m	herdsman	married
45	Thérèse	20	f	farmer	married
46	Nyirarukundo	1	f		
47	Etienne	62	m	herdsman	married
48	Sophie	57	f	farmer	married
49	Ignace Kayijaho	25	m	herdsman	single
50	Kyirabwoneje	17	f	student	single
51	Rosalie	10	m	student	
52	Seburinkembe	15	f	student	
53	Albert	28	m	herdsman	married
54	Isidore Nyakayiro	19	m	farmer	single
55	Odile Sezibera	12	f	student	
56	Emerthe Mukarusagara	48	f	farmer	married
57	Julienne	6	f		
58	Nzayisenga	6	m		
59	Aphrodis Bunyenzi	52	m	herdsman	married
60	Joséphine	49	f	farmer	married
61	Alphonsine	15	f	student	
62	Kabuyanja	19	f	student	single
63	Théonèste Mukeshimana	18	m	student	single
64	Théogène	12	m	student	
65	Félicien	9	m	student	
66	Rwamakambiza	65	m	herdsman	married
67	Alivèra	61	f	farmer	married
68	Munderere	26	m	herdsman	married
69	Thérèse	24	f	farmer	married
70	Nsengimana	6	m		
71	Kamugundu	3	m		
72	Slyvain Bizimana	63	m	herdsman	married
73	Xavéra Nyirabahutu	59	f	farmer	married
74	Uwiragiye	18	f	farmer	single
75	Uwamariya	15	f	student	
76	Julienne Mukamusoni	31	f	farmer	married
77	Nikora	5	m		
78	Jean Rwampire	53	m	farmer	married
79	Mukamudenge	50	f	farmer	married
80	Nyirampakaniye	25	f	farmer	married
81	Mukashema	20	f	farmer	married
82	Niyomugabo	17	m	student	single
83	Nyirangezahayo	15	f	student	
84	Mutuyeyezu	12	f	student	
85	Mukandayisenga	10	m	student	
86	Itegekaharinde	7	m	student	
87	Gaspard kagemana	42	m	herdsman	married
88	Mukabideri	40	f	farmer	married
89	Patricie	18	f	farmer	married
90	Mukabadege	15	f	student	
91	Mathilde	12	f	student	
92	Basile	10	m	student	
93	Mukomeza	8	m	student	
94	Nizeyimana	2	f		
95	Justin Bizimana	66	m	herdsman	married
96	Nyiramugwera	67	f	farmer	married
97	Gakwandi	25	m	farmer	married
98	Camille Ndahimana	30	m	herdsman	married
99	Thérèse Mukamunana	25	f	farmer	married
100	Nyiransengiyumva	4	f		
101	Slyvère Munyakazi	60	m	herdsman	married
102	Marie Kamberuka	58	f	farmer	married
103	Anastase Cyubahiro	20	m	farmer	single
104	Hasangwaniza	17	m	student	single
105	Bayisenge	15	m	student	
106	Nyiratebuka	70	f	farmer	married
107	Nsabwimana	9	f	student	
108	Nshyiramabere	7	m	student	
109	Ntirushwa	5	m		
110	Mukagasana	30	f	farmer	married
111	Bukumburwa	45	f	farmer	married
112	Dusabimana	19	m	farmer	single
113	Jeanne	15	f	student	
114	Thérèse Nyirabukara	30	f	farmer	married
115	Béata	5	f		
116	Jonas Matabaro	30	m	farmer	married
117	Nyirabazungu	5	f		
118	Nkeguru	3	f		
119	Ndayisaba	1	m		
120	Buhigiro	35	m	herdsman	married
121	Habimana	10	m	student	
122	Hakizimana	10	m	student	
123	Sindayiheba	6	m		
124	Nyirantabire	43	f	farmer	married
125	Nyirampumunyurwa	20	f	farmer	single
126	Nsekantibagiwe	15	m	student	
127	Mukeshimana	20	f	student	single
128	Jean Paul	7	m	student	
129	Esdras Munyansanga	32	m	tailor	married
130	Kankuyo	30	f	farmer	married
131	Furaha	9	f	student	

132	Mukashema	5	f		
133	Mugabo Habiyambere	2	m		
134	Ndayiramya	25	m	herdsman	married
135	Gasagara	42	m	farmer	married
136	Ndayiramya	5	m		
137	Hategikimana	65	m	herdsman	married
138	Adèle Nyiramana	63	f	farmer	married
139	Béata	25	f	farmer	married
140	Sarigoma	4	m		
141	Gratien	1	m		
142	Uwambaye	67	f	farmer	married
143	Chantal Nyiranturege	17	f	student	single
144	Karekezi	70	m	herdsman	married
145	Costasie Ntabareshya	68	f	farmer	married
146	François	23	m	farmer	single
147	Marie	22	f	farmer	single
148	Bikorimana	10	m	student	
149	Munyankindi	70	m	herdsman	married
150	Nyirakamondo	68	f	farmer	married
151	Casimir Kayibanda	35	m	herdsman	married
152	Murengera	25	m	farmer	single
153	Madeleine	31	f	farmer	married
154	Nyiraburyohe	12	f	student	
155	Thaddée Rucyahana	10	m	student	
156	Sebusurira	8	m	student	
157	Mukamugema	66	f	farmer	married
158	Charles	21	m	student	single
159	Gasaza	7	m	student	
160	Dative	41	f	farmer	married
161	Igirimbabazi	18	f	farmer	single
162	Debora	16	m	farmer	single
163	Nkorerimana	12	f	student	
164	Nzayisenga	8	m	student	
165	Munyantarama	61	m	farmer	married
166	Mukashingiro	23	f	farmer	single
167	Nyirabirori	18	f	farmer	single
168	Adèle	16	f	student	single
169	Rubayiza	12	m	student	
170	Nyiragumiriza	10	f	student	
171	Thérèse	8	f	student	
172	Thérèse Nyirabakina	5	f		
173	Aphrodis Murwanashyaka	40	m	farmer	married
174	Nyiramazuru	9	f	student	
175	Mukarutana	28	f	farmer	married
176	Matoroshi	12	m	student	
177	Ujyakuvuga	7	m	student	
178	Suzanne Nyiramazuru	9	f	student	
179	Ayinkamiye	12	f	student	
180	Vianney Rushingabigwi	14	m	student	
181	Joséphine	13	f	student	
182	Nyirantoki	53	f	farmer	married

1.2.2 Cellule Musasa

No.	Name	Age	Sex	Occupn.	Marital Status
1	André Sesonga	56	m	herdsman	married
2	Evérienne Mukankomeje	52	f	farmer	married
3	Gérard Karemera	16	m	student	single
4	Monique Nyirantagorama	14	f	student	
5	Azel Mukanugiye	12	f	student	
6	Didier Wihogora	10	f	student	
7	Niyomugabo	6	m		
8	Dative Nyirabugingo	29	f	farmer	married
9	Emerthe Nyinawumuntu	3	f		
10	Manirafasha	2	f		
11	Shema	14d	m		
12	Claver Gashema	26	m	herdsman	married
13	Berthilde Mnrorunkwere	20	f	farmer	married
14	Gudi Nzayisenga	7	m	student	
15	Ntakirutimana	4	m		
16	Narcisse Marara	35	m	herdsman	married
17	Pascasie Nyirabukara	28	f	farmer	married
18	Mugorewindekwe	8	f	student	
19	Thérèse Nyirabuka	4	f		
20	Etienne Ncamukega	50	m	herdsman	married
21	Félocité Kabagwiza	48	f	farmer	married
22	Madeleine Nyirahabimana	18	f	farmer	single
23	Béata Nyirabukara	15	f	student	
24	Joseph Mpakanije	37	m	herdsman	married
25	Odette Mukamuzima	35	f	farmer	married
26	Joséphine Uwitije	8	f	student	
27	Joël Yambogoreye	6	m		
28	Dorothée Mpakanije	4	f		
29	Céléstin Mnvunandinda	50	m	farmer	married
30	Julienne Mnhembasuku	55	f	farmer	married
31	Daphrose Mukantagwabira	23	f	farmer	married
32	Nyirankotsori	1	f		
33	Jean Rubyogo Bizimana	18	m	student	single
34	Modeste Rutayisire	15	m	student	
35	Marthe Mukambaraga	9	f	student	
36	Mbaraga	7	m	student	
37	Mukandinda Macibiri	5	f		
38	Chrésie Kampire	30	m	farmer	married
39	Alphonsine Uwitonze	15	f	student	
40	Yankurije	13	f	student	
41	Marcel Uhoraningoga	11	m	student	
42	Espérance Niyonshuti	9	f	student	
43	Uzabakiriho	4	m		
44	Umutesi	5	f		
45	Gasurira	6	m	student	
46	Bernadette Mukankuranga	35	f	farmer	married
47	Mukamwiza	17	f	farmer	single
48	Nyirabukara	15	f	student	
49	Habineza	13	m	student	
50	Nyirahabimana	11	f	student	
51	Emmanuel	5	m		
52	Médard Karemara	3	m		
53	Drocella Nyirampeta	1	f		
54	Aminadabu Habiyambere	60	m	herdsman	married
55	Adeline Gatimatare	42	f	farmer	married
56	Nsengiyumva	17	m	farmer	single
57	Mukasine	15	f	student	
58	Rudomoro Mbarushimana	13	m	student	
59	Bayingana	6	m	student	
60	Chresie Nyirabera	55	f	farmer	married
61	Maricianne Mukamusoni	18	f	farmer	single
62	Jonas Mbyirukira	32	m	herdsman	married
63	Berna Mukashyaka	28	f	farmer	married
64	Nsabimana	5	m		
65	Benjamin Hashakimana	32	m	herdsman	married
66	Julienne Mukarubayiza	30	f	farmer	married
67	Ngirinshuti	6	m	student	
68	Mukeshimana	14	f	student	
69	Murwanashyaka Isorole	8	m	student	
70	Mutuyemungu	4	m		
71	Boniface Ntakirutimana	28	m	herdsman	married
72	Dative Nyinawandori	26	f	farmer	married
73	Nyiramatama	1	f		
74	Nathanaël Murindabigwi	50	m	herdsman	married
75	Berthilde Nyiramuruta	35	f	farmer	married
76	Béata Uwimana	30	f	farmer	divorced
77	Nyiramazuru	4	f		
78	Nyiragwiza	18	f	farmer	single
79	Nyirarukundo	15	f	student	
80	Rubibi	7	m	student	
81	Ntakiyimana	5	m		
82	Léonidale Rugwizangoga	42	m	civil servant	married
83	Dative Nyirahategeka	35	f	farmer	married
84	Adèle Muringa	70	f	farmer	widow
85	Augustin Kabayiza	14	m	student	
86	Nyakana	30	m	farmer	single
87	Nsengiyumva	28	m	farmer	single
88	Stéphanie Nyirarubibi	55	f	farmer	widow
89	Casimir Butera	36	m	farmer	married
90	Immaculée	30	f	farmer	married
91	Niyonsenga	8	f	student	
92	Béatrice	6	f		
93	Béata	4	f		
94	Nyiramazuru	2	f		
95	Mugemana	10m	m		
96	Mathias Ndumugabo	28	m	farmer	single
97	Clément Kanakintama	45	m	herdsman	married
98	Agnès Mutumwinka	40	f	farmer	married
99	Patricie	21	f	student	single
100	Kanzayire	19	f	student	single
101	Nsingizimana	17	m	student	single
102	Alphonse	15	m	student	
103	Gasongo	10	m	student	
104	Athanase Bucyana	8	m	student	
105	Murekatete	6	f		
106	Basile Mpambara	45	m	teacher	married
107	Colette	30	f	farmer	married
108	Callixte Mpambara	2	m		
109	François Kandekwe	70	m	herdsman	widower
110	Gaspard Kamugisha	45	m	herdsman	married
111	Cécile Mukantagara	40	f	farmer	married
112	Nianney Ngarambe	22	m	shopkeeper	single
113	Canisius Hategekimana	20	m	farmer	single
114	Michel	18	m	farmer	single
115	Dorothée	15	f	farmer	single
116	Mukashyaka	13	f	student	
117	Louis Kamugisha	11	m	student	
118	Céléstin Muvunandinda	65	m	herdsman	married
119	Colette Mukantagara	60	f	farmer	married
120	Kagemana	30	m	driver	single
121	Rusingizandekwe	18	m	student	single
122	Martin Kayigema	20	m	farmer	single
123	Gratien Kabayiza	35	m	herdsman	married

No.	Name	Age	Sex	Occupation	Status
124	Thérèse	40	f	farmer	married
125	Théogène	6	m		
126	Jeannette	4	f		
127	Nyiraneza	2	f		
128	Augustin Kabarisa	30	m	herdsman	married
129	Margarite Uwontagaya	28	f	farmer	married
130	Mushimiyimana	2	m		
131	Edouard Ruvakwaya	50	m	herdsman	married
132	Agnès Mukarugomwa	46	f	farmer	married
133	Bernard Hakizimana	30	m	tailor	single
134	Xaverine Utetiwabo	18	f	student	single
135	Patrice Ngarambe	35	m	herdsman	married
136	Etienne Gasurira	21d	m		
137	Edouard Muzindutsi	50	m	teacher	married
138	Thérèse Mukarubayiza	45	f	farmer	married
139	Mukamurenzi	18	f	farmer	single
140	Murenzi	10	m	student	
141	Semuhungu	6	m		
142	Rubyagira	4	m		
143	Augustin Kageruka	55	m	herdsman	married
144	Agnès Mukarugwiza	40	f	farmer	married
145	Joséphine Uwamariya	23	f	teacher	single
146	Déogratias Muzungu	10	m	student	
147	Thérèse Narame	60	f	farmer	widow
148	Gaspard Ntirushwamaboko	30	m	farmer	single
149	Rosalie	23	f	farmer	single
150	Mukabiwana	45	f	farmer	
151	Rufuneri	7	m	student	
152	Aphrodis Rukara	20	m	farmer	single
153	Silas Kayibanda	50	f	farmer	married
154	Thamale Mukamuzima	2	m		
155	Odette	26	f	farmer	married
156	Zilipa Kanyundo	48	f	farmer	widow
157	Philomin Akimanizanye	45	m	herdsman	married
158	Anésie Nyirajyambere	40	f	farmer	married
159	Aloys Munyaneza	16	m	farmer	single
160	Gashengura Bisuru	14	m	student	
161	Yamfashije	12	f	student	
162	Mukeshimana	4	f		
163	Uwimana	2	f		
164	Jean Hategeka	45	m	herdsman	married
165	Elisanne Nyirankuriza	40	f	farmer	married
166	Ndayisaba Sebishihe	20	m	farmer	single
167	Emmanuel Ndatimana	7	m	student	
168	Ayinkamiye	4	f		
169	Rukara	5	m		
170	Xavéra Nyirankima	23	f	farmer	single
171	Bashikazi	75	f	farmer	married
172	Nshunguyinka	85	m	herdsman	married
173	Jean Rutayisire	36	m	herdsman	married
174	Monique Mukamunana	32	m	farmer	married
175	Jacqueline Mukandayisenga	9	f	student	
176	Alphonsine Niyonsaba	7	f	student	
177	Pierre	2	m		
178	Louis Rugwizangoga	28	m	herdsman	married
179	Mbarushimana	4	m		
180	Francisca Mukarubuga	60	f	farmer	widow
181	Adèle Nyirambogoye	40	f	farmer	widow
182	Béata Mukawera	20	f	farmer	single
183	Adalie Mukamwiza	18	f	farmer	single
184	Gahigiro	16	m	student	single
185	Félicitée	6	f		
186	Philomène	6	f		
187	Déogratias Nzamwita	47	m	herdsman	married
188	Marie Mukashuri	45	f	farmer	married
189	Consolée Mukangarambe	20	f	farmer	single
190	Annonciata Tuyisenge	18	f	farmer	single
191	Immaculée Mukangoga	16	f	student	single
192	Oswald Ngamije	28	m	herdsman	married
193	Médiatrice Mukandori	25	f	farmer	married
194	Auriel Karimwijabo	55	m	herdsman	married
195	Thadée Mukantagara	50	f	farmer	married
196	Samuel Habimana	35	m	herdsman	single
197	Ngarambe	25	m	herdsman	single
198	Pascal Sibomana	13	m	student	
199	Eliezel Munyantwari	8	m	student	
200	Patricie Yambabariye	30	f	farmer	married
201	Jacques Ngoga	3	m		
202	Simon Nemeyemungu	35	m	herdsman	single
203	Samuel Murwanashyaka	28	m	herdsman	single
204	Jason Ngirinshuti	23	m	herdsman	single
205	Berna Uwimana	18	f	farmer	single
206	Catherine Kankindi	40	f	farmer	widow
207	Izachar Ntakirutimana	29	m	herdsman	single
208	Edouard Iyamuremye	25	m	herdsman	single
209	Elina Mukamuhire	12	f	student	
210	Innocent Mbakuriyemo	6	m		
211	Everianne Kanyundo	77	f	farmer	widow
212	Salimani Hakizimana	50	m	herdsman	married
213	Suzanne Mukamukomeza	46	f	farmer	married
214	Esther Nyirankuriza	20	f	farmer	married
215	Phénéas Ndayisaba	17	m	student	single
216	Nkurunzia	10	m	student	
217	Athanase Makombe	60	m	herdsman	married
218	Véronique Mukabera	55	f	farmer	married
219	Donatille Mukanaho	30	f	farmer	
220	Gasihiri	18	m	student	single
221	Tuyishimire	9	f	student	
222	Rutebeza	6	m		
223	Hélène Mukankomeje	29	f	farmer	single
224	Ildephonse Ntizimira	40	m	farmer	married
225	Nzabirinda Butondwe	15	m	farmer	
226	Martin Ntizimira	10	m	student	
227	Charles Habimana	34	m	herdsman	married
228	Marie Thérèse Izabiriza	30	f	farmer	married
229	Nyiramatama	12	f	student	
230	Rose Nyirantama	10	f	student	
231	Mukamana	7	f	student	
232	Nyirarwimo	42	f	farmer	married
233	Nzarora	21	m	farmer	single
234	Kandinguri Mutuyeyezu	24	m	farmer	single
235	Monique Bazubagira	55	f	farmer	widow
236	Donatille Kansiriri	60	f	farmer	widow
237	Gaspard Gatera	35	f	farmer	married
238	Appolinaire Mpamo	37	m	herdsman	married
239	Rose Mukarukore	35	f	farmer	married
240	Kabeteri	5	f		
241	Agnès	8	f		
242	Jacqueline	2	f		
243	Jean Harerimana	28	m	herdsman	married
244	Cyprien Rugabo	70	m	herdsman	married
245	Mukamusoni	65	f	farmer	married
246	Mishel Ruhongeka	37	m	farmer	single
247	Anastasie Mukabayire	32	f	farmer	single
248	Raphaël Rutembeza	30	m	farmer	single
249	Donatien Karekezi	26	m	merchant	single
250	Casimir Ndinaniye	22	m	student	single
251	Siméon Madende	45	m	teacher	married
252	Colette Mukandinda	43	f	farmer	married
253	Damien Ugirashebuja	24	m	student	single
254	Louis Kadaraza	22	m	student	single
255	Pétronille Mukandekezi	20	f	student	single
256	Mukamwiza	18	f	student	single
257	Catherine Nyirankima	16	f	student	single
258	Donatha Nyirabukara	13	f	student	
259	Dative Nyinawumuntu	10	f	student	
260	Martin Karekezi	60	m	herdsman	married
261	Léoncie Nyirabanguka	58	f	farmer	married
262	Drocella Nyinawumuntu	41	f	farmer	
263	Damascine Nshimiyimana	33	m	merchant	married
264	Déo Rubayiza	26	f	farmer	married
265	Sophie Yamfashije	21	f	student	single
266	Matoroshi	19	m	student	single
267	Didier Ntezamaso	17	m	student	single
268	Anésie Ngenzi	27	f	farmer	single
269	Eric Nzabahimana	12	m	student	
270	Suzanne Mukarubenga	9	f	student	
271	Chrésie Kabera	4	f		
272	Buranga	65	m	herdsman	widower
273	Dorothée Nyirantoki	47	f	farmer	widow
274	Angèle	23	f	farmer	single
275	Louise	20	f	farmer	single
276	Aimé Rubunge	25	m	student	single
277	Didacienne Umurisa	28	f	farmer	
278	Francine Mukasekuru	19	f	student	single
279	Mafene Sibomana	15	m	student	
280	Casimir Sesonga	40	m	herdsman	married
291	Thaddée Sabato	42	m	herdsman	married
292	Didace Karimunda	21	m	farmer	single
293	Cécile Nyirakanyana	19	f	student	single
294	Mutsindashyaka	17	m	student	single
295	Jacqueline Uwamahoro	15	f	student	
296	Léonce Murebwayire	11	m	student	
297	Athanase Karasankima	30	m	herdsman	married
298	Ancille Mureskeyisoni	29	f	farmer	married
299	Chadrac Kanyarukiga	26	m	farmer	single
300	Alphonse Murindabigwi	16	m	student	single
301	Cansilde kanyange	13	f	student	
302	Rukeramihigo	9	m	student	
303	Kamenyero	2	m		
304	Nyiramahe	3	f		
305	Nyiranturege	1	f		
306	Caritas Kanakuze	28	f	teacher	married
307	Chrésie	1	f		
308	Martin Mafene	55	m	herdsman	married
309	Marie Nyirangendahayo	50	f	farmer	married
310	Appolinarie Nyiramana	12	f	student	
311	Jacqueline Mukarubayiza	10	f	student	
312	Nirere	8	f	student	
313	Emmanuel Itegekaharinde	3	m		
314	Faustin Munyandamutsa	60	m	herdsman	married
315	Stéphanie Nyamwituma	58	f	farmer	married

No.	Name	Age	Sex	Occupn.	Marital Status
316	Vianney Nzamutuma	27	m	farmer	single
317	Grégoire Rukaka	22	m	merchant	single
318	Victoire Mukandamage	19	f	student	single
319	Ndayisaba	14	m	student	
320	Laurent Munyarubuga	65	m	herdsman	married
321	Bernadette	60	f	farmer	married
322	Narcisse	19	m	student	single
323	Ndatimana	8	m	student	
324	Basile	14	m	student	
325	Augustin Kanamugire	38	m	herdsman	married
326	Patricie	29	f	farmer	married
327	Laurent Kanamugire	1	m		
328	François Kabera	40	f	farmer	married
329	Isolde Kanamugire	36	m	herdsman	married
330	Stéphanie	32	f	farmer	married
331	Béatrice Uwimana	9	f	student	
332	Donatha Uwimpuhwe	6	f		
333	Dismas Kanamugire	3	m		
334	Cyrille Kanamugire	3m	m		
335	Munyangabe	68	m	herdsman	married
336	Thérèse Nyirasangwa	65	f	farmer	married
337	Sophie	17	f	student	single
338	Claver	30	m	herdsman	single
339	Boniface Boyi	60	m	herdsman	married
340	Léoncie Kandanga	58	f	farmer	married
341	Pascal	26	m	farmer	single
342	Kayigema	30	m	herdsman	married
343	Aline Kayigema	1	f		
344	Catherine	28	f	farmer	married
345	Fabien Rudahunga	27	m	herdsman	married
346	Uwamariya	26	f	teacher	married
347	Espérance Rudahunga	2	f		
348	Cécile Rudahunga	7d	f		
349	François Gatera	36	m	merchant	married
350	Félicitée Mukamugenzi	55	f	farmer	widow
351	Javan	22	m	farmer	single
352	Charles Sebuzindu	60	m	judge	married
353	Esther Uzamukunda	58	f	farmer	married
354	Gertrude Mukabyagaju	24	f	farmer	
355	Fidèle	22	m	merchant	single
356	Jean Bosco	20	m	merchant	single
357	Espérance	17	f	student	single
358	François Sebisaho	45	m	teacher	married
359	Marthe Mukabuhake	42	f	teacher	married
360	Salemon Kagimbangabo	19	m	student	single
361	Damarce Nyamurangwa	16	m	student	single
362	Thamale Nyinawindinda	34	f	farmer	widow
363	Emmanuel Karibana	16	m	student	single
364	Jason Sentama	13	m	student	
365	Mukarusanga	8	f	student	
366	Cyriaque	4	m		
367	Innocent Kanamugire	52	m	herdsman	married
368	Léoncie Nyiransabimana	50	f	farmer	married
369	Julienne Karukina	29	f	farmer	married
370	Etienne Sindikubwabo	27	m	farmer	single
371	Jacqueline Kiribazayire	22	f	farmer	single
372	Alice	18	f	student	single
373	Elyse	15	f	student	
374	Habinshuti Rudomoro	7	m	student	
375	Vénant Nzamukwereka	3	m		
376	Gilbert Muhayeyezu	28	m	herdsman	married
377	Dorothée Masoyinyana	26	f	farmer	married
378	David Ribakare	4	m		

1.2.2 Cellule Musasa (continued)

No.	Name	Age	Sex	Occupn.	Marital Status
1	Jean Kaje	50	m	herdsman	married
2	Evérienne Mukadusanga	41	f	farmer	married
3	Bizimana	15	m	student	
4	Hakizimana	10	m	student	
5	Harerimana	8	m	student	
6	Niyomugabo	5	m		
7	Sekuru	3	m		
8	lette Kamurera	50	f	farmer	widow
9	Télésphore Murerandinda	22	m	farmer	single
10	Ezéchias Butera	51	m	herdsman	married
11	Emerthe Nyirantereye	47	f	farmer	married
12	Mukaremera	17	f	student	single
13	Mukantaganda	13	f	student	
14	Mukarugwiza	11	f	student	
15	Léoncie Nyiraromba	50	f	farmer	married
16	Claver Ndahimana	22	m	herdsman	single
17	Simon Gashirabake	55	m	herdsman	married
18	Vérène Nyirakinazi	50	f	farmer	married
19	Munyansanga	30	m	builder	single
20	Bikorimana	12	m	student	
21	Jacqueline Mukandirima	30	m	farmer	married
22	Umuhoza	2	f		
23	Umutesi	1	f		
24	Védaste Munyakabungo	35	m	farmer	married
25	Françoise Uwayisaba	27	f	farmer	married
26	Joseph	3	m		
27	Joséphine	18m	f		
28	Basile Mwanafunze	42	m	teacher	married
29	Madeleine Ayuruvugo	40	f	teacher	married
30	Uwineaa	14	f	student	
31	Sibomana	12	m	student	
32	Dusabe	7	m	student	
33	Dushime	6	m		
34	Nyirakaranena	5	f		
35	Boniface Ubuzinda	75	m	teacher	married
36	Euphrasie Nyiramafara	65	f	farmer	married
37	Cyrille Seminega	54	m	farmer	married
38	Anathalie Kambuga	47	f	farmer	married
39	Bernadette Mukakabayiza	22	f	farmer	single
40	Béata Mukantabana	18	f	student	single
41	Urimubenshi	17	m	student	single
42	Habimana	15	m	student	
43	Ndamage	12	m	student	
44	Bujanja	8	m	student	
45	Mukandamage	10	f	student	
46	Uwayisaba	6	f		
47	Seminega	7d	m		
48	Samuel Nkeramihigo	35	m	herdsman	married
49	Nyiranubaha	32	f	farmer	married
50	Emmanuel	3	m		
51	Uwimana	1	f		
52	Nkeramihigo	2m	m		
53	Claver Munyakaganda	45	m	herdsman	married
54	Gaudence Mukagatare	42	f	farmer	married
55	Emmanuel	18	m	student	single
56	Nyiramazuru	12	f	student	
57	François Semuhungu	45	m	herdsman	married
58	Agnès Uwayisaba	40	f	farmer	married
59	Mukandori	21	f	farmer	single
60	Odette	18	f	farmer	single
61	Sebiroro	12	m	student	
62	Kanyoni	10	m	student	
63	Uwayisaba	8	f	student	
64	Buseruka	6	f		
65	Léonidace Kanyabiga	60	m	herdsman	married
66	Anathalie Mukankusi	54	f	farmer	married
67	Kayihura	30	m	farmer	single
68	Mugoremwiza	40	f	farmer	single
69	Alexis	12	m	student	
70	Christine	10	f	student	
71	Kanyabigega	8	m	student	
72	Télésphore	8	m	student	
73	Gasigwa	5	m		
74	Athanase Buregeya	60	m	herdsman	married
75	Bernadette	50	f	farmer	married
76	Jeanne'Arc Mukamurenzi	25	f	farmer	married
77	Françoise	2	f		
78	Nyiragasigwa	30	f	farmer	married
79	Dancille Mukabahizi	35	f	farmer	married
80	Saruhara	12	m	student	
81	Bapfakurera	52	m	herdsman	married
82	Adèle	40	f	farmer	married
83	Ayirwanda	14	m	student	
84	Nyirambarara	12	f	student	

1.2.3 Cellule Nyamabuye

No.	Name	Age	Sex	Occupn.	Marital Status
1	Michel Kanyamibwa	80	m	herdsman	married
2	Rose Karuyumba	75	f	farmer	married
3	Bénoît Mucumbitsi	45	m	teacher	married
4	Félicitée	38	f	teacher	married
5	Dorothée	17	f	farmer	single
6	François Gahiga	70	m	herdsman	maried
7	Jérôme Mucungandege	55	m	nurse	married
8	Thacienne Mukarubuga	55	f	farmer	married
9	Eugène Mutuyeyezu	32	m	farmer	single
10	Jacques Rubayiza	28	m	farmer	single
11	Jacqueline Mukakabayiza	24	f	student	single
12	Jean Bimenyimana	20	m	student	single
13	Mukabyagaju	13	f	student	
14	Mafene	6	m		
15	Bernard Murasandonyi	55	m	herdsman	married
16	Alphonse Kayigema	28	m	merchant	single
17	Aphrodis Ntakirutimana	24	m	mechanic	single
18	Eugénie	17	f	farmer	single
19	Rusingiza	15	m	student	
20	Hélène	52	f	farmer	married

No.	Name	Age	Sex	Occupn.	Marital Status
21	Bernard Munyankindi	50	m	herdsman	married
22	Thérèse Mukamudenge	45	f	farmer	married
23	Consolée	17	f	farmer	single
24	Alphonsine	13	f	student	
25	Nyakazi Nyirabagira	9	f	student	
26	Uwamahoro	12	f	student	
27	Mukamutesi	6	f		
28	Sudi Kabanda	33	m	farmer	married
29	Thacienne	2	f	farmer	
30	Nyiranshuti	7	f	student	
31	Ingabire	4	f		
32	Mukarushema	45	f	farmer	widow
33	Nyiratunga	32	f	farmer	
34	Mukakinani	28	f	farmer	
35	Uwamariya	26	f	farmer	single
36	Mukamunana	24	f	merchant	single
37	Rugwiza	17	m	public servant	single
38	Sugabo	3	m		
39	Virgile	4	m		
40	Rwamanywa	70	m	herdsman	married
41	Vénérande Nyirakanuma	65	f	farmer	married
42	Claude Mutama	18	m	student	single
43	Généreuse Ruzindana	18	f	student	single
44	Nyirabugegera	40	f	farmer	widow
45	Kamana	45	m	herdsman	married
46	Kumutoyi	40	f	farmer	married
47	Karangwa	23	m	student	single
48	Mukarugwiza	20	f	student	single
49	Faïna	7	f	student	
50	Rudomoro	16	m	student	single
51	Françoise Nyirabutoraguro	5	f		
52	Nyiramazuru	3	f		
53	André Mahuku	82	m	herdsman	married
54	Nyirabukeye	90	f	farmer	married
55	Njakazi	14	f	student	
56	Nyiramucyo	17	f	student	single
57	Busizori	9	f	student	
58	Agnès	17	f	student	single
59	Monique Karubero	42	f	merchant	divorced
60	Butyerezi	6	m		
61	Bénoît Mucumbitsi	53	m	teacher	married
62	Félicitée	45	f	teacher	married
63	Martin Mazimpaka	34	m	builder	married
64	Daphrose Mukarasi	28	f	farmer	married
65	Kayitesi	13	f	student	
66	Umurisa	11	f	student	
67	Kibwa	10	m	student	
68	Sarigoma	7	m		
69	Cyrille Mazimpaka	5	m		
70	Damascène Mazimpaka	2	m		
71	Michel Kayihura	45	m	herdsman	married
72	Thérèse Mukaruhunga	3	f	farmer	
73	Xaveri	18	m	farmer	single
74	Rupari	14	m	student	
75	Mukamana	8	f	student	
76	Nyirabusoya	4	f		
77	Athanase Mukaragandekwe	40	m	herdsman	married
78	Appolinaire Mukasangwa	34	f	farmer	married
79	Uwimana	18	f	farmer	single
80	Mukamana	15	f	student	
81	Mukamutesi	10	f	student	
82	Madeleine	55	f	farmer	widow
83	Mukandori	20	f	student	single
84	Bifata	14	m	student	
85	Claver Munyampundu	40	m	herdsman	married
86	Cécile Nyirandutiye	37	f	farmer	married
87	Rutabana	23	m	herdsman	single
88	Canisius	20	m	herdsman	single
89	Pierre	18	m	herdsman	
90	Candide	25	f	teacher	single
91	Isabelle Mutanguha	20	f	student	single

1.2.4 Cellule Rwabirembo

No.	Name	Age	Sex	Occupn.	Marital Status
1	Martin Majene	55	m	herdsman	married
2	Marie Nyirangendahayo	50	f	farmer	married
3	Appolinarie N.gendahayo	50	f	student	student
4	Jacqueline Mukarubayiza	10	f	student	
5	Nirere	8	f	student	
6	Faustin Munyandamutsa	60	m	herdsman	married
7	Stéphanie	58	f	farmer	married
8	J. M Vianney Nzamutuma	27	m	farmer	single
9	Grégoire Rukaka	22	m	shopkeeper	single
10	Victorie Mukandamage	19	f	student	single
11	Xavier Ndayisaba	14	m	student	
12	Laurent Mumyarubuga	65	m	herdsman	married
13	Bernadette M.mukomeza	60	f	farmer	married
14	Narcisse Rutiyomba	19	m	student	single
15	Basile	14	m	student	
16	Ndatimana	8	m	student	
17	Augustin Kanamugire	32	m	herdsman	married
18	Patricie Bayisenge	29	f	farmer	married
19	Laurent Kanamugire	1	m		
20	François Kalera	40	m	farmer	single
21	Isidore Kanamugire	36	m	herdsman	married
22	Stéphanie	32	m	farmer	married
23	Béatrice Uwimana	9	f	student	
24	Donatha Uwimpuhme	6	f	student	
25	Dismas Kanamugire	3	m		
26	Cyrille Kanamugire	3 m	m		
27	Eric Kanamugire	1	m		
28	Gabriel Munyagabe	68	m	herdsman	married
29	Thérèse Nyirasangwa	65	f	farmer	married
30	Claver Kabanda	30	m	farmer	married
31	Boniface Boyi	60	m	herdsman	married
32	Léoncie Kandanga	26	m	farmer	single
33	Pascal Kabagema	26	m	farmer	single
34	Gaspard Kayigema	28	m		
35	Elias	29	m	student	single
36	Fabien Rudahunga	27	m	herdsman	married
37	Anne-Marie Uwanyiligira	26	f	teacher	married
38	Espérance Rudahunga	2	f		
39	Cécile Rudahunga	7d	f		
40	Augustin Gatera	36	m	shopkeeper	married
41	Charles Buzindu	60	m	judge	married
42	Astérie Uzamukunda	58	f	farmer	married
43	Gertrude Mukobwagaju	24	f	shopkeeper	
44	Fidèle Rurangirwa	22	m	shopkeeper	single
45	Jean Bosco	20	m	shopkeeper	single
46	Espérance Murekatete	19	f	student	single
47	François Sebisaho	45	m	teacher	married
48	Marthe Mukabuhake	42	f	teacher	married
49	Javan	22	m	herdsman	single
50	Pascal Nsabimana	42	m	shopkeeper	married
51	Emile Kamilindi	70	m	farmer	married
52	Théodore Habiyambere	50	m	farmer	married
53	François Myandagona	55	m	farmer	married
54	Bernard Muberuka	32	m	farmer	married
55	Adela Mukabadege	60	f	farmer	widow
56	Anne-Marie Mukarugwiza	30	f	farmer	

1.2.4 Cellule Rwabirembo (continued)

No.	Name	Age	Sex	Occupn.	Marital Status
1	Didace	45	m	herdsman	married
2	Patricie	42	f	farmer	married
3	Mukashyaka	8	f	student	
4	Martin	7	m	student	
5	Son of Didace	3	m		
6	Vianney Rutaganira	42	m	farmer	married
7	Eugénie	34	f	farmer	married
8	Nyiranzage	4	f		
9	Dative	2	f		
10	Mukasekuru	1	f		
11	Rushingabigwi	72	m	herdsman	married
12	Uwambaye	65	f	farmer	married
13	Louis	22	m	farmer	single
14	Kajabo	70	m	herdsman	married
15	Gaudence	62	f	farmer	married
16	Busugugu	15	m	farmer	single
17	Augustin Kayigana	40	m	herdsman	married
18	Nyirankware	9	f	student	
19	Candide	4	f		
20	Mukimbiri	2	m		
21	Burimwinyundo	45	m	herdsman	married
22	Sylvestre	7	m	student	
23	Muzehe	5	m		
24	Nyiraneza	2	f		
25	Denis	54	m	herdsman	married
26	Rosalie	48	f	farmer	married
27	Michel	25	m	farmer	single
28	Béata	17	f	student	single
29	Vérène	12	f	student	
30	Rubyogo	6	m		
31	Son of Denis	4	m		
32	Eudosie	40	f	farmer	widow
33	Catherine	25	f	farmer	single
34	Esther	26	f	student	single
35	Mbaraga	40	m	herdsman	married
36	Laurencie	32	f	farmer	married
37	Pacifique	8	m	student	
38	Virginie	6	f		
39	Louis Mbaraga	4	m		

40	Théonèste Mbaraga	2	m		
41	Gabriel	28	m	herdsman	married
42	Dancile	20	f	farmer	married
43	Son of Gabriel	1	m		
44	Fidèle	30	m	farmer	married
45	Adèle	27	f	farmer	married
46	Baby of Fidèle	1	m		
47	Kageruka	52	m	herdsman	married
48	Ngarambe	2	m		
49	Kwishima	20	f	farmer	single
50	Musabyimana	17	m	farmer	single
51	Gakwavu	50	m	herdsman	married
52	Anésie	47	f	farmer	married
53	Eugénie	20	f	farmer	single
54	Ribuba	17	f	student	single
55	Alfred	35	m	herdsman	married
56	Caritas	32	f	farmer	married
57	Son of Alfred	4	m		
58	Rwamanywa	60	m	herdsman	married
59	Marthe	54	f	farmer	married
60	Nzatona	22	f	farmer	single
61	Marianne	45	f	farmer	widow
62	Uwamariya	21	f	farmer	single
63	Emmanuel	19	m	student	single
64	Garambe	37	m	herdsman	married
65	Caritas	31	f	farmer	married
66	Niyomugabo	4	m		

1.3 Sector Gishyita

1.3.1 Cellule Nganzo

No.	Name	Age	Sex	Occupn.	Marital Status
1	Eliezer Ngendahayo	57	m	herdsman	married
2	Azelle Nyirabukacari	52	f	farmer	married
3	Ezéchias Ndekezi	33	m	teacher	single
4	Jonas Ruhumuliza	25	m	farmer	single
5	Assiel Rutaganda	22	m	student	single
6	Jacqueline Mukamana	13	f	student	
7	Denis Mutarambirwa	60	m	teacher	married
8	Julienne	45	f	farmer	married
9	Rose Mukashyaka	16	f	student	single
10	Erina Nyiraneza	18	f	farmer	single
11	Jérôme	11	m	student	
12	Edith	8	f	student	
13	Adalie Mukagatare	40	f	farmer	widow
14	Israël Habineza	18	m	farmer	single
15	Phanuel Bayiringire	13	m	student	
16	Mukamusana	10	f	student	
17	Paul Bitega	85	m	married	
18	Julie	60	f	farmer	married
19	Esther	26	f	student	single
20	Esdras Ruzindana	50	m	herdsman	married
21	Thabithe	47	f	farmer	married
22	Tuyisenge	19	m	student	single
23	Antoine	22	m	student	single
24	Antoinette	24	f	student	single
25	Nshimiye	6	m	student	
26	Nsengamihigo	56	m	herdsman	married
27	Mukankusi	50	f	farmer	married
28	Thérèse	26	f	farmer	single
29	Anésie	24	f	farmer	single
30	Anastase	22	m	farmer	single
31	Assiel Ngoboka	20	m	farmer	single
32	Xavere Nkundumukiza	18	m	farmer	single
33	Mukamudenge	16	f	student	single
34	Mukankundiye	14	f	student	
35	Jean Hitimana	45	m	herdsman	married
36	Chrésia	40	f	farmer	married
37	Gratien Ruhumuliza	20	m	student	single
38	Ntihemuka	18	m	farmer	single
39	Alphonse	4	m		
40	Marie	9	f	student	
41	Nsengiyumva	12	m	student	
42	Ildephonse Hitimana	4m	m		
43	Eliezer Seromba	55	m	priest	married
44	Judith Mukankiko	47	f	farmer	married
45	Jakson Seromba	25	m	student	single
46	Ndagije	32	m	teacher	single
47	Nelson Ndizeye	22	m	student	single
48	Théophile Byiringiro	18	m	student	single
49	Jason Ngirumwami	51	m	nurse	married
50	Marthe Mukantagara	48	f	farmer	married
51	Ismaël Ntawuyirusha	26	m	teacher	single
52	Wilson	24	m	student	single
53	Tite Muvunyi	20	m	student	single
54	Charlotte Ngirumwami	9	f	student	
55	Charles Habayo	45	m	teacher/farmer	married
56	Nyiraneza	35	f	teacher	married
57	Karemera	45	m	herdsman	married
58	Judith Nyirantoki	40	f	farmer	married
59	Karekezi	45	m	herdsman	married
60	Daniel Habyarimana	48	m	herdsman	married
61	Rose	44	f	farmer	married
62	Son of Gashugi	2	m		
63	Rugaragara	5	m		
64	Thomas Niyitegeka	19	m	student	single
65	Sahabo	42	m	builder	married
66	Nyirakadari	14	f	student	
67	Niyonzima	11	m	student	
68	Bayiringire	16	m	student	single
69	Reya	82	f	farmer	widow
70	Sophie Mukandekezi	60	f	farmer	widow
71	Seth Bayingana	24	m	student	single
72	Anathalie	30	f	farmer	widow
73	Tuyishime	11	m	student	
74	Alex Ruhumuliza	25	m	farmer	single
75	Evérienne Mukakayijuka	52	f	farmer	married
76	Sylvain Nzisabira	29	m	student	single
77	Joël Bizirurema	14	m	student	
78	Bucurindinga	75	f	farmer	widow
79	Murisa	22	f	farmer	married
80	Thomas Sentama	57	m	herdsman	married
81	Nyiranuma	50	f	farmer	married
82	Cécile Nyirandizihiwe	20	f	farmer	single
83	Benjamin	13	m	student	
84	Kanyamugara	48	m	herdsman	married
85	Ana Marie	37	f	farmer	married
86	Muhire	13	m	student	
87	Adèle Mukandutiye	62	f	farmer	widow
88	Charles Gashugi	45	m	herdsman	married
89	Mukashema	40	f	farmer	married
90	Marcel Ndayisaba	20	m	farmer	single
91	Eugénie	17	f	student	single
92	Espérance	15	f	student	
93	Marie	11	f	student	
94	Alphonse	9	f	student	

1.3.2 Cellule Mpatsi

No.	Name	Age	Sex	Occupn.	Marital Status
1	Ndahayo	8	m	student	
2	Simon Muvunyi	6	f		
3	Gasagara's daughter	2	f		
4	Mathias Rutaganira	25	m	herdsman	married
5	Mukabideri's wife	22	f	farmer	married
6	Karekezi	65	m	herdsman	married
7	Louise Rutaganira	2	f		
8	Ndabiruzi	78	m	herdsman	married
9	Nyiragashonga	67	f	farmer	married
10	Kwizera	14	m	herdsman	
11	Azelle Nyirakidederi	67	f	farmer	widow
12	Gasasira	25	m	herdsman	single
13	Cyprien	14	m	herdsman	
14	Claver Mugema	32	m	herdsman	married
15	Mukabutera	23	f	farmer	married
16	Mugema	2	m		
17	Rwigema	35	m	herdsman	married
18	Dorothée	32	f	farmer	married
19	Béata	11	f	student	
20	Gasaza	8	m	student	
21	Rwigema	5	f		
22	Alice Rwigema	2	f		
23	Etienne Habimana	45	m	herdsman	married
24	Nyinawumwami	42	f	farmer	married
25	Damien	12	m	student	
26	Habimana	2	m		
27	Kajisho Hategeka	52	m	herdsman	married
28	Felicitée Mukangwije	47	f	farmer	married
29	Nsengiyimva	18	m	farmer	single
30	Antoine Ngiruwonsanga	54	m	farmer	widower
31	Ildephonse Shingiro	23	m	teacher	single
32	Patricie Mukamasabo	20	f	student	single
33	Pascasie Mukaruyonza	14	f	student	
34	Vérène	10	f	student	
35	Denis Ngiruwonsanga	4	m		
36	Cyprien Munyakazi	60	m	farmer	married
37	Nyirakajangwe	57	f	farmer	married
38	Eline Uwimana	22	f	student	single
39	Jean Nsengayire	40	m	farmer	married
40	Mukanyangezi	38	f	farmer	married

No.	Name	Age	Sex	Occupn.	Marital Status
41	Nsengiyaremye	13	m	student	
42	Nsengiyumva	10	m	student	
43	Jeannette	7	f	student	
44	Nsengimana	5	m		
45	Jean, son of Nsengayire	3	m		
46	Sayinzoga	67	m	herdsman	married
47	Kanyanja	62	f	farmer	married
48	Faïda	6	f		
49	Pascal Nzahumunyurwa	21	m	herdsman	married
50	Mukansanga	19	f	farmer	married
51	Nélie	51	f	farmer	widow
52	Mukansanga	12	f	student	
53	Marie	15	f	student	
54	Munyandekwe	60	m	herdsman	married
55	Esther Mukarugwiza	52	f	farmer	married
56	Seth	40	m	farmer	married
57	Jonas Muvunandinda	24	m	farmer	single
58	Mukamurenzi	20	f	farmer	single
59	Seth Niyomuremyi	15	m	student	
60	Sophie	47	f	farmer	married
61	Vincent Ruhumuliza	14	m	student	
62	Assiel Kabanda	52	m	herdsman	married
63	Rose	49	f	farmer	married
64	Julienne	24	f	student	single
65	Ousiel Ndikubwimana	20	m	student	single
66	Nirere	15	f	student	
67	Sindayigaya	12	m	student	
68	Jason Ngeruka	33	m	herdsman	married
69	Alphonsone	27	f	farmer	married
70	Tumishime	5	m		
71	Donatha Ngeruka	2	f		
72	Mathias	28	m	farmer	married
73	Marie Mukangoga	35	f	farmer	married
74	Damascène Uwayo Mafene	11	m	student	
75	Dusabimana	6	f	student	
76	Mujawimana	3	f		
77	Son of Basomingera	3d	m		
78	Athanase Semakwavu	62	m	herdsman	married
79	Nyirandizanya	57	f	farmer	married
80	Mukamunana	19	f	farmer	single
81	Samuel Kampayana	32	m	herdsman	married
82	Thèrèse Mukabera	35	f	farmer/	marred
83	Odette Mukamurenzi	11	f	student	
84	Kampayana	6	m		
85	Louis Kampayana	3	m		
86	Ngarambe	42	m	herdsman	married
87	Madeleine	31	f	farmer	married
88	Chrésie Nyirabashyitsi	61	f	farmer	married
89	Déo Ngarambe	5	m		
90	Sugabo Ngarambe	2	m		
91	Muhutu	65	m	herdsman	married
92	Muheha	62	f	farmer	married
93	Ndikumuzima	45	m	farmer	single
94	Nyinawandori	25	f	student	single
95	Philomen Mugemana	31	m	farmer	married
96	Mukarwego	28	f	farmer	married
97	Uwamahoro	5	f		
98	Domatille Mugemana	2	f		
99	Gérard Mavugwa	49	m	farmer	married
100	Mukakarera	45	f	farmer	married
101	Mukangwije	18	f	student	single
102	Niyonzima	14	m	student	
103	Rutaburingoga	11	m	student	
104	Mukarunyange	30	f	farmer	married
105	Cassien Nibigira	5	m		
106	Drocella Nibigira	2	f		
107	Mukakabera	54	f	farmer	widow
108	Karanguza	49	m	farmer	single
109	Diolace Karangira	15	m	student	
110	Nyirambabazi	65	f	farmer	widow
111	Herdion Iyamuremye	30	m	toiler	single
112	Silas Kageruka	46	m	builder/herdsman	married
113	Marthe Mukangoga	41	f	farmer	married
114	Rachel	21	f	student	single
115	Nyirabashyitsi	20	f	farmer	single
116	Nikuze	14	f	student	
117	Samuel	12	m	student	
118	Elianne Ngendahimana	34	m	builder	married
119	Elina Musanandori	31	f	farmer	married
120	Niyongira	13	f	student	
121	Pierre	19	m	student	single
122	Jean Ndikubwimana	27	m	builder	married
123	Mukashyaka	22	f	farmer	married
124	Jeanne Ndikubwimana	2	f		
125	Kajabo	62	m	herdsman	married
126	Habyarimana	24	m	student	single
127	Joséphine	19	f	student	single
128	Emmanuel Nkurikiyinka	45	m	builder	married
129	Elina	41	f	farmer	married
130	Muvunyi	14	m	student	
131	Marguerite	12	f	student	
132	Bugingo	9	m	student	
133	Epiphanie Muhoracyeye	7	f	student	
134	Marcianne	5	f		
135	Rugamba	3	m		
136	Rubayiza	27	m	farmer/builder	married
137	Judith Mukazitoni	29	f	farmer	married
138	Rubayiza	2	m		
139	Karekezi	65	m	herdsman	married

1.3.3 Cellule Bugina

No.	Name	Age	Sex	Occupn.	Marital Status
1	Kabanyana	34	f	farmer	married
2	Jean Kanyenkwere	49	m	builder	married
3	Patricie Bayisenge	22	f	farmer	married
4	Pascasie Bamurebe	20	f	student	single
5	Pétronille Bazubagira	17	f	student	single
6	Perpétuée Niyirema	16	f	student	single
7	Marie Mukarushema	38	f	farmer	married
8	Emmanuel Sibomana	6	m		
9	Lerideri Kayitera	38	m	herdsman	married
10	Odette Mukabutera	35	f	farmer	married
11	Mathieu Ruhamyambuga	11	m	student	
12	Eric Kagabo	8	m	student	
13	Olive Nyirabucinkeri	6	f		
14	Shabungori	3	m		
15	Abiyingoma	52	m	herdsman	married
16	Adèle Mukangofero	43	f	farmer	married
17	Mukamukomeza	12	f	student	
18	Jeanne Nyirasogi	32	f	farmer	single
19	Gaspard	6	m		
20	Immaculée Mukangwije	50	f	farmer	widow
21	Niyomugabo	5	m		
22	Aloys Kayinamura	49	m	builder	married
23	Appolinaire Mukarugina	48	f	farmer	married
24	Uwamahoro	16	f	student	single
25	Nyirarugira	12	f	student	
26	Gaspard Ndikuyeze	14	m	student	
27	André Rwatambuga	68	m	farmer	widower
28	Denis Nduwamungu	35	m	herdsman	married
29	Nyampinga	5			
30	Uwimana	12	f	student	
31	Sibomana	3	m		
32	Nyiransanabandi	7	f	student	
33	Nduwamungu	9	m	student	
34	Mukarubirika	53	f	farmer	married
35	Bidederi	38	m	herdsman	married
36	Suzanne	33	f	farmer	married
37	Nsengiyumva	11	m	student	
38	Mbindigiri	4	f		
39	Marcianne	13	f	student	
40	Tuyizere	6	m		
41	Vincent Kanamugire	46	m	herdsman	married
42	Thérèse Nyirabatemberezi	42	f	farmer	married
43	Mukeshimana	17	f	farmer	single
44	Sibomana	15	m	student	
45	Martin Munyampenda	42	m	herdsman	married
46	Mukariyaka	7	f	student	
47	Hakizimana	3	m		
48	Thadée	60	f	farmer	widow
49	Marcel	26	m	herdsman	single
50	Munyakayanza	35	m	herdsman	married
51	Patricie	50	f	farmer	married
52	Nyiraromba	8	f	student	
53	Christophe	5	m		
54	Cyprien Munyankindi	33	m	herdsman	married
55	Xavéra	28	f	farmer	married
56	Nyirabagenimana	18	f	farmer	single
57	Mukarugwiza	14	f	student	
58	Marthe	43	f	farmer	widow
59	Evérienne	18	f	farmer	single
60	Joseph Munyanshongore	70	m	teacher	married
61	Cécile Nyirabwinturo	60	f	farmer	married
62	Pierre Nsabimana	27	m	herdsman	married
63	Emmanuelle Mujawamariya	17	f	farmer	single
64	Gasana	50	m	herdsman	married
65	Agnès Uwimana	24	f	farmer	married
66	Nyirabagirishya	46	f	farmer	widow
67	Mukankusi	23	f	farmer	single
68	Kirizani	10	m	student	
69	Béata Mukamusoni	17	f	student	single
70	François Ndayisaba	68	m	farmer	widower
71	Munyangabe	42	m	farmer	widower
72	Bucyana	29	m	herdsman	married
73	Winniphrida	21	f	farmer	married
74	Bucyana	1	m		

No.	Name	Age	Sex	Occupn.	Marital Status
75	Ignace Habiyambere	49	m	herdsman	married
76	Murekatete	6	f		
77	Pascasie	4	f		
78	Mukasine	3	f		
79	Perpétuée	56	f	farmer	widow
80	Damien	21	m	farmer	single
81	Eugénie	18	f	student	single
82	Catherine	56	f	farmer	widow
83	Anésie	22	f	farmer	single
84	Kirizani	10	m	student	
85	Munyandamutsa	45	m	herdsman	widower
86	Mukandori	20	f	farmer	single
87	Karangwa	16	m	farmer	single
88	Nyirimpeta	67	m	herdsman	married
89	Consolée	53	f	farmer	married
90	Isaïe	17	m	farmer	single
91	Aimé-Marie	15	f	farmer	single
92	Emmanuelle	20	f	farmer	single
93	Gakeri	71	m	herdsman	widower
94	Edouard	49	m	tailor	single
95	Karegeya	25	m	farmer	single
96	Mukandori	21	f	farmer	single
97	Monique	32	f	farmer	single
98	Mukangwije	56	f	farmer	widow
99	Annonciata	15	f	student	single
100	Mukarusanga	13	f	student	
101	Vénancie Nyiramafaranga	40	f	farmer	widow
102	Mukarugwiza	14	f	student	
103	Mukotanyi	10	m	student	
104	Marie Mukarutabana	60	f	farmer	widow
105	Vincent Munyambibi	30	m	civil servant	single
106	Gorette	20	f	farmer	single
107	Uwamahoro	6	f		
108	Bélie Kabagwiza	70	f	farmer	widow
109	Cyprien Munyurangabo	40	m	herdsman	married
110	Béatrice	30	f	farmer	married
111	Berna	65	f	farmer	widow
112	Mathias	40	m	herdsman	married
113	Xaverine Mukareta	30	f	farmer	married
114	Marie	17	f	farmer	single
115	Pierre	18	m	farmer	single
116	Musabende	10	f	student	
117	Rusezera	7	m	student	
118	Martin Sindayiheba	40	m	herdsman	married
119	Marguerite Kanziga	30	f	farmer	married
120	Alphonsine	18	f	farmer	single
121	Rukara	10	m	student	
122	Kanyamaswa	45	m	herdsman	married
123	Bernadette	30	f	farmer	married
124	Rudomoro	18	m	farmer	single
125	Kadugu	10	m	student	
126	Isacar Ruhumuliza	35	m	herdsman	married
127	Dina Mukarugwiza	30	f	farmer	married
128	Emmanuel	13	m	student	
129	Ruhumuliza	9	m	student	
130	Cécile Ruhumuliza	7	f	student	
131	Mathias Muhire	50	m	herdsman	married
132	Chrésie	23	f	farmer	single

1.3.4

No.	Name	Age	Sex	Occupn.	Marital Status
1	Kanyaviekwe	61	m	herdsman	married
2	Nyirandeme	53	f	farmer	married
3	Appolinaire Nyirasangwa	32	f	farmer	single
4	Jean	26	m	farmer	single
5	Musabyimana	21	f	farmer	single
6	Emmanuelle Mukeshmana	14	f	student	
7	Athanase Makaka	37	m	civil servant	married
8	Athanasie Mukeshimana	84	f	teacher	married
9	Tuyisenge	12	m	student	
10	Marguerite Ishimwe	9	f	student	
11	Emmanuel Rukundo	5	m		
12	Makaka	2	m		
13	Gorette	38	f	farmer	
14	Florence Nyirabikara	17	f	farmer	single
15	Nzayisenga Matoroshi	14	m	student	
16	Twagiramungu	12	m	student	
17	Mathias Nsabimana	37	m	civil servant	married
18	Munyantarama	40	m	herdsman	single
19	Amon Gahigi	45	m	farmer	single
20	Marc Nturo	58	m	herdsman	married
21	Pauline Nyirajyambere	49	f	farmer	married
22	Habimana	27	m	farmer	single
23	Aron Nsabimana	25	m	farmer	single
24	Thomas	22	m	professor	single
25	Gaudence	20	f	student	single
26	Munyabarame	54	m	herdsman	married
27	Pauline Nyiramanyana	48	f	farmer	married
28	Babenia	20	m	student	single
29	Matorshi	15	m	student	
30	Munyantarama	13	m	student	
31	Xavéra Mukabutera	32	f	farmer	married
32	Denise	2	f		
33	Emmanuel Muhayimana	32	m	shopkeeper	married
34	Ishimwe	30	f	farmer	married
35	Claudine Niyodusenga	9	f	student	
36	Nzayisenga	6	m		
37	Claudine Tumushime	3	f		
38	Charles Gashugi	61	m	herdsman	married
39	Monique Mukamusoni	52	f	farmer	married
40	Alfred Niyongaba	23	m	shopkeeper	single
41	Annonciata	38	f	farmer	married
42	Emmanuelle Mukeshimana	16	f	student	single
43	Gashugi	12	f	student	
44	Raphaël	17	m	student	single
45	Jeanne	14	f	student	
46	Alexandre Nsengiyumva	6	m		
47	Cansilde	25	f	farmer	single
48	Nyirambagariye	81	f	farmer	widow
49	Mukamusoni	15	f	student	
50	Uwimbabazi	12	f	student	
51	Mukesharurema	18	f	farmer	single
52	Camir Ngezahayo	44	m	farmer	single
53	Mukantagara	48	f	farmer	married
54	Kabibi	21	f	farmer	single
55	Ntigurirwa Sekaganda	27	m	herdsman	married
56	Suzanne	26	f	farmer	married
57	Athanasie	9	f	student	
58	Ndahimana	4	m		
59	Ntigurirwa	5m	m		
60	Dominique Nturo	62	m	herdsman	married
61	Madeleine Nyirakigarama	52	f	farmer	married
62	Cyriaque Sarasi	12	m	student	
63	François Munyankambi	61	m	herdsman	married
64	Bernadette	55	f	farmer	married
65	Xavéra Nkori	19	f	student	single
66	Angélique	14	f	student	
67	Niyonsaba	25	f	farmer	single
68	Kamugwera	69	f	farmer	widow
69	Charles Munyakazi	49	m	farmer	single
70	Patricie Uwantege	29	f	teacher	single
71	Musirikari	27	m	farmer	single
72	Nyirasinbwabo	24	f	farmer	single
73	Marie Niyigena	5	f		
74	Pascasie Mukankusi	35	f	farmer	widow
75	Ndayisaba	11	m	student	
76	Mukankusi	5	f		
77	Pasteur Ntagara	49	m	herdsman	married
78	Gaudence	45	f	farmer	married
79	Philbert Karangwa	24	m	student	single
80	Marcel	20	m	student	single
81	Martin Karekezi	52	m	herdsman	married
82	Agnès Mukantagara	49	f	farmer	married
83	Buhungiro	21	m	student	single
84	Cansilde	27	f	farmer	sngle
85	Thérèse	15	f	student	single
86	Daphrose	25	f	farmer	single
87	Thomas	60	m	herdsman	married
88	Rose	54	f	farmer	married
89	Odette	26	f	farmer	single
90	Athanasie	24	f	student	single
91	Son of Odette	4	m		
92	Thomas Rutabana	62	m	shopkeeper	single
93	Edouard Gakwaya	55	m	herdsman	married
94	Bernadette	52	f	farmer	married
95	Ignace	34	m	shopkeeper	single
96	Agnès	27	f	farmer	single
97	Ngarambe	24	m	farmer	single
98	Claver Ndagije	21	m	student	single
99	Déo	65	m	herdsman	married
100	Esther	60	f	farmer	married
101	Mukakayiro	31	f	farmer	single
102	Gaudence	24	f	farmer	single
103	Dominique Nsabimana	5	m		
104	Nsanzurwimo	52	m	herdsman	married
105	Evérienne Kamayogi	53	f	farmer	married
106	Gaspard	15	m	student	
107	Mukangwije	30	f	farmer	
108	Habayo	12	m	student	
109	Bernard Gakwaya	57	m	herdsman	married
110	Xaveri	16	m	student	single
111	Marie Nyirangirimana	12	f	student	
112	Gakwaya	8	m	student	
113	Abel Gakwaya	5	m		
114	Tite Gakwaya	2	m		
115	Mutemberezi	53	m	herdsman	married
116	Odette	56	f	farmer	married
117	Thérèse	18	f	farmer	single

No.	Name	Age	Sex	Occupn.	Marital Status
118	Eugénie	16	f	farmer	single
119	Mutemberezi	12	m	student	
120	Dugiri	9	m	student	
121	Mukangarambe	7	f	student	
122	Banyangiriki	50	f	farmer	widow
123	Nyiranteziryayo	32	f	farmer	single
124	Nyirabakiga	25	f	farmer	single
125	Segatashya	40	m	farmer	married
126	Banamwana	32	f	farmer	married
127	Nyirabucinkeri	12	f	student	
128	Sugabo	5	m		
129	Nyirarukundo	14	f	student	
130	Alphonse	10	m	student	
131	Callixte Sindayiheba	32	m	shopkeeper	married
132	Nyirahabimana	31	f	farmer	married
133	Nsabimana	7	m	student	
134	Mukabagire	10	f	student	
135	Rusihiri	7	m	student	
136	Sindayiheba	5	m		
137	Louis Sindayiheba	2	m		
138	Anésie	37	f	farmer	married
139	Théogène	20	m	student	single
140	Dodori	18	m	farmer	single
141	Théobald	16	m	farmer	single
142	Théonèste	14	m	student	
143	Muzehe	12	m	student	
144	Nkecuru	7	f	student	
145	Mukamusoni	30	f	farmer	single
146	Nyabwana	14	m	student	
147	Nkecuru	8	f	student	
148	Gatera	37	m	herdsman	married
149	His wife, Eugénie	28	f	farmer	married
150	Nsengiyumva	14	m	student	
151	Gibyori	11	m	student	
152	Jean-Paul	9	m	student	
153	Claudine	5	f	student	
154	Anathalie	38	f	civil servant	married
155	Paul Muzungu	39	m	shopkeeper	married
156	Cyrille Muzungu	5	m		
157	Pauline Muzungu	2	f		
158	Claudine Muzungu	1	f		
159	Madeleine Nikuze	18	f	student	single
160	Emmanuel	26	m	nurse	single
161	Triphine Nyirabukara	32	f	inspector	married
162	Nzamurambaho	4	f		
163	Déo Nzamurambaho	1	m		
164	Anésie	21	f	servant	single
165	Donatien	32	m	farmer	single
166	Rwabashi	68	m	farmer	widower
167	Xaverine Nyiraromba	35	f	farmer	single
168	Lidie Nyiragiraneza	31	f	civ. servant	married
169	Kimonyo	21	m	farmer	single
170	Aloys Ndahayo	45	m	herdsman	married
171	Cléophaste Ndahayo	14	m	student	
172	Cécile Ndahayo	12	f	student	
173	Denis Ndahayo	9	m	student	
174	Rubyogo Ndahayo	5	m		

1.4 Sector Mubuga

1.4.1 Cellule Gihira

No.	Name	Age	Sex	Occupn.	Marital Status
1	Annonciata Nyirabahunde	63	f	farmer	widow
2	Augustin Rugwizangoga	35	m	herdsman	single
3	Claudine Barazagwire	7	f	student	
4	Izabayo	5	m		
5	Cyprien Nzamurambaho	8	m	student	
6	Ntaganira	40	m	farmer	married
7	Agnès	12	f	student	
8	Marthe Ntaganira	10	f	student	
9	Alphonse Ntaganira	5	m		
10	Denis Ntaganira	3	m		
11	Canisius Gabiro	50	m	herdsman	married
12	Caritas Mukamunana	42	f	farmer	married
13	Xavier Mashaka	32	m	farmer	single
14	Pascal Ndori	14	m	student	
15	Jeanne Kabagwira	22	f	farmer	single
16	Nyiramadibongo	10	f	student	
17	Rugamba	9	m	student	
18	Munyangabe	65	m	herdsman	married
19	Athanasie Mukamusoni	50	f	farmer	married
20	Vénuste	35	m	tailor	single
21	Emmanuel Rutayisire	24	m	trader	single
22	Mukamunana	20	f	farmer	single
23	Vianney Munyangabe	25	m	herdsman	single
24	Jean Nzamutuma	13	m	student	
25	Emmanuelle Rutaysire	30	f	farmer	married
26	Marie Uwimana	22	f	student	single
27	Immaculée Mukamurigo	58	f	farmer	widow
28	Mukarutabana	14	f	student	
29	Rubunda	9	m	student	
30	Pascasie Uwimana	12	f	student	
31	Nyirafaranga	7	f	student	
32	Martin Munyankindi	55	m	herdsman	married
33	Marie-Thérèse Mukangamije	42	f	farmer	married
34	Nyirarigoga	12	f	student	
35	Vincent Banamwana	15	m	student	
36	Uwera	16	f	farmer	single
37	Théodore Ngarambe	23	m	herdsman	single
38	Vincent Rubiringa	12	m	student	
39	Emile Bayingana	16	m	student	single
40	Evariste	35	m	herdsman	married
41	Colette Uwimana	30	f	farmer	married
42	Nzamurambaho	12	m	student	
43	Zimenyi	19	m	student	single
44	Uwineza	5	f		
45	Alphonsine	17	f	student	single
46	Gakirage	10	f	student	
47	Uwamahoro	15	f	student	
48	Athanase Benimana	60	m		married
49	Angéline Mukakurigo	42	f	farmer	married
50	Assumpta Benimana	30	f	teacher	single
51	Marie Pierre	22	f	teacher	single
52	Agnès Benimana	20	f	teacher	single
53	Rubunda	9	m	student	
54	Bernard Kabera	35	m	farmer	married
55	Murakaza	12	m	student	
56	Jean Rudakubana	59	m	herdsman	married
57	Agnès Kandamage	42	f	farmer	married
58	Clarisse	52	f	farmer	widow
59	Jacqueline Ingabire	15	f	student	
60	Agnès Mukamwiza	16	f	student	single
61	Félicitée Mukamwiza	17	f	student	single
62	Marie Louise Bamurange	10	f	student	
63	Niyigena	7	f	student	
64	Marie Mukarwego	20	f	student	single
65	Habinshuti	14	m	student	
66	Phocas Segasagara	50	m	builder	married
67	Thacienne Nyirabatwa	48	f	farmer	married
68	Mukamwiza	35	f	farmer	widow
69	Athanase Bikorimana	14	m	student	
70	Eugénie Mushimiyimana	12	f	student	
71	Jacqueline Mukabaziki	8	f	student	
72	Cécile	30	f	teacher	widow
73	Aimé Gashema	3	m		
74	Raphaël Kayigema	45	m	teacher	married
75	Anastasie Mukantagara	37	f	farmer	married
76	Césalie	14	f	student	
77	Jacques Kayigema	16	m	student	single
78	Justine	20	f	student	single
79	Déo Mukarurangwa	36	m	civil servant	married
80	Bibianne Musaniwabo	28	f	farmer	married
81	Jean d'Arc Muhayemungu	15	m	student	
82	Valence Twayigira	13	m	student	
83	Aimé Semuhanuka	10	m	student	
84	Providence Muhayemungu	7	f	student	
85	Emmanuel Rudakenga	29	m	herdsman	single
86	Bonaventure Gasarasi	42	m	herdsman	married
87	Liberata Mukarugero	37	f	farmer	married
88	Sébastien Rwigema	13	m	student	
89	Marie-Claire Uwamurera	11	f	student	
90	Mwavita	14	f	student	
91	Jean-Damascène Seribateri	8	m	student	
92	Agnès Nyinawumwami	5	f		
93	Caritas Mukabatesi	21	f	teacher	single
94	François Nyarwanda	37	m	herdsman	married
95	Berthe Mukabatesi	27	f	farmer	married
96	Clementine Uwamahoro	3	f		
97	Stanislas Mbonimana	1	m		
98	Alexis Kayitsinga	37	m	herdsman	married
99	Marie Mukasine	32	f	farmer	married
100	Joseph Kayitsinga	8	m	student	
101	Justine Uwimana	5	f		
102	Epimaque	28	m	herdsman	single
103	Ladislas Gakwavu	60	m	herdsman	married
104	Gaudence Nyirabititaweho	54	f	farmer	married
105	Ngarambe	12	m	student	
106	Claudien Gakwavu	9	m	student	
107	Thacien Ngimbanyi	49	m	herdsman	married
108	Mutabaruka	70	m	herdsman	married
109	Costasie	62	f	farmer	married
110	Valence Ndamyambi	42	m	vet	married
111	Thacienne Mukabutera	37	f	farmer	married
112	Clément	17	m	soldier	single
113	Agnès Uwihaye	14	f	student	

114	Cyuzuzo	10	f	student	
115	Madeleine Akayezu	8	f	student	
116	Ignace Nkezabayo	24	m	preist	single
117	Marthe Mukangango	23	f	nurse	married
118	Damien	47	m	herdsman	married
119	Dative Mukantagwabira	35	f	farmer	married
120	Athanase Nsabimana	9	m	student	
121	Wenceslas Munyambo	70	m	herdsman	married
122	Dancille Karuyonga	67	f	farmer	married
123	Béata Uwimana	16	f	student	single
124	Drocella Mukakibibi	22	f	farmer	single
125	Muvoma	20	m	farmer	single
126	Murebwayire	14	f	student	
127	Damien Hakizimana	40	m	teacher	married
128	Mukabera	47	f	farmer	widow
129	Anaclet Rugirwa	19	f	trader	single
130	Agnès Uwayisaba	13	f	student	
131	Chantal Mukandori	10	f	student	
132	Cécile Uwera	50	f	farmer	widow
133	Ignace Shingiro	23	m	teacher	single
134	Colette karmpire	42	f	farmer	widow
135	Jules Ndamage	14	m	student	
136	Marie Chantal Mukandori	14	f	student	
137	Casimir	37	m	herdsman	married
138	Christine	46	f	farmer	married
139	Frédéric Bikerinka	62	m	herdsman	married
140	Marie-Thèrèse Nyiramariza	54	f	farmer	married
141	Amiel Bayingana	38	m	secretary	married
142	Thérèse Nyiramariza	33	f	farmer	married
143	Nyirarudomoro	5	f		
144	Rudomoro	8	m		
145	Augustine Rwasibo	41	m	herdsman	married
146	Kanyundo	32	f	farmer	married
147	Gakwaya	5	m		
148	Olive Nyiranjagari	38	f	farmer	married
149	Mujawamariya	18	f	student	single
150	Uwamariya	18	f	student	single
151	Joséphine Uwase	14	f	student	
152	Joseph Cadet	6	m		
153	Gato	3	m		
154	Gakuro	3	m		
155	J.M.V Nyakarundi	70	m	herdsman	married
156	Venancie Nyirantagorama	58	f	farmer	married
157	Laurent	50	m	herdsman	married
158	Rosaline Ntakabonye	46	f	farmer	married
159	Emmanuel Ndayisaba	18	m	farmer	single
160	Etienne Ndamage	15	m	student	single
161	Gashema	12	f	student	
162	Tite Rutiyomba	35	m	herdsman	married
163	Agnès Mukandinda	32	f	farmer	married
164	Sendamage	14	m	student	
165	Nzuruzaba	6	m		
166	Ukobizaba	2	m		
167	Eugène Nshizirungu	28	m	farmer	married
168	Xaverine Musabyemariya	23	f	farmer	married
169	Emile Mushinzemungu	14	m	student	
170	Stanislas Kanimba	49	m	herdsman	married
171	Josephina Nyiramipira	43	f	farmer	married
172	Corneille Mafene	12	m	student	
173	Béata Nyiramafene	7	f	student	
174	Vérédienne Nyinawandori	60	f	farmer	married
175	Médard Kanimba	58	m	herdsman	married
176	Agnès Kampire	53	f	farmer	married
177	Ikimanimpaye	16	f	student	single
178	Ujeneza	12	f	student	
179	Louis Tena	46	m	farmer	married
180	Eugènie Nyiranshuti	41	f	farmer	married
181	Jeanne Kamariza	5	f		
182	Philbert Ruterana	2	m		
183	Edouard Kanamugire	24	m	herdsman	married
184	Emile Biterisenge	45	m	herdsman	widower
185	Evariste	49	m	herdsman	married
186	Félicitée Mukabaziga	40	f	farmer	married
187	Rukebesha	58	m	teacher	widower
188	Claire Bamukunde	19	f	student	single
189	Françoise Bamukunde	11	f	student	
190	Florence Bayisenge	15	f	student	
191	Oreste Batsinda	11	m	student	
192	Pascal Rucyebesha	39	m	teacher	widower
193	Léonidas Butaza	72	m	teacher	married
194	Thérèse Nyiramahe	63	f	farmer	married
195	Antoine Rugeruza	17	m	student	single
196	Alphonse Butaza	33	m	farmer	single
197	Justine Butaza	30	f	farmer	single
198	Madeleine Uwimana	18	f	student	single
199	Alphonse Uwera	21	f	student	single
200	Mawo	7	m	student	
201	Camille Kayigamba	39	m	civil servant	married
202	Agnès Kamariza	27	f	teacher	married
203	Olivier Kayigariza	10	m	student	
204	Thomas Gatana	67	m	herdsman	married
205	Vérédienne Kamatamu	60	f	farmer	married
206	Clément Nkurikiyinka	42	m	teacher	single
207	Annonciata Mukamunana	33	f	teacher	single
208	Gloriose Uwamahoro	30	f	nurse	single
209	Adrien Kamoso	29	m	farmer	single
210	Jean Rwasibo	25	m	builder	single
211	Agnès Mukakimanuka	62	f	farmer	widow
212	Emmanuel Muyenzi	32	m	civil servant	married
213	Adèle Nyirangije	30	f	farmer	single
214	Tharcisse Rukerikibaye	15	m	student	
215	Denis Senkerekere	68	m	farmer	married
216	Louis Nyakayiro	28	m	herdsman	single

1.4.2 Cellule Rwamiko

No.	Name	Age	Sex	Occupn.	Marital Status
1	Alphonsine Kayitesi	32	f	farmer	married
2	Christine Mukantaganzwa	35	f	farmer	widow
3	Ugiraneza	13	m	student	
4	Mukeshimana	8	f	student	
5	Antoine Ngango	65	m	herdsman	married
6	Christine Nyinawandori	50	f	farmer	married
7	Ntagwabira	35	m	herdsman	single
8	Gasagara	33	m	herdsman	single
9	Mukandori	23	f	farmer	single
10	Jean Rutebuka	37	m	herdsman	married
11	Immaculée Uwamahoro	35	f	farmer	married
12	Jeanne Mushimiyimana	12	f	student	
13	Eugénie Nzamutuma	9	f	student	
14	Emmanuel Ndamage	7	m	student	
15	Marie Mukarwego	38	f	farmer	widow
16	Justine Nsabimana	16	m	student	single
17	Emmanuelle Nyiragukura	14	f	student	
18	Emmerence Nyirabera	12	f	student	
19	Jean Gasigwa	40	m	herdsman	married
20	Xaverine Nyirabera	35	f	farmer	married
21	Jules Kanamugire	14	m	student	
22	Nzamutuma	11	m	student	
23	Casimir Kagenza	42	m	herdsman	married
24	Béata Nyiranzitonda	40	f	farmer	married
25	Dancille Uwera	14	f	student	
26	Ancille Mukeshimana	12	f	student	
27	Mukandori	10	f	student	
28	Rukara	8	m	student	
29	Ilibagiza	4	f		
30	Claudien Kabanda	45	m	herdsman	married
31	Caritas Mukandanga	39	f	farmer	married
32	Charles Kayiranga	28	m	businessman	single
33	Dorothée Mukamurigo	24	f	student	single
34	Ignace Niyomugabo	18	m	student	single
35	Antoine Uzabumwana	36	m	civil servant	married
36	Justine Mukarukaka	32	f	farmer	married
37	Pascal Nshimiye	12	m	student	
38	Ilibagiza	14	f	student	
39	Urayaneza	12	f	student	
40	Abraham	66	m	herdsman	widower
41	Marie-Thérèse N.gahombo	72	f	farmer	widow
42	Charles Karangwa	45	m	herdsman	widower
43	Zitoni Gaspard	58	m	herdsman	widower
44	Louis Mugesera	69	m	herdsman	widower
45	Anastasie Nyinawindinda	47	f	farmer	widow
46	Antoinette Mukantwari	44	f	teacher	widow
47	Tharcisse Ngezahayo	54	m	herdsman	married
48	Anastasie Nyinawandori	48	f	farmer	married
49	Cécile Nyirashongore	18	f	student	single
50	Jean-Paul Nsabayezu	47	m	nurse	married
51	Catherine Nyiranjishi	45	f	farmer	married
52	Marie- Louise Uwimana	15	f	student	
53	Aimé Kararwa	9	f	student	
54	Stanislas Twagiramusinga	48	m	herdsman	married
55	Paul Kayihura	51	m	herdsman	married
56	Xavéra Mukankusi	42	f	farmer	married
57	Gaspard Gasasira	16	m	student	
58	Rutaganda	14	m	student	
59	Ujeneza	8	m	student	
60	Gihura	12	m	student	
61	Kayiranga	5	m		
62	Pascasie Mukarugwiza	37	f	farmer	married
63	Justine Kagoyire	7	f	student	
64	Joséphine Musomandera	39	f	farmer	widow
65	Donatille Uwera	17	f	student	single
66	Gorette Uwimana	15	f	student	
67	Odette Uwitonze	13	f	student	
68	Aloys Ntezimana	11	m	student	
69	Joséphine Kabagwiza	10	f	student	
70	Kwitonda	8	m	student	
71	Mashyaka	5	m		

No.	Name	Age	Sex	Occupn.	Marital Status
72	Uwikunda	3	m		
73	DaphroseYankurije	29	f	farmer	married
74	Tuyizere	6	f		
75	Uwimpuhire	2	m		
76	Bernadette Mutamuriza	27	f	farmer	married
77	Jean Ruhumuliza	17	m	student	single
78	Mpinganzima	40	f	farmer	single
79	Marie	35	f	farmer	married
80	Mathieu Masabo	26	m	farmer	single
81	Consolée Mukarubibi	42	f	farmer	married
82	Donatille Bayisenge	34	f	farmer	married

1.5 Sector Ngoma

1.5.1 Cellule Uwingabo

No.	Name	Age	Sex	Occupn.	Marital Status
1	Cyprien Mugemana	74	m	herdsman	married
2	Foyibi Mpogazi	70	f	farmer	married
3	Claudette Uwera	10	f	student	
4	Marie Mukamuyango	30	f	farmer	married
5	Mukasine	7	f	student	
6	Esdras Ngirindamutsa	45	m	responsable	married
7	Mukandoli	40	f	farmer	married
8	Seth Bayiringire	21	m	farmer	single
9	Jacques Niyitegeka	19	m	student	single
10	Pierre Ntivuguruzwa	17	m	student	single
11	Mbarushimana	13	m	herdsman	
12	Odette Mukamana	20	f	farmer	married
13	Samuel Mulindahabi	47	m	herdsman	married
14	Emerithe	22	f	farmer	married
15	François Mushimiyimana	16	m	student	single
16	Jeanette Mukamuhizi	14	f	student	
17	Aimable	12	m	student	
18	Twagirayezu	10	m	student	
19	Isacar	15	m	herdsman	
20	Ezéchiel Ruhigisha	55	m	caretaker	married
21	Félicitée	50	f	farmer	married
22	Edouard	27	m	technician	single
23	Jamaika	23	m	student	single
24	Julius Mbabazi	17	m	student	single
25	Murekatete	20	f	student	single
26	Uwamariya	10	f	student	
27	Thérèse	15	f	servant	
28	Jean Ngango	30	m	mechanic	single
29	Marthe Nyirahabimana	35	f	nurse	married
30	Eric Bigirimana	13	m	student	
31	Dina	10	f	student	
32	Yvette	8	f	student	
33	Josué Nzamwita	50	m	tailor	married
34	Esther	48	f	farmer	married
35	Gérard	23	m	student	single
36	Birori	20	m	student	single
37	Furaha	25	m	student	single
38	Isacar Kajongi	52	m	accountant	married

1.5.1 Cellule Uwingabo (continued)

No.	Name	Age	Sex	Occupn.	Marital Status
1	Zachée Rukara	60	m	herdsman	married
2	Pauline Busasa	55	f	farmer	married
3	Euphrasie Mukamusoni	30	f	farmer	single
4	Julie	28	f	seamstress	single
5	Nyiramana	26	f	student	single
6	Elie Ndayisaba	24	m	herdsman	single
7	Aloys	45	f	farmer	married
8	Ntagara	28	m	builder	single
9	Rwabudadara	47	m	herdsman	married
10	Mukangarambe	30	f	farmer	married
11	Nyiransengiyumva	19	f	farmer	single
12	Murasandonyi	60	m	farmer	married
13	Mukasine	10	f	student	
14	Mukabera	8	f	student	
15	Nyirabuyange	60	f	farmer	widow
16	Hakizimana	28	m	herdsman	single
17	Eliézer Musayidizi	30	m	herdsman	single
18	Donat Ngarambe	35	m	herdsman	married
19	Félicitée Nyirahabayo	30	f	farmer	married
20	Casimir	32	m	herdsman	married
21	Mukarwema	30	m	herdsman	married
22	Habineza	7	m	student	
23	Hesron Gahizi	60	m	herdsman	married
24	Lidie Mukandutiye	55	f	farmer	married
25	Kayigema	23	m	student	single
26	Mukamana	20	f	student	single
27	Senyoni	16	m	herdsman	single
28	Edison Kayijuka	32	m	farmer	married
29	Mukarutabana	30	f	farmer	married
30	Mukantagara	48	f	farmer	married
31	Joséphine	15	f	student	
32	Umutesi	12	f	student	
33	Eugénie	29	f	farmer	single
34	Géneviève	24	f	farmer	single
35	Bizimungu	30	m	farmer	married
36	Edith Mukamtwali	26	f	farmer	married
37	Tabeya	68	f	farmer	widow
38	Julienne	50	f	farmer	married
39	Mukasine	25	f	nurse	single
40	Joséphine	22	f	teacher	single
41	Emmanuel	20	m	herdsman	single
42	Charles Kobizaba	50	m	accountant	married
43	Musonera	32	m	farmer	single
44	Nzamukunda	45	f	farmer	married
45	Osée	28	m	student	single
46	Vérène	20	f	student	single
47	Mariane Nyirambuye	78	f	farmer	married
48	Uwamariya	10	f	student	
49	Rwadigiri	65	m	herdsman	married
50	Keziya	60	f	farmer	married
51	Thomas	20	m	student	single
52	Nyiransabimana	18	f	student	single
53	Amos Karera	50	m	secretary	married
54	Edith	48	f	farmer	married
55	Jeanette	25	f	teacher	single
56	Eugénie	22	f	teacher	single
57	Jean-Louis	18	m	student	single
58	Albert	16	m	student	single
59	Chantal	14	f	student	
60	Alexis	20	m	herdsman	single
61	Bugwete	60	m	herdsman	married
62	Murasandonyi	60	m	farmer	married
63	Muhire	16	m	student	single
64	Rosalie	60	f	farmer	married
65	Nsanzimfura	12	m	student	
66	Nsengimana	14	m	student	
67	Dominique Matingiri	38	m	nurse	married
68	Caritas	30	f	teacher	married
69	Erina	15	f	servant	
70	Esther	40	f	farmer	married
71	Benjamin	24	m	student	single
72	Edison	22	m	student	single
73	Makuza	20	m	student	single
74	Ngarambe	18	m	student	single
75	Uwayo	16	m	student	single
76	Ndayishimiye	14	m	student	
77	Joshua Mbuguje	55	m	preacher	married
78	Nyiramongi	30	f	farmer	married
79	Joseph	27	m	teacher	single
80	Nyiragwiza	31	f	farmer	married
81	Emmanuel	17	m	student	single
82	Mukarubingo	80	f	farmer	widow
83	Nyirabagirishya	68	f	farmer	widow
84	Ndekezi	30	m	farmer	single
85	Jonas Ngendahayo	45	m	accountant	married
86	Elena Nsabwimana	42	f	worker	married
87	Vera	25	f	teacher	married
88	Bitahurugamba	35	m	shopkeeper	married
89	Mukarutabana	38	f	worker	married
90	Uwizeye	10	f	student	
91	Uwamahoro	8	f	student	
92	Byiringiro	6	m	student	
93	Gaspard	16	m	herdsman	single
94	Sindayigaya	38	m	tailor	married
95	Nyiragwiza	35	f	teacher	married
96	Jean d'Amour	9	m	student	
97	Philippe Mwitegeri	70	m	tailor	married
98	Debora	65	f	farmer	married
99	Mukabaziga	17	f	student	single
100	Etienne Sirikari	7	m	student	
101	Rudakubana	24	m	farmer	single
102	Yuwana	22	m	farmer	single
103	Musemakweli	12	m	student	
104	Mukashimana	15	f	student	
105	Thomas Rukara	48	m	farmer	married
106	Mukagatare	40	f	farmer	married
107	Mukabutera	25	f	farmer	single
108	Muhire	11	m	student	
109	Aminadabu Kabenga	50	m	nurse	married
110	Tamari Mukawera	45	f	farmer	married
111	Manzi	32	m	nurse	single
112	Vérène	22	f	teacher	single
113	Rwagasore	60	m	farmer	married
114	Karwoga	50	f	farmer	married
115	Colette Mukamujara	30	f	farmer	married

116	Samuel	36	m	farmer	married
117	Muhayimana	12	m	student	
118	Dina	8	m	student	
119	Claver Nsangimfura	32	m	farmer	married
120	Mukabutera	30	f	farmer	married
121	Iyamuremye	45	m	farmer	married
122	Nyirabuseruka	42	f	farmer	married
123	Munyandamutsa	28	m	driver	single
124	Thérèse	25	f	teacher	single
125	Mukangarambe	22	f	student	single
126	Iyamuremye	17	m	student	single
127	Jason Kayibanda	50	m	teacher	married
128	Erina	45	f	worker	married
129	Ngirumwami	45	m	worker	married
130	Zibiya	42	f	farmer	married
131	Nyirahabimana	18	f	student	single
132	Nyiraneza	16	f	student	single
133	Annonciata	14	f	student	
134	Odette	12	f	student	
135	Racherl	10	f	student	
136	Emmanuel	8	f	student	
137	Pierre	6	m	student	
138	Kabuto	80	m	farmer	widow
139	Rukara	35	m	farmer	single
140	Mukakarori	30	f	farmer	married
141	Danny Mushimiyimana	11	m	student	
142	Usabwimana	9	f	student	
143	Niyongira	7	f	student	
144	Kayijamahe	50	m	farmer	married
145	Nyirabagisha	45	f	farmer	married

1.5.2 Cellule Kigarama

No.	Name	Age	Sex	Occupn.	Marital Status
154	Félicitée	15	f		
155	Bisengimana	33	m	farmer	married
156	Kayijuka	30	m	farmer	single
157	Mwizerwa	17	m	student	single
158	Habyarimana	15	m	student	
159	Vincent Kayishema	53	m	accountant	married
160	Colette	44	f	farmer	married
161	Valérie	15	f	student	
162	Valence	12	m	student	
163	Vestine	10	m	student	
164	Gapfizi	56	m	responsable	married
165	Nshimyumukiza	30	m	farmer	single
166	Ntihemuka	20	m	student	single
167	Nyiranshuti	12	f	student	
168	Yamuragiye	55	m	builder	married
169	Twagirayezu	17	m	student	single
170	Muhayimana	13	m	student	
171	Nyirabukara	12	f	student	
172	Musabyimana	7	m	student	
173	Nyirabiraro	70	f	farmer	widow
174	Nyirabuseruka	35	f	farmer	single
175	André	65	m	farmer	married
176	Nzitukuze	68	f	farmer	widow
177	Dancille Mukagatare	37	f	farmer	married
178	Adèle Kanyanja	60	f	farmer	married
179	Mukangwije	10	f	student	
180	Ntibugirumye	45	m	carpenter	married
181	Anselme	40	m	herdsman	married
182	Cyubahiro	24	m	student	single
183	Uwimpuhwe	18	f	student	
184	Jacques	13	m	student	
185	Erina	9	f	student	
186	David	35	m	farmer	married
187	Bernadette	25	f	farmer	married
188	Nyirandekwe	63	f	farmer	widow
189	Muhire	24	m	carpenter	single
190	Mukaruberwa	22	f	farmer	single
191	Gafaranga	12	m	student	
192	Mushimiyimana	45	m	farmer	married
193	Nyirarukundo	43	f	farmer	married
194	Nyirabugingo	16	f	student	single
195	Mukamwiza	14	f	student	
196	Uwilingiyimana	12	f	student	
197	Hagenimana	7	m	student	
198	Ndamyimana	35	m	farmer	married
199	Mukagasore	30	f	farmer	married
200	Eric	7	m	student	
201	Birara	70	m	farmer	married
202	Kambibi	60	f	farmer	married
203	Adiriya	34	f	farmer	married
204	Ndayizeye	12	m	student	
205	Emmanuelle	7	f	student	
206	Nyamwigendaho	65	m	farmer	married
207	Agnès	50	f	farmer	married
208	Nyiragaruka	45	f	farmer	married
209	Léonard	70	m	farmer	married
210	Uwamahoro	13	f	student	
211	Uwimana	28	f	farmer	widow
212	Harindintwali	7	m	student	
213	Marcel Habinshuti	30	m	farmer	married
214	Ayinkamiye	25	f	farmer	married
215	Athanase Gashugi	25	m	farmer	married
216	Mukabarore	30	f	farmer	married
217	Ndayisaba	14	m	student	
218	Béata	10	f	student	
219	Nyiramaningiri	7	f	student	
220	Mwimuka	45	m	farmer	married
221	Mukamazimpaka	40	f	farmer	married
222	Innocent	26	m	farmer	single
223	Mukamudenge	24	f	farmer	single
224	Louis	21	m	student	single
225	Mukankundiye	16	f	student	single
226	Mukamwiza	13	f	student	
227	Rubayiza	8	m	student	
228	Gakwaya	38	m	farmer	married
229	Mukamutesi	34	f	farmer	married
230	Joseph Matabaro	16	m	student	single
231	Pascasie	18	f	farmer	single
232	Mukamana	35	f	farmer	married
233	Espérance	16	f	student	single
234	Ntakuritimana	14	m	student	
235	Faustin	12	m	student	
236	Caritas	8	f	student	
237	Mukandamage	34	f	farmer	married
238	Kamali	12	m	student	
239	Hakizimana	9	m	student	
240	Nsanzurwimo	35	m	farmer	married
241	Mukanjabali	33	f	farmer	married
242	Jacques	14	m	student	
243	Bosco	11	m	student	
244	Chantal	7	f	student	
245	Harolimana	35	m	farmer	single
246	Murutankwaya	38	m	farmer	married
247	Mukangofero	34	f	farmer	married
248	Munyantwali	22	m	farmer	single
249	Mukeshimana	18	f	student	single
250	Bizimungu	14	m	student	
251	Berthilde	14	m	student	
252	Utetiwabo	7	f	student	
253	Nyilidandi	70	m	herdsman	married
254	Izabiriza	38	f	farmer	married
255	Nyiransengimana	21	f	shopkeeper	single
256	Nyirakanani	8	f	student	
257	Bugingo	15	m	student	
258	Gérard	9	m	student	
259	Gasherebuka	45	m	agronomist	married
260	Mukahigiro	40	f	farmer	married
261	Virginie	30	f	farmer	married
262	Charles	25	m	student	single
263	Martha	20	f	student	single
264	Uwamahoro	16	f	student	single
265	Bucyeye	60	f	farmer	married
266	Gakwerere	36	m	herdsman	single
267	Prosper	33	m	farmer	single
268	Françoise	26	f	farmer	single
269	Mbanda	30	m	herdsman	single
270	Kabanda	26	m	herdsman	single
271	Kabandana	18	m	herdsman	single
272	Gaëtan	35	m	herdsman	single
273	Odette	55	f	farmer	widow
274	Vénuste	28	m	shopkeeper	single
275	Jean Marie-Vianney	30	m	herdsman	single
276	Rutaremara	26	m	farmer	single
277	Rutabana	24	m	farmer	single
278	Innocent	22	m	herdsman	single
279	Mukeshimana	18	f	farmer	single
280	Devota	15	f	student	
281	Nyamaswa	50	m	farmer	married
282	Kankuyo	45	f	farmer	married
283	Ignace	35	m	herdsman	single
284	Kayitera	36	m	herdsman	single
285	Gatera	38	m	herdsman	single
286	Olive Mukangoga	22	f	farmer	single
287	Muhayimana	20	m	herdsman	single
288	Habinshuti	16	m	student	single
289	Mukamana	14	f	student	
290	Simon Kalimunda	60	m	herdsman	married
291	Adèle Mukankanika	40	f	farmer	married
292	Bayingana	13	m	student	
293	Zingiro	11	m	student	
294	Ngamije	7	m	student	
295	Gasamagera	30	m	farmer	married
296	Musengimana	26	f	farmer	married

297 Odette	40	f	farmer	married
298 Nyirahabimana	20	f	farmer	married
299 Laurent	24	m	farmer	single
300 Nyirankuzana	10	f	student	
301 Nsengiyumva	40	m	herdsman	married
302 Mukarudahunga	35	f	farmer	married
303 Nyirahakizimana	15	f	student	
304 Niyomwungeli	12	f	student	
305 Madeleine	9	f	student	
306 Clément	58	m	herdsman	married
307 Thérèse	52	f	farmer	married
308 Ruhimbana	30	m	herdsman	single
309 Emmanuel	24	m	herdsman	single
310 Ndayiringiye	18	m	herdsman	single
311 Sophie	47	f	farmer	married
312 Kanyabashi	60	m	herdsman	married
313 Belline	55	f	farmer	married
314 Gloria	28	m	herdsman	single
315 Mathilde	20	f	farmer	single
316 Danny Kayibanda	49	m	farmer	married
317 Aimable	20	m	student	single
318 Erina	24	f	tailor	single
319 Bahati	18	f	student	single
320 Mugiraneza	12	f	student	
321 Furaha	8	f	student	
322 Eliézer	36	m	herdsman	married
323 Bernadette	30	f	farmer	married
324 Appolinaire	11	f	student	
325 Sophie	30	f	farmer	married
326 Izabiriza	38	m	herdsman	widower
327 Akumuremyi	38	f	farmer	widow
328 Maboko	14	m	student	
329 Hakizimana	12	m	student	
330 Mukabatare	45	f	farmer	married
331 Kamegeri	25	m	herdsman	single
332 Habyarimana	21	m	herdsman	single
333 Mayira	18	m	herdsman	single
334 Mukeshimana	15	f	student	
335 Buregeya	11	m	student	
336 Zaburoni	41	m	herdsman	married

1.5.4 Cellule Kamaliba

No.	Name	Age	Sex	Occupn.	Marital status
1	Anselme	40	m	herdsman	married
2	Adrien	34	f	farmer	married
3	Pascasie	18	f	farmer	single
4	Félicitée	15	f	farmer	
5	Appolinaire	11	f	student	
6	Nyirakanani	8	f	student	
7	Ntigurirwa	60	m	builder	single
8	Nyiranshara	55	f	farmer	single
9	Nkundimana	26	m	herdsman	single
10	Mukandoli	25	f	farmer	single
11	Ndatimana	19	m	shop keeper	single
12	Mukeshimana	12	f	student	
13	Uwimana	15	f	student	
14	Nkundimana	37	m	herdsman	single
15	Jurida	34	f	farmer	married
16	Nkundimana	14	m	herdsman	
17	Donat	9	m	student	
18	Mukeshimana	7	f	student	
19	Musonera	17	m	student	single
20	Gashema	60	m	herdsman	married
21	Mukantagara	60	f	farmer	married
22	Nyilidandi	50	m	farmer	married
23	Nyirakijè	50	f	farmer	married
24	Bamurange	25	f	farmer	single
25	Mukamana	22	f	farmer	single
26	Ndahimana	20	m	farmer	single
27	Macondo	15	m	student	
28	Akimana	10	f	student	
29	Karengera	55	m	herdsman	single
30	Kanamugire	45	m	farmer	married
31	Yamfashije	40	m	herdsman	married
32	Dativa	30	f	farmer	married
33	Niyonsenga	23	m	herdsman	single
34	Emmanuel	20	m	herdsman	single
35	Adèle Nyirakamondo	40	f	farmer	married
36	Mukamuganga	6	f	student	
37	Kamayugi	65	f	farmer	married
38	Camille	36	m	herdsman	single
39	Uwambaye	26	f	farmer	single
40	Iyakaremye	20	m	herdsman	single
41	Caritas	30	f	farmer	single

1.6 Sector Mpembe

1.6.1 Cellule Gisoro

No.	Name	Age	Sex	Occupn.	Marital Status
1	Elias Buhanga	82	m	herdsman	married
2	Anésie Kamunazi	73	f		married
3	Bruno Munyankindi	45	m	herdsman	single
4	Habarugira	1	m		
5	Claver Kayiranga	17	m	student	single
6	Marie-Jeanne Mukandoli	22	f	farmer	single
7	Jeannette Mukandayisenga	9	f	student	
8	Mathilde Mukashyaka	24	f	farmer	single
9	Marie Nyirabukara	12	f	student	
10	André Sebuturumba	80	m	herdsman	married
11	Vérédiane	72	f		married
12	Catherine Mukandoli	38	f	farmer	single
13	Fidèle Yambabariye	33	m	herdsman	single
14	Stanislas Shema	48	m	herdsman	single
15	Gaspard Kaberuka	68	m	herdsman	married
16	Mukantaganda	2	f	farmer	married
17	Albert Yambabariye	16	m	herdsman	single
18	Philbert Karangwa	20	m	herdsman	single
19	Félicien Gasana	15	m	herdsman	single
20	Twagirayezu	11	m	student	
21	Donatha Uwanyiligira	9	f	student	
22	Géneviève Mukarutakwa	30	f	teacher	single
23	Damien Zanindi	52	m	herdsman	married
24	Xavéra Nyiranshimiyimana	40	f	farmer	married
25	Jeanne D'arc Uwizeyimana	20	f	farmer	single
26	Jean-Paul Mugabonejo	12	m	student	
27	Appolinaire Mukasine	25	f	farmer	single
28	Léopold Niyomwungeli	9	m	student	
29	Mbabazi	5	m	student	
30	Emmanuel	2	m		
31	Vianney Rugira	28	m	herdsman	married
32	Césalie Mukamukomeza	50	f	farmer	single

1.6.1 Cellule Gisoro (continued)

No.	Name	Age	Sex	Occupn.	Marital Status
1	Ferdinand Kabera	65	m	herdsman	married
2	Patricie Nyirarubungo	60	f	farmer	married
3	Thérèse Mukangamije	48	f	farmer	widow
4	Evariste Kayigire	26	m	herdsman	single
5	Déo Iyamuremye	23	m	farmer	single
6	Iyamumpaye	18	f	farmer	single
7	Gabriel Hitimana	10	m	student	
8	Béata Nyirabugingo	8	f	student	
9	Samuel Ruhumuliza	70	m	farmer	married
10	Chrésie Mukamacumu	67	f	farmer	married
11	Augustin Kamanzi	32	m	farmer	single
12	Julienne Yankurije	25	f	farmer	single
13	Mukeshimana	35	m	herdsman	married
14	Gaudence Nyirangohe	25	f	farmer	married
15	Aloys Mukeshimana	2	m		
16	Anastasie Bugirimfura	80	f	farmer	married
17	Innocent Niyitegeka	30	m	farmer	married
18	Habimana	27	m	farmer	single
19	Augustin Ngamije	35	m	herdsman	married
20	Marie Ngamije	2	f		
21	Innocent Uwayisaba	50	m	teacher	married
22	Bernadette Mukansanga	42	f	farmer	married
23	Muhire	2	m		
24	Augustin Mugenga	35	m	farmer	married
25	Béata Mukayuhi	28	f	farmer	married
26	Eric Mugenga	10	m	student	
27	Angélique Mukamugenga	13	f	student	
28	Téléphone Imanimurinde	4	f		
29	Erina Yankurije	22	f	farmer	married
30	Nkoreyimana	50	m	farmer	widower
31	Nzayisenga	12	m	student	
32	Nyirabugingo	9	f	student	
33	Boniface Renzaho	70	m	farmer	married
34	Zimuyange	60	f	farmer	married
35	Emmanuel Habiyambere	35	m	farmer	single
36	Ildephonse Hitimana	35	m	farmer	single
37	Erina Nikuze	30	f	farmer	single
38	Papias Nduwamungu	40	m	farmer	married
39	Vénancie Kanyanja	35	f	farmer	married
40	Kibwega	11	m	student	
41	Antoinette Nduwamungu	9	f	student	

42	Consolée	5	f		
43	Mujawamariya	35	f	farmer	widow
44	J. Paul Ndayisaba	12	m	student	
45	Julienne Uwayezu	30	f	farmer	widow
46	Nyiransengimana	1	f		
47	Mbanzarugamba	35	m	farmer	widower
48	Nsabimana	11	m	student	
49	Rwatingamba	50	m	herdsman	widow
50	Muzehe Rwatingamba	10	m	student	
51	Saruhara	10	m	student	
52	Ndayisaba	12	m	student	
53	Jacques Migeri	32	m	herdsman	married
54	Catherine Migeri	30	f	farmer	married
55	Rubyogo	10	m	student	
56	Ntakuritimana	8	m	student	
57	Léonidas Twagirayezu	50	m	herdsman	married
58	Mukankuranga	40	f	farmer	married
59	Epiphanie Mujawayezu	12	f	student	
60	Théophile Bugenimana	9	f	student	
61	Iyamumpaye	16	m	student	single
62	Juvénal Simbizi	60	m	herdsman	married
63	Caritas Nagahweje	50	f	farmer	married
64	Nzamutuma	20	m	farmer	single
65	Murekatete	28	f	farmer	single
66	Nyiramwamira	2	f		
67	Léonard Habiyambere	56	m	herdsman	married
68	Généreuse Mukazitoni	50	f	farmer	married
69	Léonidas Ndayisaba	18	m	student	single
70	Béatrice Dusabimana	15	f	student	
71	Marie Uwizeye	12	f	student	
72	Martin Sezibera	54	m	herdsman	married
73	Mukankwaya	50	f	farmer	married
74	Augustin Ruzindana	26	m	farmer	single
75	Bernard Nteziryayo	8	m	student	
76	Consolée Bayisenge	20	f	farmer	single
77	Christine Mukamana	14	f	student	
78	Caritas Nyirahabimana	16	f	student	single
79	Jean Nsengiyumva	7	m	student	
80	Namuhoranye	35	f	farmer	widow
81	Mukashema	12	f	student	
82	Alexia	6	f		
83	Rusingizandekwe	80	m	farmer	married
84	Nyiransengimana	28	f	farmer	married
85	Adèle Nyinawumuntu	10	f	student	
86	Fidèle Iraguha	5	m		
87	Félix Mugisha	1	m		
88	Ignace Hageniyaremye	18	m	student	single
89	Tuyisenge	14	f	student	
90	Augustin Ndayizeye	12	m	student	
91	Bigirimana	10	m	student	
92	Ndayambaje	8	m	student	
93	Rwasabahizi	60	m	herdsman	married
94	Pauline Karwera	55	f	farmer	married
95	Zigiranyirazo	12	m	student	
96	Seth Habineza	10	m	student	
97	Céléstin Simbikangwa	50	m	herdsman	married
98	Nyirabizimana	7	f	student	
99	Gena	5	m		
100	Nyirabutaza	8	f	student	
101	Kabera	60	f	farmer	widow
102	Ngezahoguhora	20	m	farmer	single
103	Uwayisaba	3	f		
104	Mathias Hagenimana	30	m	herdsman	married
105	Uwamahoro	4	f		
106	Sibomana	2	m		
107	Mukanoheri	1	f		
108	Marianne Nyiramagufi	50	f	farmer	widow
109	Nzayisenga	20	m	farmer	single
110	Donatha Habinshuti	25	f	farmer	married
111	Vénant Rubaduka	65	m	herdsman	married
112	Rose Kakuze	60	f	farmer	married
113	Nyiranuma	15	f	student	
114	Kibwa	10	m	student	
115	Aloys	55	m	farmer	married
116	Marthe Mukandekezi	45	f	farmer	married
117	Agnès Mukagatare	30	f	nurse	single
118	François Mukeshimana	13	f	student	
119	Marie Uwimana	10	f	student	
120	Chrésie Mukaruziga	40	f	farmer	widow
121	Françoise Mukeshimana	13	f	student	
122	Thomas Muhayimana	10	m	student	
123	Jean-Paul Munyakazi	7	m	student	
124	Anathalie Mukamana	3	f		
125	Consolée Munyakizi	1	f		
126	Jean Kayiranga	52	m	herdsman	married
127	Alphonsine Nyirabugingo	45	f	farmer	married
128	Jeanne Nyiransengimana	16	f	student	single
129	Emmanuel Hakizimana	14	m	student	
130	Joseph Hategikimana	12	m	student	
131	Nyiramana	10	f	student	
132	Matoroshi Kayiranga	5	m		
133	Kayiranga Rubyogo	7	m	student	
134	Jean Havuga	67	m	herdsman	married
135	Mukamurigo	40	f	farmer	married
136	Nyirabukara	15	f	student	
137	Mukangoga	14	f	student	
138	Gasamagera	9	m	student	
139	Kanziga	4	m		
140	Daniel Havuga	67	m	herdsman	married
141	Amos Ngiraguseswa	36	m	farmer	married
142	Daphrose Mukamugema	30	f	farmer	married
143	Rubyogo	3	m		
144	Etienne Rutiyomba	45	m	herdsman	married
145	Alphonsine Mukasine	35	f	farmer	married
146	Rutiyomba	18	m	student	single
147	Cassien Rutiyomba	16	m	student	single
148	Bernadette Rutiyomba	14	f	student	
149	Damien Rutiyomba	11	m	student	
150	Suzanne Rutiyomba	5	f		
151	Nyirandibikiye	60	f	farmer	widow
152	Obed Kabirigi		m	farmer	widower
153	Thomas Nzamutuma	35	m	farmer	widower
154	Harorimana	5	m		
155	Nyirabukara	6	f		
156	Anglebert Iyamuremye	40	m	herdsman	married
157	Dancilla Kabazinga	42	f	farmer	married
158	Colette Nyiranzabahimana	15	f	student	
159	Thérèse Niyigena	13	f	student	
160	Angelebert Gasore	39	m	herdsman	married
161	Jeanne Nyiransengimana	35	f	farmer	married
162	Pascal Uwamariya	4	m		
163	Emmanuel Mbanziriza	5	m		
164	Erina Yankurije	22	f	farmer	married
165	Mukarwaka	40	f	farmer	married
166	Elière Hagenimana	5	m	student	
167	Nsabyimana	7	f	student	
168	Ukwitegetse	3	f		
169	Muzindutsi	54	m	herdsman	married
170	Thérèse Mukamunana	33	f	farmer	married
171	Mukamusoni	15	f	student	
172	Munyandamutsa	35	m	herdsman	married
173	Léoncie Muzindutsi	10	f	student	
174	Nikuze	8	f	student	
175	Chadrac Kagabo	60	m	herdsman	married
176	Mukantanda	45	f	farmer	married
177	Nshimyikiza	12	m	student	
178	Joséphine Uwimana	10	f	student	
179	Muturakazi	8	f	student	
180	Charles Kagabo	4	m		
181	Niyomugabo	11	m	student	
182	Rusaya	30	m	farmer	single

2. Commune Gisovu

2.1 Sector Rwankuba

2.1.1 Cellule Bisesero

No.	Name	Age	Sex	Occupn.	Marital Status
1	Stéphanie Nyirangezahayo	54	f	farmer	married
2	Narcisse Rwagasana	24	m	student	single
3	Vincent Rutaganira	20	m	student	single
4	Pascasie Mukagasana	16	f	student	single
5	Cécile Mukasonga	14	f	student	
6	Odette Mukamurenzi	12	f	student	
7	Immaculée Mukamunana	11	f	student	
8	Nyirahategeka	44	f	farmer	married
9	Alphonse Hakizimana	25	m	farmer	single
10	Mukangoga	21	f	farmer	married
11	Uwiturije	19	f	student	single
12	Uwiragiye	17	f	student	single
13	Nyiransengiyumva	18	f	student	single
14	Karimwijabo	74	m	herdsman	widow
15	Kangabe	54	f	farmer	married
16	Mukarusanga	26	f	farmer	single
17	Nyirahabineza	23	f	farmer	single
18	Nyiraneza	21	f	farmer	single
19	Bagambiki	22	m	farmer	single
20	Joseph Segikwiye	31	m	herdsman	married
21	Mukaribanje	29	f	farmer	married
22	Sindabyemera	8	m	student	
23	Mukankomeje	6	f		

24	Nyirabagiriki	5	f		
25	Nyirabucandage	40	f	farmer	married
26	Mukabutera	20	f	farmer	single
27	Mukamukomeza	18	f	student	single
28	Uwimana	16	f	student	single
29	Musabyimana	7	f	student	
30	Rwemarika	45	m	herdsman	married
31	Innocent Nsengimana	24	m	student	single
32	Rose Nyirahategeka	35	m	farmer	married
33	Hélène Nyirahategeka	40	f	farmer	single
34	Kanamugire	10	m	student	
35	Nyirambindigiri	7	f	student	
36	Maronko	8	f	student	
37	Nyiramana	6	f		
38	Rwambuga	80	m	herdsman	married
39	Nyiramugwera	75	f	farmer	married
40	Nyiramashashi	28	f	farmer	married
41	Nyirambegeti	10	f	student	
42	Nyirahabimana	9	f	student	
43	Uwamahoro	6	f		
44	Rwanyagatare	50	m	herdsman	married
45	Mukangamije	42	f	farmer	married
46	J. Damascène Muhajimana	14	m	student	
47	Eugénie	12	f	student	
48	Mukashema	10	f	student	
49	Nkunzurwanda	30	m	herdsman	married
50	Mukamuganga	25	f	farmer	married
51	Nyirandegeya	12	f	student	
52	Nyirambeba	10	f	student	
53	Nyiramatama	8	f	student	
54	Habimana	6	m		
55	Munyaneza	30	m	farmer	married
56	Matoroshi	6	m		
57	Habimana	4	m		
58	Mukandutiye	40	f	farmer	married
59	Habiyambere	30	m	farmer	married
60	Nyirankumbuye	22	f	farmer	married
61	Nsengimana	2	m		
62	Ntagozera	50	m	farmer	married
63	Ntagara	12	m	student	
64	Kamagaza	25	f	farmer	single
65	Utetiwabo	18	f	farmer	single
66	Nikuze	15	f	student	
67	Gatorano	2	m		
68	Ntampuhwe	35	m	herdsman	single
69	Mukagashema	29	f	farmer	single
70	Nsabimana	9	m	student	
71	Uwamahoro	7	m	student	
72	Gapiripiri	15	m	farmer	
73	Sebugunzu	15	m	student	
74	Kazungu	40	m	herdsman	married
75	Mukansonera	30	f	farmer	married
76	Kanamugire	10	m	student	
77	Marceline Uwimana	8	f	student	
78	Nyiramashashi	7	f	student	
79	Nyiraneza	6	f		
80	Kankindi	70	f	farmer	married
81	Munyarubuga	80	m	herdsman	widower
82	Augustin Bivara	47	m	herdsman	married
83	Mukankwaya	40	f	farmer	single
84	Havugimana	24	m	farmer	
85	Muzehe	16	m	student	
86	Jean-Damascène Gihanga	12	m	student	
87	Nyirakanani	6	f		
88	Mukamana	4	f		
89	Bimenyimana	28	m	farmer	married
90	Uwimana	20	f	farmer	married
91	Utetiwabo	38	f	farmer	married
92	Niyomugabo	14	m	student	
93	Nsengiyumva	10	m	student	
94	Kazungu	6	m		
95	Mukankomeje	3	f		
96	Rwabununga	65	m	herdsman	married
97	Mukaruburika	35	f	farmer	married
98	Mukarubayiza	35	f	farmer	single
99	Nyiramazuru	8	f	student	
100	Akizanye	22	f	farmer	single
101	Uwimana	7	f	student	
102	Mukashema	4	f		
103	Uwayisaba	3	f		
104	Mukankomeje	35	f	farmer	married
105	Mukamana	30	f	farmer	single
106	Mukashema	28	f	farmer	married
107	Ayinkamiye	10	f	student	
108	Gasagara	70	m	herdsman	married
109	Uwambaye	60	f	farmer	married
110	Mukashyaka	30	f	farmer	married
111	Nyirabunuma	3	f		
112	Uwihoreye	1	f		
113	Ruhanga	55	m	herdsman	married
114	Uzamukunda	49	f	farmer	married
115	Ahishakiye	8	f	student	
116	Iyamuremye	67	m	herdsman	married
117	Ndayisaba	26	m	farmer	single
118	Rutiyomba	24	m	farmer	single
119	Sinzayisebya	21	m	farmer	single
120	Kagabo	18	m	farmer	single
121	Mukabideri	22	f	farmer	married
122	Mukamuhire	2	f		
123	Rutayisire	30	m	farmer	married
124	Mukamuhire	25	f	farmer	married
125	Mukamusoni	2	f		
126	Dismas	52	m	herdsman	married
127	Mukantaganda	47	f	farmer	married
128	Ndahimana	24	m	farmer	married
129	Nyirahabimana	26	f	farmer	married
130	Masabo	6	m		
131	Marcel Mushimiyimana	4	m		
132	Mukashyaka	2	f		
133	Havugimana	15	m	student	
134	Nyirabideri	79	f	farmer	married
135	Kayumba	26	m	farmer	married
136	Mukadefanyi	24	f	farmer	married
137	Mukamana	2	f		
138	Seromba	17	m	farmer	single
139	Vuguziga	2	f		
140	Mukashema	38	f	farmer	married
141	Nirere	15	f	farmer	
142	Mukaruziga	8	f	student	
143	Mukabera	4	f		
144	Nzitukuze	32	f	farmer	married
145	Harorimana	11	m	student	
146	Mukangango	7	f	student	
147	Mukankaka	5	f		
148	Mukamudenge	5	f		
149	Sankweri	3	f		
150	Mukansonera	1	f		
151	Mukabideri	34	f	farmer	married
152	Nyirabwerinuma	10	f	student	
153	Nyiransengiyumva	8	f	student	
154	Gashirabake	5	m		
155	Ingabire	3	f		
156	Nyirangezahayo	36	f	farmer	married
157	Kananura	55	m	farmer	married
158	Nyiramayombo	52	f	farmer	married
159	Muhayimana	25	m	farmer	single
160	Yamuragiye	9	f	student	
161	Mukamuhigirwa	35	f	farmer	married
162	Nziyumvira	14	m	student	
163	Nzabitega	12	f	student	
164	Mukankundiye	9	m	student	
165	Nyirahabimana	7	f	student	
166	Sebugunzu	70	m	herdsman	married
167	Nyirabumende	65	f	farmer	married
168	Mushingwamana	72	m	herdsman	married
169	Mukarusine	50	f	farmer	married
170	Rushema	87	m	herdsman	married
171	Kamashara	80	f	farmer	married
172	Nyirankundwa	95	f	farmer	widow
173	Mukarwego	65	f	farmer	married
174	Mukankubito	25	f	farmer	single
175	Mangara	55	m	herdsman	married